SETUP

What the Air Force Did in Vietnam and Why

by

Earl H. Tilford, Jr.

Air University Press
Maxwell Air Force Base, Alabama 36112-5532

June 1991

Library of Congress Cataloging-in-Publication Data

Tilford, Earl H.
    Setup: what the Air Force did in Vietnam and why/by
Earl H. Tilford, Jr.
        p. cm.
    "June 1991."
    Includes index.
    1. Vietnamese Conflict, 1961-1975—Aerial operations, American. 2. United States.—Air
Force—History— Vietnamese Conflict, 1961-1975. I. Title.
DS558.8.T55 1991
959.704'348—dc20   91-10956
ISBN 1-58566-038-8   CIP

First Printing June 1991
Second Printing July 2002

DISCLAIMER

For Sale by the Superintendent of Documents
US Government Printing Office
Washington, DC 20402

*To Grace
for giving me faith*

Contents

Chapter		Page
	DISCLAIMER	ii
	FOREWORD	ix
	ABOUT THE AUTHOR	xiii
	PREFACE	xv
1	IN THE TIME OF ATOMIC PLENTY	1
	Air Power Fulfilled	1
	The Road to a Separate Service	2
	The Atomic Bomb and the New Air Force	7
	Preludes to Vietnam	15
	The "New Look" and the Air Force	24
	Notes	40
2	SITUATIONS OF A LESSER MAGNITUDE	45
	The Kennedy Administration, the Cold War, and the Air Force	45
	The Laotian Factor	53
	In at the Beginning	60
	At War with the Army	68
	Notes	83
3	ROLLING THUNDER AND THE DIFFUSION OF HEAT	89
	The Dark before the Storm	90
	The Air Force that Flew Rolling Thunder	95
	Rolling Thunder Begins	102

Chapter   *Page*

Bombing the North 106
The Bombing Escalates 115
Rushing to Meet Our Thunder 121
Switch in Strategy or in Targets? 133
Toward a Bombing Halt 146
Tet and the Bombing Halt 149
Notes 156

4   "HOWEVER FRUSTRATED WE ARE" 165

Shifting Gears in 1968 166
Search for Tomorrow 171
Operation Commando Hunt 172
Productivity as Strategy 182
The Air War in Northern Laos 186
Cambodia 194
Back to Laos 198
Lam Son 719 Fallout 204
Frustrations Continue 205
Proud Deep Alpha 208
Notes 210

5   "IT WAS A LOSER" 215

Marking Time along the Ho Chi Minh Trail 217
Spring in the Air 221
The Shoe Falls 224
Deciding to Go North Again 227
Linebacker One 233
Bombing and Diplomacy 237
Linebacker One as a Tactical Success 238
Saigon Balks 248
Linebacker Two 253
Notes 265

Chapter		Page

6   COMPLETING THE SETUP 271

    Laos: Coming Full Circle 271
    Cambodia 274
    Mayaguez as a Microcosm of the War 280
    The Setup Completed 282
    Why Did Air Power Fail? 283
        History 284
        Doctrine 285
        Technology 285
        Management 286
        Decreased Intellectual Acumen 286
        Some Generic Reasons 287
    Unhealthy Myths 288
    Notes 297

   INDEX 301

Illustrations

B-29s 10
Gen Curtis E. LeMay 12
B-36 13
B-52 32
F-105 Thunderchief 33
F-105s in Joint Maneuvers 37
Secretary of the Air Force Eugene M. Zuckert .. 46
XB-70 48
President John F. Kennedy with
   Gen Curtis E. LeMay 51
F-4 Phantom 52
Joint Chiefs of Staff 63

T-28 65

B-26 65

A-1 Skyraider 66

F-100 80

F-104 96

B-58 Hustler 96

XB-70 97

Hanoi Petroleum Storage Site 119

North Vietnamese Antiaircraft Artillery Site . . . 122

North Vietnamese Surface-to-Air Missile Site . . 123

F-105 Thunderchief 128

F-4 Phantom 128

Interdiction Strike on a River Bridge
    in North Vietnam 134

Secretary of the Air Force Harold Brown 136

Secretary of Defense Robert S. McNamara 137

Gen William W. Momyer 143

Secretary of the Air Force
    Robert C. Seamans, Jr 166

Army Mechanized Infantry on Patrol 170

Air Strike in the Republic of Vietnam 208

B-52 Releases Bombs during Linebacker 229

F-4 Equipped with Air-to-Air Missiles 244

MiG–21 244

B-52 Crews on Guam 258

B-52 Taking Off on Bombing Mission
    in Southeast Asia 259

Foreword

The United States Air Force of the 1990s faces perhaps the single greatest challenge to its institutional weltanschauung since it became an independent service in 1947. The specter of a hostile, expansionist Soviet Union—which, for the last 45 years, has justified the maintenance of a large strategic air force over-whelmingly oriented to the western European theater—is fading fast with no similarly immense threat on the immediate horizon to take its place. As a result, the USAF, perhaps more than any other US military service, faces the prospect of losing the foundation upon which it has based its entire institutional identity and even its very existence.

Strategic bombing is not mere doctrine to the USAF; it is its lifeblood and provides its entire raison d'être. Strategic bombing is as central to the identity of the Air Force as the New Testament is to the Catholic church. Without the Gospels there would be no pope; and without strategic bombing there would be no Air Force. The theology of strategic bombing has influenced every aspect of the Air Force's development since well before World War II. This system of belief too often has led the keepers of the USAF's institutional memory to dismiss as aberrant, peripheral, and irrelevant anything that fell outside the narrow confines of its strategic concepts. The USAF's uncritical approach to its own past has enabled it to declare strategic bombing decisive where it was not (Europe, 1943–45); to claim victory where there was none (Vietnam, 1972); and to neglect those air operations that, indeed, proved indispensable and potentially decisive (tactical air campaigns in the European and Pacific theaters during World War II and in Korea during 1950 and 1951). This inability of the USAF to assess realistically the lessons and implications of its wartime experiences—failures along with successes—not only keeps it from facing the more difficult and sometimes painful implications of the Vietnam experience, but in the long run enervates all Air Force doctrine, strategic as well as tactical.

Outside the context of traditional Air Force concepts and hidebound-institutional assumptions, Dr Earl H. Tilford provides in this volume the sort of critical self-appraisal of USAF strategy in Vietnam that has been too long in coming. Uniformed Air Force historians, while relatively prolific generally have demonstrated a distressing lack of skepticism; as a result, their efforts too often lack the critical analysis necessary to challenge unhealthy myths and to derive meaningful lessons from past operational experience. The Air Force has never produced a body of internal critics comparable to those Army officers who, through the late 1970s and 1980s, often risked their military careers to challenge prevailing ground force strategies in Southeast Asia in the 1960s. Dr Tilford, along with a small but growing number of his former USAF colleagues, has begun the belated process of questioning the underlying assumptions of the USAF's strategy in Southeast Asia.

Tilford—a retired Air Force officer and a widely respected historian in his own right—is not squeamish about demolishing the myths that abound concerning the air war in Southeast Asia. He is forthright in challenging both the USAF's strategic tunnel vision and the cherished misconceptions of many civilian historians whose criticisms of the air war in Vietnam are long on politics and short on facts. The integrity of Dr Tilford's research, his knowledge of air power theory and technology, and his expertise as a historian all contribute to a high quality effort that proves, among other things, that neither the Air Force nor its civilian critics have yet secured a monopoly on truth.

In his analysis of the air war against North Vietnam, Tilford presents one overwhelming lesson: that USAF strategic bombing doctrine is ethnocentric and Eurocentric, and is conceived utterly without regard to important cultural and political variations among potential adversaries. This lesson, more than any other, is one that today's Air Force must learn if it is to establish any relevance in a post-cold war world in which the global, superpower war for which it has planned almost exclusively since 1945 becomes an evermore remote possibility. Whatever the Air Force's operational role in the twenty-first century turns out to be, it seems likely that an air technocracy geared toward fighting a general war against a modern, industrialized major power will become even less relevant than it proved to be in Korea and Vietnam. At the very least, the Air Force of the future will do well to heed Dr Tilford's other major conclusion that because war is more than sortie generation and getting ordnance on targets, statistics are a poor substitute for strategy.

Military organizations have accepted the value of official history ever since the elder Helmuth von Moltke invented the genre in the 1870s. Too often, however, the effort to highlight successes and rationalize, or worse yet, expunge failures overshadows the value of official history as an organ of self-evaluation and improvement. While it is perhaps going too far to suggest that military historians should study only failures, a more balanced treatment of operational shortcomings from within the military services would be a refreshing and ultimately beneficial change.

Official histories with such an orientation would have a much greater impact on the mainstream of military history because they would be more difficult to dismiss as public relations rather than scholarship.

Official military history was born as a learning exercise, and in this book Dr Tilford has returned to those roots. He proceeds from the assumption that it is more important to understand what went wrong in Vietnam and why, than it is to manipulate the record and paint failure as victory. At the very least, Tilford's work joins earlier studies—most notably, Mark Clodfelter's *The Limits of Air Power* and Barry Watts's *The Foundations of US Air Doctrine* in what many students of air power hope is "the new Air Force history": honest appraisals of the historical record, free from the service biases, conceptual limitations, and strategic dogmatism that have tended to cloud the USAF's interpretation of its past. The already high quality of the histories that appeared under the imprint of the Office of Air Force History and the Warrior Studies Series can improve only when their historians—uniformed and civilian—feel free to ask, and answer, the difficult questions that the USAF has evaded for the past 40 years. Many within the Air Force will not like what Earl Tilford and his breed have to say, but one can only hope that in the best interests of the institution they will listen anyway.

CAROLINE F. ZIEMKE, PhD
Arlington, Virginia
May 1990

About the Author

Dr Earl H. Tilford, Jr.

Dr Earl H. Tilford, Jr., is an associate professor of history at Troy State University in Montgomery and visiting professor of military history at the Air Command and Staff College. He earned his BA and MA degrees in history at the University of Alabama and his PhD in American military history at George Washington University. Dr Tilford retired from the Air Force in 1989 after a career that included tours as an intelligence officer in Thailand and at Headquarters Strategic Air Command. From 1975 to 1979, he was part of a team of military and civilian historians writing the official history of Air Force operations during the Vietnam War. Dr Tilford taught history at the US Air Force Academy before becoming associate editor and then editor of the *Air University Review*. He began writing *Setup* in 1987 during an assignment as a research fellow at the Air University Center for Aerospace Doctrine, Research, and Education. Dr Tilford is the author of *The United States Air Force Search and Rescue in Southeast Asia, 1961–1975* and more than 20 articles pertaining to the Vietnam War. He teaches courses on the Vietnam War at Troy State University in Montgomery, Auburn University at Montgomery, and the University of Alabama. Dr Tilford pioneered elective courses on the Vietnam War at the Air Force's Air War College and the Air Command and Staff College. He has lectured extensively at numerous colleges and universities in the United States and Europe. Dr Tilford lives in Prattville, Alabama, with his wife, three children, and a cat named Clausewitz.

Preface

The primary mission of Headquarters Seventh/Thirteenth Air Force, located at Udorn Royal Thai Air Force Base, Thailand, was to coordinate and support Air Force operations over northern Laos. In 1970 and 1971, as a new second lieutenant, I served there as an intelligence briefer. My job was to prepare and deliver the morning intelligence briefing to the commander, a major general.

The headquarters director of intelligence (DI) provided strict ground rules for his briefers to follow. A briefing script had to be prepared and, once approved, adhered to almost exactly. Negative words, like *lost*, *ambushed*, *retreat*, although increasingly appropriate by 1971, were anathema.

By mid-March 1971, South Vietnam's invasion of Laos to cut the Ho Chi Minh Trail, Operation Lam Son 719, had fallen apart. What was left of an invasion force of over 15,000 soldiers of the Army of the Republic of Vietnam (ARVN) crumbled before a concerted North Vietnamese counterattack comprised of more than four divisions. ARVN troops, stalled along Route 9 leading from Khe Sanh to Tchepone, Laos, the transshipment point at the center of the trail, were either surrendering, fading into the jungle, or desperately boarding (and often clinging to) US Army helicopters attempting to ferry them to safety.

One morning it fell to me to brief this debacle to the general. First, at 7:00 A.M., I had to brief the director of intelligence to get his approval for what would be said to the general an hour later. As the briefing developed, I said, "Sir, the ARVN is retreating along Route 9 back toward Khe Sanh." The colonel looked up from his copy of the script and said, "Tilford, you know better than that. Get another word for 'retreating.'"

As I briefed the general at the eight o'clock briefing, I said, "Turning our attention to Operation Lam Son 719 . . . the ARVN is fleeing along Route 9 back toward Khe Sanh."

"What do you mean, 'fleeing'?" the general asked.

"Sir, as the colonel indicated earlier, this is not a retreat. Retreats have cohesion. Lam Son 719 has turned into a rout. The South Vietnamese who haven't surrendered are either running off into the jungle or piling into helicopters—even clinging to their skids—to get out of Laos."

The general turned to the director of intelligence, "Dan, is that right?"

"Yessir, that seems to be right."

Then the general turned to another colonel, the Seventh/ Thirteenth Air Force director of operations (DO) and ordered, "All planes not used to support troops in contact [firefights] in northern Laos are to be turned over to Seventh Air Force [our Southeast Asia headquarters in Saigon] for Lam Son 719."

When the briefing concluded the two colonels followed me back to my office. There they delivered a severe tongue lashing, which, while only one of many I was to get during my 20-year Air Force career, was nonetheless among the most memorable. After the colonels had finished with me and departed, a wiser and more experienced first lieutenant said, "You know what you did, don't you? You took away the DO's planes. That's an embarrassment and a big loss of prestige for him." The ARVN be damned, the colonel had been embarrassed.

By 1971 the Vietnam War had been lost long ago. Our involvement no longer had anything to do with stemming the tide of communism or even ensuring the right of the Republic of Vietnam to exist. Without a clearly defined objective, the US military services in Indochina focused on larger institutional issues which might affect them in the postwar years. Power struggles abounded at the highest levels among the White House, Congress, the Department of Defense, and the Department of State and at a lower level among the Air Force, Navy, and Army. Within the Air Force, the Strategic Air Command competed with the Tactical Air Command (TAC), and within TAC the jet mafia with their high-technology fighters competed with the special operations mafia and their propeller-driven gunships and fighter-bombers. What the colonels who chewed me out were concerned with was part of an internal struggle within Air Force units assigned to Southeast Asia revolving around prerogatives reserved for the Seventh Air Force and those designated to the Seventh/Thirteenth Air Force.

- - - - - - - - -

The Vietnam War has been over for nearly two decades. Generally, American military professionals have had a difficult time understanding their role in this nation's most ignominious defeat. The US Air Force has had more difficulty assessing the Vietnam War than the other services. For instance, the US Army has identified problems with leadership, morale in the ranks, and its doctrines in the early 1970s which both compelled and resulted from the defeat in Vietnam. The Air Force, on the other hand, believed (and still believes) it won the war. Ask many airmen about air power in Vietnam, and they will relate the myth of Linebacker Two: how using B-52s over Hanoi and other major cities for 11 days in December 1972 brought the North Vietnamese to their collective knees. The myth of Linebacker Two is reassuring because it reinforces accepted doctrinal precepts and bolsters an institutional commitment to the manned bomber. The myth also perpetuates misunderstanding and, because it is widely accepted and believed by airmen, prevents the Air Force from gaining the valuable insights that an objective study of the Vietnam War could provide.

The Vietnam War, as Thomas C. Thayer states in his book *War without Fronts*, was primarily an air war, at least in terms of resource allocation. More than half of the hundreds of billions of dollars spent on the Vietnam War went to support Air Force, Army, and Navy aerial operations. The Air Force built up its forces the fastest of any service, reaching near peak strength by mid-1966, and then remained in Southeast Asia longer than any other service, not closing down its Thailand-based headquarters until January 1976. The United States dropped eight million tons of bombs on Vietnam, Laos, and Cambodia between 1962 and 1973—the Air Force accounting for nearly 80 percent of those bombs. Total US aircraft losses, fixed wing and helicopter, came to 8,588. The Air Force lost 2,257 aircraft and more than 2,700 Air Force men died while hundreds of airmen endured torture in captivity. For all that expenditure of treasure, firepower, and lives, air power, while occasionally pivotal, was *never* decisive in the Vietnam War.

The Air Force flew into Vietnam on the wings of a doctrine devised to fight industrial powers like Nazi Germany, Imperial Japan, and the Soviet Union. That North Vietnam was a preindustrial agricultural society which was simply not susceptible to strategic bombing is only part of the reason that air power failed. This book explains additional factors leading to the "setup" which not only resulted in a failure for air power, but also contributed to the fall of South Vietnam, Laos, and Cambodia to Communist forces in 1975. The reasons behind this failure are important and relevant to the present and future.

Nearly half a century has passed since American air power was used effectively to win a war. Indeed, some pundits revel in pointing out that the United States has not won a war since it acquired an independent Air Force. Korea and Vietnam were more than unhappy exceptions to the true course of strategic air power doctrine developed in the 1930s and advanced during and immediately after World War II. These limited wars are indicative of the kinds of conflicts the United States likely will fight in the future. For that reason, airmen need to open their eyes and minds to the unpleasant realities of the limited applicability of strategic bombing. Airmen ought to ask difficult questions about the Vietnam War and about the doctrinal foundations rooted so firmly in the prophesies of strategic bombing which form the basis of an independent Air Force. Not to do so virtually assures that others outside the air power community will ask these questions and their answers are likely to be unpalatable for enthusiasts of the strategic air offensive.

The central thesis that I develop in *Setup* is that the failure of American air power in the Vietnam War cannot be blamed entirely on politicians "who tied our hands," a pernicious and "wayward" press, or the antiwar movement. Air Force leaders, especially the air commanders in Saigon, Honolulu, and Washington between 1964 and 1972, share much of the blame. In the final analysis, they could not—indeed, did not—develop a strategy appropriate to the war at hand. In fact, they failed to articulate any coherent strategy at all. In Vietnam the Air Force fell victim to its own brief history and to the unswerving commitment of its leadership to the dubious doctrine of strategic bombing.

- - - - - - - - -

This book could never have been written without the help and encouragement of many people. I deeply appreciate the support of Col Dennis M. Drew, director of the Airpower Research Institute (ARI) at the Air University Center for Aerospace Doctrine, Research, and Education at Maxwell AFB, Alabama. Colonel

Drew, a former graduate student of mine, paid his teacher the highest compliment by encouraging me to write this book and then providing an assignment in a place where I could work with little distraction. Dr David MacIsaac, ARI's director of research, helped me with detailed critiques of the early chapters. After he had pronounced them "oscar foxtrot sierra hotel," I knew I could press on. My office mate, Lt Col Frank P. Donnini, in addition to suffering through three years of having copies of *Ms* magazines left on his desk and other manifestations of my often warped sense of humor, read each chapter twice in an attempt to catch spelling and grammatical errors. I owe a great deal to Dr Stanley Spangler, ARI's distinguished visiting professor from 1986 to 1989, for his insights and comments and for educating me in the field of coercive diplomacy. Tom Lobenstein of the Air University Press improved the readability and accuracy of this book through his diligent editing. Marshall Brooks was extremely helpful in providing maps to illustrate this work. Patricia Boyle, Joan Dawson, Mary Moore, Jeni Thares, and Marcia Williams, also of the Press, along with Lula Barnes, Sue Carr, Katie Ladd, and Carolyn Ward, helped put the manuscript in publishable form.

The staff at the Air Force Historical Research Center, also located at Maxwell, was helpful. Senior historian Warren Trest read drafts of the first three chapters and offered suggestions which kept me from straying from my desired thesis. Judy Endicott, Presley Bickerstaff, and James H. Kitchens located documents and responded quickly to my requests for declassification. The staff at the John F. Kennedy Library in Boston, especially Suzanne K. Forbes, was very helpful in locating documents and suggesting areas for research.

Other friends and colleagues offered critical comments and suggestions. Dr Anthony Short of the University of Aberdeen, Scotland, read the entire manuscript. Dr Wesley P. Newton, professor emeritus of history at Auburn University, offered detailed criticisms at each stage of the manuscript's development. University of Alabama history professor and friend Dr Maarten Ultee gave me the benefit of the kind of critique that only a scholar of eighteenth-century French intellectual history can provide. Dr Jeffrey Record of BDM International and Dr Caroline Ziemke of the Institute for Defense Analysis read portions of the manuscript, offered critiques, and kept my spirits high. My friend and colleague Lt Col Suzanne B. Gehri, who as a captain introduced the first course on the Vietnam War at the US Air Force Academy, read most of the chapters and encouraged me to stay in the course. Dr Donald D. Chipman, education advisor at the Squadron Officer School (SOS) at Maxwell AFB, encouraged me to write this book after he had fought for a place for the study of the Vietnam air war in the SOS curriculum. Finally, I owe a great deal to Maj Mark Clodfelter, an associate professor of history at the Air Force Academy. Mark responded to my often frantic requests for information and advice. He shared ideas as well as facts he had gathered while researching his masterful book *The Limits of Air Power* (1989).

My family deserves more credit than I could ever pay. My father, a Presbyterian minister, taught me what moral courage was all about when, nearly three decades ago, he took the position that the fatherhood of God implied the brotherhood of mankind. That was a difficult and potentially dangerous stand for a Southerner to take in Alabama in 1962. Without the values passed on to me by Mom and Dad, I do not think that I would have substituted "fleeing" for "retreating" and the seeds that bore fruit in this book may never have taken root. My wife, Grace, and my children, Victoria, Michael, and Ellen, have loved me despite myself. This book is dedicated to them in the hope that it will, in some small way, make up for too many missed weekends.

EARL H. TILFORD, JR.
Troy State University in Montgomery
Spring 1990

Chapter 1

In the Time of Atomic Plenty

In 1961, on the eve of America's involvement in the Vietnam War, Gen Curtis E. LeMay stated, "I think we have been consistent in our concepts since the formation of GHQ [General Headquarters] Air Force in 1935. Our basic doctrine has remained generally unchanged since that time."[1] Three years later, when President Lyndon Johnson asked for a plan to bomb North Vietnam, the Air Force's response was a list of 94 targets—with airfields to be bombed first, then petroleum manufacturing and storage facilities, followed by the industrial system, and finally the road and transportation network. The Air Force was prepared to fly into Vietnam against guerrilla forces on the wings of the same conventional strategy used in bombing Nazi Germany in 1944. The reasons for this incoherence between the Air Force's conventional strategy and the unconventional war at hand in Vietnam were many and must be gleaned from the Air Force's doctrinal and institutional past and from the flush of victory that the first generation of Air Force leaders felt in the postwar period.

Air Power Fulfilled

When, on 15 September 1945, Japanese diplomats and military officers signed the articles of surrender on board the USS *Missouri* in Tokyo harbor, the US Army Air Forces had good reason to be proud of its contributions to the Allied victory in the Second World War. Indeed, the future for American air power looked bright. After two decades of struggle against an Army leadership that insisted on keeping air power in a subordinate role, the air enthusiasts felt vindicated in their beliefs in efficacy of air power.

1

The wedding of the right weapon to the right delivery system—the atomic bomb to the B-29 bomber—made air power a potentially decisive weapon in war.

Those Army Air Forces officers who had longed for independence had propagated the idea that the strategic bombing of Japanese industrial centers and cities had brought about the capitulation of Japan. What they had failed to recognize was that Japan was defeated before the atomic bombs fell on Hiroshima and Nagasaki. Years of war—culminating in the interdiction of the Japanese oil line from Southeast Asia and the naval blockade, along with the aerial campaign carried out by the B-29s of the Twentieth Air Force—had brought Japan to the verge of surrender by August 1945. The firebombing of Japanese cities and the two atomic bombs had provided the final pushes that forced acknowledgment of defeat by the Japanese leadership.[2] The role that air power had played in the defeat of Japan and Germany was instrumental to the creation of the Air Force as an independent branch of the armed services in 1947. To its enthusiasts, air power had finally proven that it was more than pie-in-the-sky fantasizing.

The Road to a Separate Service

In the two decades before the Second World War, the true believers among these air power enthusiasts had been inspired by the theories of the Italian prophet of air power Giulio Douhet and the crusader of American aviation William ("Billy") Mitchell. Like Douhet and Mitchell, these latter-day proponents of air power were convinced that when used independently air power could conclude most wars quickly. Aerial warfare, they argued, had eclipsed all other forms of struggle waged by armies and navies. Indeed, as they asserted, the idea that wars *must* be won by combat between land armies had become obsolete. In their eyes, the intransigent adherence of the old-line Army generals to this notion of combat was a last-ditch effort to stave off the inevitable rise of strategic air power. With the development of the atomic bomb and a powerful strategic bombing capability, the air power enthusiasts were sure that the air force could lay siege to and then destroy any potential enemy's war-making industries, thereby denying that nation its "very means of living" and causing its "complete capitulation."[3]

The journey to independence, completed in 1947, had not been an easy one. Before the Great War (World War I), only a few dreamers, like science-fiction writer H. G. Wells, believed that aircraft would ever play a decisive role in warfare. At the end of that war, Douhet, Mitchell, Basil Liddell Hart, Hugh Trenchard, and a few others adopted the dream. For most soldiers and military thinkers, air power was still at best a curiosity and at worst a threat to Army and Navy institutional prerogatives. While the concepts of air power were a source of promise to those disposed to believe in them, in the end Germany and its armed forces had collapsed from exhaustion.[4]

In the aftermath of the First World War, Trenchard, Douhet, and Mitchell were among those offering alternatives to the bloodletting in the trenches. Douhet, in his 1921 book, *The Command of the Air*, proposed that aerial operations conducted autonomously behind an enemy nation's lines could cause its will to collapse due to the destruction wreaked on the "heartland." Theoretically, when national will collapsed, the army in the field would soon give up. Mitchell Americanized Douhet in two very important ways.

First, Mitchell's concepts of air power were more tactical than strategic. Certainly he believed in bombing the "vital centers"— the factories in the heartland of the enemy nation. However, the fabric-covered, wood-framed airplanes of the 1920s hardly inspired confidence for rooting out major industrial cities. Unless those cities happened to be Windsor, Ontario, or Tijuana, Mexico, US planes were not going to get there. On the other hand, if the enemy were to sail a fleet into range of land-based bombers, even the flimsy airplanes of that era could wreak havoc on the ships and at a fraction of the cost of the Navy. When Mitchell's planes sank four captured German warships off the Virginia capes in 1921 and then carried out successful attacks on the obsolete US battleships

3

Alabama, *Virginia*, and *New Jersey*, he proved his point—
tactically. Like Douhet and, in subsequent years, the men who
built the separate United States Air Force, Mitchell believed in the
efficacy of the offensive. He certainly endorsed Douhet's doctrine
of bombing the industrial centers. Mitchell wrote: "War is the
attempt of one nation to impress its will on another. . . . The attempt
of one combatant . . . to so control the vital centers of the other that
it will be powerless to defend itself."[5] He sounded this theme more
often during the period after his court-martial and resignation than
while on active duty. He refined Douhet's concept of air power to
encompass elements other than bombing vital centers.

Second, unlike Douhet, Mitchell believed a modern air force
would include ground attack and fighter planes as well as "battle
planes" capable of fighting their way through enemy defenses to
the vital centers.[6] He envisioned bombers and pursuit planes
striking targets at a distance something like 25,000 yards in front
of the army to destroy the enemy's "means of supply." Mitchell
also advocated hitting airfields and air defense headquarters to help
win "command of the air" so that supply dumps, lines of
communications, and reserve forces could be attacked without
interference from opposing aircraft.[7]

Mitchell's court-martial and conviction weighed heavily upon
his fellow air power enthusiasts, restraining their rhetoric if not
their commitment to the prophetic concepts of strategic
bombardment and, ultimately, an independent air force. The two
concepts were, in their minds, related. Those officers at the Army
Air Corps Tactical School who advocated strategic bombardment
overshadowed those who thought and wrote about air power in
support of ground forces and about pursuit aviation. To the air
power purists, ground support aviation legitimized the Army's
institutional claim that the purpose of airplanes was to support the
infantry. If pursuit advocates were correct in their theory that
pursuit planes could engage and destroy bombers, then the
argument for an independent air force might be undermined.
Hence, air power enthusiasts believed as an essential article of faith

that the bomber could always get through to destroy the vital centers.

The Army as an institution continued to maintain that the purpose of the Air Corps was to support ground forces. That position disputed the contention of air power enthusiasts that air power could, by itself, win wars. During the 1930s, when military budgets were lean and aircraft increased in both sophistication and cost, the proponents of strategic bombing claimed that placing expensive aircraft, which were procured in fewer numbers, in jeopardy by flying them low in support of ground troops was foolish. How much better it would be to go directly to the vital centers to end the conflict with a minimum of bloodshed and expense.

Moreover, rapid advances in aeronautical technology in the thirties favored the development of bombers rather than pursuit aircraft. Multiengine aircraft were faster and could fly higher than single-engine planes. In 1935 the Martin B-10 twin-engine monoplane bomber had a top speed of just over 200 miles an hour. Most pursuit planes were slower. The Boeing P-26—a single-engine, all metal monoplane fighter—was barely as fast as a B-10. For a pursuit plane to intercept and destroy a bomber, the fighter had to find the bomber, overtake it, and then get into position for a kill. Further complicating the problem, pursuit planes were lightly armed, usually carrying only a pair of 30-caliber machine guns. Even if a pursuit plane found and caught up with a bomber, it might not be able to shoot it down. All things considered, bomber advocates had good reason to boast that "the bomber will always get through."

In the 1930s American air enthusiasts could point to Douhet's doctrine, the pace of technological change, and economic circumstance as favoring their concept of what an air force should be—an independent service built around aircraft that could fly to the enemy's heartland to lay waste the vital centers. In 1934 the Army Air Corps submitted a requirement for a bomber that could fly more than a thousand miles hauling a 2,000-pound bomb load at a speed of 200 miles an hour. The following year the Boeing

Aircraft Corporation produced the prototype, four-engine model 299. It flew the 2,100 miles from Seattle to Wright Field in Dayton, Ohio, at a speed of 252 miles an hour. In 1936 the Army ordered 13 of these planes, designated as the B-17.[8]

Doctrine and technology seemed to have come together in 1936. But was this really the case? Arguments to procure the B-17 had been couched in defensive rather than offensive terms. As good as it was, the B-17 did not have the range to fly to the heartland of any country other than Mexico, Canada, or Cuba—each of which was more or less friendly and had little in the way of vital centers. Additionally, the isolationist climate in public opinion did not favor building an air force that could devastate foreign cities. The B-17, therefore, was advertised as a means for providing a relatively inexpensive way to defend America's shores from enemy fleets and to protect the Panama Canal.

Within a few years, however, B-17s were bombing Nazi-occupied Europe and Germany. The results of strategic bombing in the Second World War seemed to vindicate all the passionate claims of the air power enthusiasts. The combined bomber offensive had the Royal Air Force bombing German cities at night and the US Army Air Forces bombing industries by day. The "Big Week" campaign, conducted at the end of February 1944, and the bombing of Berlin in February and March more than decimated the Luftwaffe by blasting aircraft industries and by shooting down Messerschmitts and Focke-Wulfs in aerial combat. The bombing of German petroleum manufacturing centers cut oil production substantially, forcing the Luftwaffe to curtail training, which, in turn, degraded the quality of pilots who challenged the American and British aircrews toward the end of the war. Bombing contributed substantially to attaining air superiority, which facilitated the Normandy invasion in June 1944.

None could deny that air power had done more than its part but it was just that, a part of the war effort. The fact remained that the Red Army offensive from the east coupled with the British and American ground offensives from the west determined the fate of the Third Reich. Bombing had not exactly realized the promise prophesied by Douhet and Mitchell. German will had not broken under the weight of Allied bombs. While bombing the cities to "de-house" the German population probably did hurt morale, the Nazis had ways to coerce acceptable behavior, meaning that lowered morale did not significantly change the way workers performed.[9]

In the Pacific theater, land, sea, and air forces appeared to share more equitably in the credit for defeating Japan. Gen Henry H. Arnold created the Twentieth Air Force to give air operators a more equal relationship with naval and ground operators. The Twentieth Air Force answered only to the Joint Chiefs of Staff through General Arnold, going over the heads of Adm Chester Nimitz, Gen Douglas MacArthur, and Gen Joseph Stilwell. The strategic bombing survey, commissioned by President Franklin Roosevelt in 1944, concluded that Allied air power had been instrumental in ruining the German war economy and "in all probability" could have ended the war with Japan by the end of 1945 even if atomic bombs had not been dropped and no invasion had been contemplated. At the end of the war, the Twentieth Air Force served as the model for the new Strategic Air Command (SAC), which was placed under the Joint Chiefs of Staff as an equal with theater commanders.[10]

The Atomic Bomb and the New Air Force

The strategic implications of the atomic bomb coincided with the self-perception developing within the soon-to-be-independent Air Force that a well-planned and well-executed air offensive would decide the outcome of future wars. Strategic bombing campaigns, enhanced by the dropping of the atomic bombs, had forced a quick and conclusive end to the conflict and, thereby, had demonstrated the salience of strategic bombing.[11] The atomic bomb, its B-29 delivery system, and the independent Air Force came together during a period favorable to the growth of an institution that offered a relatively inexpensive alternative to mass mobilization during a major war, even if that alternative was to obliterate the enemy's military-industrial complex with an "air atomic" attack.

Atomic weapons fitted very well into the evolving air power doctrine focused as it was on fighting a war with the Soviet Union. Certainly the USSR did its part to sustain the spirit that drove the strategic orientation of the Air Force. The civil war in Greece, the blockade of Berlin, the Communist coup in Czechoslovakia, the victory of Communist forces in China, and the Korean War reinforced and legitimized the need for a Strategic Air Command. Indeed, in the late 1940s, the United States atomic capability seemed to be all that constrained the Soviet juggernaut. Lt Col Frank R. Pancake, in an article in the *Air University Quarterly Review* in 1948, wrote, "If we are to have peace in our time it will have to be a Pax Americana. There has been further awakening to the fact that the instrument of Pax Americana must be Air Power."[12] As the Iron Curtain descended upon Europe and the cold war became a reality, the Soviet Union, and later Red China, became, in the minds of the American military and many political leaders, "outside instigators" capable of fostering virtually any and every form of international mischief.[13]

At the same time that the Soviet threat was burgeoning, the Air Force was faced with drastic cuts in its budget and fighting strength. Less than two years after the conclusion of the Second World War, at about the time it gained its independence, the Air Force had been reduced from 2.2 million people to 303,000 officers and enlisted personnel, including just over 24,000 aircrew members.[14] Hence, the new and much smaller Air Force had to emphasize those areas that not only provided the kind of defense the nation needed but also served the service's institutional ends.

Between the end of World War II and the outbreak of hostilities in Korea, the Strategic Air Command, such as it was, dominated the Air Force. In 1946 Gen Carl A. Spaatz, the Army Air Forces' commanding general, defined his branch's primary mission as that of a long-range striking power capable of destroying any enemy's industrial and war-making capacity. He "gave first priority to 'the backbone of our Air Force—the long-range bomber groups and their protective long-range fighter groups organized in our Strategic Air Force.'"[15] In the 48-wing Air Force of the late 1940s, the tactical air forces, those units used to support the Army, nearly disappeared as they were reduced to small cadres and subordinated to the Continental Air Command (ConAC).[16] The lines between tactical and strategic missions seemed to blur, with the predominant direction of that blur being into the strategic spectrum. In the winter of 1950, in an article entitled "Air Power Indivisible," Col Dale O. Smith and Maj Gen John DeForest Barker stated that the tactical mission was supplemental to the strategic mission and that "interdiction—the squeezing off of communication arteries to the battle zones—is merely a phase of the strategic bombing mission."[17] Furthermore, strategic bombing constituted the "interdiction of *all* enemy strength" and "the interdiction mission of tactical aviation is essentially a part of the long range mission of strategic employment."[18]

Smith and Barker agreed with Douhet, who had written, "Viewed in its true light, aerial warfare admits no defense, only offense."[19] In comparison with the bombers, the fighters had little or no worth in the immediate postwar Air Force. Smith even questioned whether jets would be as useful for intercepting bombers as the propeller planes of the Second World War. He concluded, "In fact, it is even likely that the jet will be less effective."[20] Smith reasoned that the speed differential between jets and the piston-engine bombers of the late forties would offer jets less time to bring their guns to bear and, therefore, result in fewer hits. Additionally, jets consumed fuel at a higher rate than propeller-driven fighters and would have less time to locate and dispatch their prey.[21] Even though ConAC had absorbed the missions, planes, and men of the Tactical Air Command (TAC), ConAC had far less support than SAC and, therefore, languished in the backwaters of the newly separate Air Force.

Air power enthusiasts, however, failed to recognize that the strategic striking power of SAC immediately after the war was relatively puny. Only limited numbers of atomic bombs were available from 1945 to 1950. In 1947, just as the cold war was getting under way, SAC had only 27 "silverplate" B-29s (bombers specially modified to carry the atomic bomb). Two developments, however, ensured that things were going to get better.[22]

First, the Air Force finally began the building and purchase of a true long-range strategic bomber. In the postwar Air Force, the Convair B-36 was to be the airplane that enforced the efficacy of strategic bombing by making it possible to fly to the enemy's heartland to destroy vital centers. The B-36 had been conceived in 1940 before the United States entered the Second World War. At that time the possibility that England would fall to the forces of Nazi Germany had seemed quite real. The B-36 had been designed to fly from the United States to Germany, drop a hefty bomb load, and return. It was to have six pusher engines and enough defensive

B-29s. The Air Force had only a handful of B-29s capable of delivering atomic bombs during the late 1940s and early 1950s. These medium-range bombers would have needed overseas bases to reach targets in the Soviet Union.

armament to shoot its way through German defenses, at least theoretically. As it turned out, England did not fall to the Germans, but the B-36 was developed anyway and began entering the SAC inventory in 1948.

Second, on 16 October 1948 General LeMay, a strong believer in strategic bombing, took command of SAC. His stated conviction was that "'the fundamental goal of the Air Force should be the creation of a strategic atomic striking force capable of attacking any target in Eurasia from bases in the United States and returning to the points of take-off.'"[23] The B-36, although relatively slow, could do that. However, the low speed and high price of the B-36 made it vulnerable to criticisms that were a part of the heated competition for limited dollars in the defense budget. Although the addition of twin jet pods beneath each wing boosted the top speed of the B-36 to close to 400 miles an hour at higher altitudes, the criticism, particularly from the Navy, did not slacken.

The B-36 upset the relationship between the Air Force and the Navy that had allowed each service to perpetuate its traditional missions even at the dawn of the time of atomic plenty. Atom bombs were big and quite heavy and only large aircraft could lift them. The normal aircraft carrier could not accommodate an airplane large enough to carry the atomic bomb. Therefore, the Navy needed to build larger aircraft carriers while developing planes, including a seaplane bomber, that could haul atomic bombs. The Navy planned to build the USS *United States*—an 80,000-ton carrier that was central to the Navy's plan for staying competitive with the Air Force in the nuclear mission. Additionally, the B-36 threatened another of the Navy's missions: securing and holding overseas bases from which bombers could fly. The B-36 made such bases unnecessary, which meant fewer ships for the Navy, further undermining its institutional integrity, threatening its future, limiting promotion opportunities, and menacing its share of the budget.

On 23 April 1949 Secretary of Defense Louis Johnson, a former assistant secretary of war for air, reacting to pressures to cut defense spending while maintaining support for the Air Force,

Gen Curtis E. LeMay. As commander in chief, General LeMay shaped the
Strategic Air Command around the doctrine of strategic bombing.

cancelled the USS *United States* five days after its keel was laid.[24] This action inspired the "revolt of the admirals," which focused criticism on the B-36 and the way the Air Force procured the plane. The B-36 controversy came when Johnson was trying to form the sprawling Defense Department into an agency with a semblance of unity. On 14 April, hoping to keep the various services from airing their grievances in public, he issued Consolidation Directive 1, stating that all information emanating from the Pentagon would be reviewed by censors not only for security but also for policy and propriety.[25]

The Air Force claimed that the B-36, particularly when modified with the addition of jet pods, could fly higher than the operational interceptors of the day. The Navy held that its F2H Banshee jets and the Soviet Union's new MiG-15s could intercept the bombers. The issue was never really resolved, however. In

B-36. During the late 1940s, the Consolidated-Vultee B-36 was at the center of squabbles between the Air Force and Navy. The B-36 had a long enough range that it could strike targets in the Soviet Union from bases in the United States. This capability threatened the Navy's traditional role of projecting power overseas.

March 1949 the Air Force's Senior Officers Board, realizing that the B-36 eventually would become obsolete, moved toward buying a follow-on bomber, Boeing's B-52.[26]

While moving toward purchase of even more capable bombers for the future, the Air Force mounted a counterattack to the Navy's efforts to discredit not only the B-36 but, by extension, strategic bombing. The Air Force Association took the point in the counterattack, publishing articles and editorials critical of the Navy and supportive of the B-36. James H. Straubel, an editor of *Air Force Magazine*, the publication of the Air Force Association, wrote that the Navy had become irrelevant because "Russia [had] no Navy" and, being self-sufficient in resources, was not susceptible to a naval blockade. Furthermore, carrier planes were short-range aircraft that could not reach targets deep inside the Soviet Union even if they could carry atomic bombs. Only long-range, land-based bombers, he claimed, could strike at the Soviet heartland: "Therefore, the need for a powerful U.S. surface Navy [could not] be defended."[27]

The next month, in March 1949, just as the Air Force announced that the B-36s would be modified with the addition of jet pods, *Air Force Magazine* published an article praising the bomber entitled, "Exposing the Milk Wagon," and featuring a photograph of a carrier task force in the Gulf of Alaska around a quote from Vice Adm Gerald Bogan, "I don't know how a B-29 could have seen us, much less knocked us out."[28] After the addition of four jet engines increased the performance of the B-36, the Navy switched its attack from operational capabilities of the bomber to personalities, criticizing the procurement policies and intimating impropriety on the part of Secretary of the Air Force W. Stuart Symington.

The B-36 controversy seemed to set a precedent for the way the Air Force would respond to controversy in the future.[29] Consolidation Directive 1 seems to have initiated what became a suffocating policy of censorship that, over the years, was practiced more enthusiastically by the Air Force than by the other services. In a larger sense, the Air Force, in future controversies, often followed an approach similar to the one established for dealing with the B-36 flap; namely, hunkering down to claim that any problems that might exist were fixed yesterday while the Air Force Association and the public affairs office mounted the counterattack through articles in *Air Force Magazine.*

Despite vindication over the B-36, all did not go well for the nation's newest service in its budget battles. A 1949 budget restriction cut the planned 70-group Air Force to one of 48 groups. Orders for airplanes placed in 1948 had to be rescinded. When the Air Force managed to recapture nearly $270 million in supplemental funds, LeMay was able to have the money applied to the purchase of additional B-36s. All he had to do was to appeal to the Senior Officers Board, which, in March 1949, granted an increase in aircraft complements for each B-36 and RB-36 group from 18 to 30.[30] SAC was indeed dominant.

Preludes to Vietnam

Then, on 25 June 1950, the North Korean People's Army attacked across the 38th parallel into South Korea. American vital interests were not readily apparent in Korea and reasons for fighting there lacked the cogency of the goals for which Americans had died in the Second World War. Korea was, from the American perspective, a limited war. For the Koreans, however, it was a total war fought on the one side to unify the country under a single Communist system and on the other side to maintain independence. For the United States, because the enemy was a small agricultural country that was not a microcosm of American society, the war had to be "limited." The Air Force, likewise, conceived of the war in limited terms because of the kinds of weapons it could and could not use and because of the types of targets it could or could not strike. The same dichotomy would mark the nation's and the Air Force's experiences in Vietnam a decade later.

Furthermore, as in Vietnam, America's reasons for committing its forces to Korea and the way in which these forces were used were determined by factors that had little to do with actual events or issues at stake in the war at hand. Secretary of the Air Force Thomas K. Finletter called Korea a "very special situation" that, though peripheral to America's global strategy, was, nonetheless, a test of national will and determination.[31]

During the summer of 1950 American air power was vital to the survival of the retreating South Korean and American forces. Air cover by F-51 Mustang fighters of World War II vintage and by newer F-80 jets kept the North Korean air force away from the beleaguered South Koreans and Americans. Meanwhile, attacks on the increasingly lengthening North Korean supply lines weakened their offensive thrust. Lt Gen James M. Gavin of the Army later testified that during the first weeks of the Korean War, air power seemed so effective that there were some who believed the war might end before United Nations (UN) forces could intervene.[32]

In the first stages of the war, air interdiction proved somewhat more effective than close air support. The latter was problematic because the Air Force and the Army had not properly coordinated their activities in the postwar years. The problem was an outgrowth of the interservice rivalries that had only been agitated by the National Security Act of 1947 and the March 1948 "Functions Papers," more popularly known as the Key West agreement. The National Security Act attempted to integrate some missions of the three services. This action led to conflict among the services over their various roles. The Key West agreement was supposed to clarify each service's understanding of functions and responsibilities. The "Functions Papers" outlined three main Air Force responsibilities toward the Army:

> 1. To furnish close combat and logistical air support to the Army, to include airlift, support, and resupply of airborne operations, aerial photography, tactical reconnaissance, and interdiction of enemy land power and communications.

2. To provide air transport for the Armed Forces except as otherwise assigned.

3. To develop, in coordination with the other Services, doctrines, procedures, and equipment employed by Air Force forces in airborne operations.[33]

The proverbial stone in the shoe was one sentence that appeared in the Army portion of both documents, section 205 (E) of the National Security Act of 1947, and section IV of the "Functions Papers." That statement read as follows: "The United States Army includes land combat and service forces and *such aviation* and water transport as may be organic therein."[34]

The close air support problems were resolved by the necessity of combat effectiveness in the face of an immediate threat: the North Korean army. In the summer of 1950 interdiction worked better for several reasons. From 25 June through 17 September a classic setup for effective interdiction existed. The North Koreans were on the offensive, consuming supplies at an accelerated rate over ever lengthening lines of communications that, because of the nature of the terrain and the fair summer weather, were susceptible to attack. The role played by air power in the summer of 1950 became clearer when, after the landing at Inchon and the breakout of UN forces from Pusan, the North Korean armies crumbled.

As the United Nations forces crossed the 38th parallel and moved into North Korea, air power in the close air support role was vital to the success of the ground offensive advancing on the Yalu. In late September, Soviet-made MiG-15 fighters appeared in the skies over Korea. After Chinese troops were committed to the war in November, the number of MiGs increased dramatically as the Communists tried to keep American planes from bombing and strafing the advancing Chinese armies. The United States rushed its newest jet fighter, the F-86 Sabre to Korea to combat the MiG-15s.

Korea was the first war in which jets played a major role. During the course of the fighting, Gen Hoyt S. Vandenberg, Air Force chief of staff, lauded the performance of the jets, holding that "jets are superior for every conceivable job . . . including flying at

17

tree-top level to silence one machine gun." Vandenberg insisted that jets were proving more reliable because they were "easier to maintain in the field."[35] Furthermore, while flying 25 percent more sorties than propeller-driven Mustangs, only 21 F-80s had been lost to ground fire at the beginning of 1951 as against 50 F-51s.[36]

As the fighting developed in 1951 and 1952, UN forces used various tactical aircraft for ground support missions. Before the stalemate developed along the 38th parallel, the tactical situation had been relatively fluid. A system of coordinating air-ground support evolved that used forward air controllers in T-6 trainers and ground teams working as air guides to direct fighters and fighter-bombers. Of all the air power missions, close air support probably proved to be the most crucial throughout the Korean War. Strategic bombing was limited by the number of appropriate targets. Still, SAC's B-29s flying from Okinawa destroyed most of what industry there was in North Korea. B-29s were also used against railway marshalling yards and in carpet bombing attacks whenever Chinese forces concentrated. Additionally, B-29s kept Korean airfields that might have been used by the Chinese in a state of constant disrepair.[37]

In the postwar analysis of air power in Korea, interdiction became the most controversial of missions. What would later be termed battlefield air interdiction worked quite well, particularly when North Korean forces were chasing the South Korean and American troops down the peninsula. In the campaign against lines of communications, the Air Force claimed to have destroyed 15,000 railcars, 1,000 locomotives, and many thousands of trucks.[38] Indeed, the various interdiction campaigns slowed down the movement of supplies, but to what degree and to what end is a matter of debate.

In Korea, as in Vietnam over a decade later, the United States military assumed that because the US Army needed a well-defined and smoothly functioning supply line, the North Korean and Chinese armies would too. As it turned out, they were not as dependent on their logistical base as the Americans and their allies. A Chinese division, for instance, could fight on 50 tons of supplies a day, or about 25 truckloads. Additionally, the Koreans and the Chinese were very clever in sustaining supply lines despite the bombing. They developed a diversified supply network that proved difficult to define, and they were able to move supplies in bad weather and at night with impunity.[39] By concentrating their antiaircraft guns along railroads, near bridges, and at vital transshipment points, the Communists exacted a high price in planes destroyed and damaged.[40]

Air-to-air action was intense and, for the Air Force, provided a focal point of postwar analysis. F-86 Sabre jets had a kill ratio of nearly 15 to 1 against the MiGs, although a long-standing rumor within the Air Force is that many of those MiGs were shot down when they were low on fuel and in the landing pattern at airfields in Manchuria. Still, the figures piled up. In the Air Force of the post-Korean War era, this mystique of the air-to-air victories cast a spell on the younger pilots who later fought in Vietnam. Air-to-air action there would be rare, but the impulse to seek it and to judge oneself and one's colleagues by eagerness for and skill in aerial combat persisted.

As they would after losing in Vietnam, many Air Force officers, particularly the generals, complained that in Korea air power was not used properly. If only given its full rein, many cried, the war could have been won quickly and decisively. Writing in the *Air University Quarterly Review*, Col Dale O. Smith (a regular contributor over the years) and Maj Gen John DeF. Barker lamented that the Air Force should have been allowed to strike at the enemy across arbitrary boundaries (the Chinese border) and that the Chinese were able to mount their forces for attacks into Korea with impunity because targets in China were off-limits.[41] Seven years after the Korean armistice, Gen Frederic H. Smith, Jr., bemoaned the wasted effort in attempting to destroy the Yalu River bridges with conventional bombing. "Precisely what expenditure of nuclear bombs would have equaled the destructive effect of the high explosives (HE) dropped upon the Yalu River bridges could be readily computed . . . but it becomes apparent . . . that with the nuclear weapons the total effort . . . could have been very greatly reduced." [42]

General Smith's article reflected an attitude that became dominant among Air Force officers after the Korean War, namely that warfare is nothing more than an exercise in weapons employment and targeting and atomic bombs were merely another weapon of choice. The political implications of using atomic bombs to destroy bridges between North Korea and the People's Republic of China did not enter into Smith's calculations. In his mind the issue was merely what bomb was right for the target. However, sound strategic, political, and tactical reasons argued against using nuclear weapons in Korea. First, the Joint Chiefs of Staff, along with just about everyone else in Washington, were convinced that the attack in Korea was a diversion preceding Soviet aggression elsewhere. If that were the case, the limited number of atomic bombs in the stockpile had to be conserved for the coming war with the Soviets. Second, North Korea contained few targets for which atomic weapons would have been appropriate. Third, based on analysis of bombs dropped on Hiroshima and Nagasaki, many believed that steel and concrete bridges were relatively invulnerable to atomic strike. A girder bridge less than a hundred yards from ground zero in Nagasaki survived the explosion with little more than superficial damage, leading many to think that atomic bombs had little effect on such structures.[43] General Smith indicated little understanding of either immediate and tactical or long-range and strategic effects of fallout when he suggested that "for airburst, a minimum distance of 4500 feet separation of friendly troops from the perimeter of weapon effects is advisable."[44] In the same article, as General Smith turned his attention from the war in Korea to a possible scenario in Indochina, he suggested that 16 medium-yield atomic or nuclear weapons could close down a jungle infiltration system 67 nautical miles in length.[45] No mention was made of what effect fallout from atomic blasts in either Korea or Southeast Asia might have on the people of Japan or the Philippines.

General Smith's remarks concerning the use of nuclear weapons indicate that he had not paid adequate attention to what might have been learned from the Korean War. He was not alone among Air Force generals in that failing. The official Air Force policy that cast the Korean War as an anomaly was more than somewhat to blame. For example, in 1955 Thomas Finletter, former secretary of the Air Force, wrote, "The Korean War was a special case, and airpower can learn little from there about its future role in United States foreign policy."[46] According to the report issued by the Far East Air Forces, Korea was "unlike wars in the past and was not necessarily typical of the future."[47]

If "nuke 'em" was the essence of what the Air Force thought before and after Korea, it is probably a good thing that the war prompted the question of whether the United States ought to fight in limited wars at all. Indeed, the overwhelming opinion after Korea was that such wars could and should be avoided. Fighting a limited war against Soviet or Chinese surrogates was "dancing to Moscow and Peking's tune," and the way to prevent such wars was to maintain political and military superiority over those two potential instigators.[48] This attitude was based on a weltanschauung that assumed the Soviets and the Chinese were behind all the world's problems. That belief was a basic tenet of cold war thinking and was a key factor in determining the way American policymakers approached international problems and crises.

As the Korean War was ending, the nation was faced with another crisis: How to prevent a Communist takeover of Southeast Asia. In French Indochina, Ho Chi Minh's Vietminh was on the verge of victory over the French colonial forces. The siege at Dien Bien Phu in the spring of 1954 took place at the same time that the authors of the "New Look" were putting the finishing strokes on the defense strategy that would dominate the next decade and that, in large part, would determine how the Air Force approached its own combat experience in Vietnam. As the French situation at Dien Bien Phu deteriorated, the Pentagon and the White House discussed the degree and nature of possible American intervention. The Joint Chiefs, with the exception of Adm Arthur W. Radford, the chairman, were united in their lack of enthusiasm for direct American involvement.[49]

The Air Force was particularly reluctant to have ground combat units deployed to a place where only limited air support might be needed.[50] In January 1954 President Dwight Eisenhower established an ad hoc committee consisting of Walter Bedell Smith, Allen Dulles (the director of the Central Intelligence Agency—CIA), Col Edward G. Lansdale (the Air Force's expert on unconventional warfare), and the Joint Chiefs of Staff to study the kinds of support the United States might offer the French. The consensus was that whatever was done ought to be at a very low level of effort. The recommendation was to send 200 Air Force technicians, augment the Civil Air Transport (the Taiwan-based CIA subsidiary air line) with a few planes, and dispatch some additional B-26s to raise the total number available to the French to 25.[51]

Admiral Radford's view of communism was that of the classic cold warrior—monolithic. Since local issues were only tangential to the struggle, reaction to situations like the one at Dien Bien Phu called for something beyond reinforcement of friendly forces caught in a dangerous predicament. What was needed was "deterrent power of strong counteroffensive forces . . . for devastating counter blows deep into enemy territory."[52]

Meanwhile, Brig Gen Joseph D. Caldara and a team of staffers from the Far East Air Forces, working from Saigon, planned a 98-plane, B-29 carpet-bombing mission targeted against Vietminh troop encampments and supposed concentrations around Dien Bien Phu.[53] After a more detailed briefing from French intelligence and a flight over the besieged garrison, Caldera came to the conclusion "that there were 'no true B-29 targets'" in the vicinity. He then suggested using B-29s to "put the required tonnage on the roads and supply areas" leading up to the entrenched Communist positions that surrounded the French.[54]

In 1954, as would be the case in 1964, the alternative to sending American ground troops to Indochina was to use air power. The possible use of atomic weapons, as a part of Operation Vulture, did not evolve beyond preliminary talks. Vulture, as proposed by Admiral Radford to Gen Paul Ely, the French chief of staff, would have had 60 B-29s and 150 carrier aircraft in direct support of the French garrison.[55] The way in which planners thought of using air power was prosaic at its conventional best and scary at its atomic worst. Bernard Fall was probably correct in asserting that a few small atomic explosions might have saved the garrison at Dien Bien Phu but, in the long run, would not have changed the outcome of the French Indochina War.[56] While planning for any American intervention focused on air power, it did not go beyond the conceptual stage. Eisenhower, like Harry S. Truman in Korea and Lyndon Johnson in Vietnam 10 years later, was forced to adopt a restrained policy by considerations that lay outside Indochina, and which had more to do with domestic and international factors.[57]

The war in Indochina could have provided many lessons. The French had decided that the massive use of air power, even if they had possessed the means to employ it, would have been irrelevant. The Vietminh had learned to cope with French air power. Through exploitation of natural cover, the Vietminh had become adept at dispersal and camouflage, enabling them to travel along roads, pathways, and waterways in comparative safety.[58] As it was, air power had been limited to direct and indirect support of ground action. Additionally, the French had employed aircraft that were only marginally useful, including a preponderance of single-seat fighters. Certainly more transports and a larger number of twin-engine, light to medium bombers would have been more useful but probably not decisive.[59]

The *Air University Quarterly Review* staff studied the French Indochina War in light of the Korean conflict. According to the *Review* staff, air power was not, in fact could not have been, used effectively in the kind of conflict that developed in Indochina. The best use of air power was in peripheral roles like transport, medical evacuation, and psychological warfare. Air power's contributions to the French cause had been minimal. "They . . . bombed highways and supply dumps. But the highways [were] repaired quickly, and most of the supply dumps [were] too small to cause serious loss to the Communists." [60] The report concluded that the French use of air power in the terrain and against the kind of forces fielded by the Vietminh had been a failure indicative of "the difficulty which confronts an enlarged air campaign *confined to Indo-China and to conventional weapons*" (emphasis added).[61]

The implication was that if atomic or nuclear weapons had been used beyond Indochina to strike at the cause of the problem in China, the war might have turned out differently. That theme was pursued in an April 1954 edition of *Air Force Magazine* in an article "Some Reflections on the 'New Look,'" which asked, "What would happen if we bombed Chinese airfields and supply dumps near the Indochina border to halt Ho Chi Minh's aggression?" [62] That logic assumed that the Vietminh movement had its origins with an outside instigator, in this case China, without whose support it could not survive. The suggested bombing of airfields was a response to an enemy perceived as being a mirror image of the United States or USSR—as though the Vietminh were dependent on airfields as a part of their logistical system. Out of the cold war mind-set emerged an enemy with which the Air Force was comfortable—one using airfields and possessing targets suitable for air atomic attack: petroleum refineries, heavy industries, and a sophisticated rail and highway system. The reality, however, had been far different.

The "New Look" and the Air Force

The Korean War had ended and its lessons and the lessons that might have been learned from the French Indochina War were deemed irrelevant or, worse, were misunderstood. The French had little understood the enemy they had faced, and, at that time, the US Air Force had ignored the Vietminh altogether. The Air Force looked to its future unhampered by its immediate past. In fact, Korea had not been bad for the Air Force. During the war its size increased from 43 wings and 400,000 officers and enlisted members to 106 authorized wings, 93 of which were operational, and nearly a million individuals.[63]

It was in the 1950s, probably more than in any other period of its existence, that the Air Force had set itself up to lose the war in Vietnam. The confluence of circumstances that fostered the setup was not simply the result of shortsightedness in foreign or defense policy, nor was it completely a result of individuals or institutions looking toward their own self-interests. In fact, the way the nation and the Air Force reacted to the Korean War and the course they pursued in the 1950s made good sense. How the Air Force approached the war in Vietnam a decade and a half later was determined by the Air Force that evolved after the Korean War.

The New Look defense policy that emerged early in the Eisenhower administration generally favored the Air Force at the expense of the other services. The United States, according to the tenets of the New Look, would provide a nuclear umbrella in defense of the free world. The Eisenhower administration envisaged military operations short of a "nukefest" and employed such uses of force several times in the 1950s to protect America's allies and friends—friend being defined as anyone opposed to communism—in places and situations as diverse as Lebanon and the Formosa Strait. Another aspect of the New Look policy was that the United States, at least theoretically, was supposed to prepare smaller friendly nations to fight their own local wars.[64] This approach made sense. After all, the fighting in Korea had been costly—34,000 Americans killed and 105,000 wounded.[65] The American people and their government blamed the Soviet Union and the People's Republic of China as the outside instigators of the Korean conflict and the war in Indochina.

According to the way cold warriors looked at the world, the Soviets were being true to form when on 20 August 1953, not even a month after the armistice in Korea was concluded, the Kremlin announced that the USSR had detonated a hydrogen bomb successfully. The National Security Council (NSC) issued NSC-162, which stated that atomic striking power should "provide the nation's first line of defense and that the Joint Chiefs" ought to plan to use atomic weapons whenever and wherever necessary.[66] When the anticipated thrust elsewhere did not materialize following the outbreak of the Korean War, Pentagon analysts decided that the Soviet military-industrial complex was still recovering from the Second World War.

At the same time, they feared that the Soviets, rather than embarking on a costly rearmament program, might use their current armaments—most of which had been manufactured during World War II and were nearing obsolescence—before they became useless. If the Soviets opted to use their inventory, the analysts reasoned, war would occur within two years—1955 being the "year of maximum danger." Preparing for 1955 was going to be expensive. In April 1953 the Eisenhower administration decided that rather than prepare for war at a specific time, American policy would be "to get . . . ready and stay ready."[67] In January 1954, in a speech before the Council on Foreign Relations, Secretary of State John Foster Dulles articulated the administration's evolving policy. America would enforce collective security by placing "more reliance on deterrent power and less dependence on local defensive power." The way America would respond to any future aggression would be to do so "vigorously at places and with means of its own choosing."[68]

The Air Force and the policy of massive retaliation epitomized the proverbial "marriage made in heaven." Former Air Force secretary Finletter, writing in 1954, set the tone:

> Under this concept all targets from the enemy front lines through his communication and supply lines, his airfields and storage, back to and including the sources of production and government direction would be the objective of Atomic-Air's attack. In the time of atomic plenty there will be enough bombs to do all this.[69]

The delivery system, for the most part, would belong to the Air Force. Furthermore, Air Force doctrine, adhered to by air power enthusiasts since the days of Billy Mitchell, was amenable to massive retaliation. It was assumed in the decade after 1954 that if the United States went to war it would do so as it had in World War II, seeking total victory through a grand crusade. The Air

Force could replay 1944 and 1945 by attacking the industrial, economic, and social foundations of the potential enemy.

The potential enemy was right for the time of atomic plenty. The Soviet Union was an industrialized nation. It was in the minds of cold warriors, a behemoth motivated by an "evil" world view that specified both the inevitability of war between capitalist and Communist systems and the certainty of the outcome. In the 1950s emotions about the Soviet Union showed no shades of coloration. Since 1941 the United States had emerged from isolation to become the leader of the free world; it would not be surprised by a Pearl Harbor–like atomic attack.

As the obsession with the threat posed by the Soviet Union increased so did the absolute nature of the response. Under the aegis of massive retaliation, forces could be concentrated and focused on a definable objective: the war-making capability of an industrialized nation. This doctrine made it easy to take and retain the initiative in atomic air warfare. Additionally, a doctrine constructed around the assumption that instant retaliation would be "by means and at places of its own choosing" implied the rejection of any limits on warfare.[70] If war came, it would be nuclear war, "eyeball-to-eyeball and toe-to-toe with the Rooskies," as Maj King Kong, the demented B-52 pilot in the satirical novel *Dr. Strangelove* put it.

As the decade progressed and intelligence-gathering capabilities improved to the point that Soviet forces could be located and their magnitude assessed with greater accuracy, the Air Force could have turned away from doctrines based on Douhet and Mitchell to focus on a more Clausewitzian strategy aimed at enemy forces. While the Air Force did not reject this approach entirely, SAC's leadership was not enthusiastic about it. According to SAC, "retardation" of enemy forces would occur simultaneously with the attack on industrial centers. Since vital military targets were located near major industrial centers (cities), the use of larger yield nuclear weapons would provide a "bonus effect" by destroying many targets in a single attack.[71]

Air Force doctrine—as articulated in the Air Force 1-series manuals, *United States Air Force Basic Doctrine*—changed very little from 1953 through 1964.[72] In the 1953 and 1954 editions the emphasis was on decisive action to destroy the enemy's war-making capacity. "The conclusive effects obtained by attacks on the heartland targets, which represent the greatest threats, require the priority commitment of air forces to this task."[73] Attacks on targets other than those associated with the heartland were called peripheral actions. According to AFM 1-2 (1953), peripheral and heartland targets were not mutually exclusive. If the heartland was destroyed, the reasoning went, the enemy's ability to conduct conventional operations at or near the front—peripheral actions—would also be impeded.[74]

Throughout the 1950s and into the 1960s, those who dreamed of rooting out the Soviet Union from Minsk to Khabarovsk with one glowing nuclear effort kept experiencing a recurring nightmare: limited war might rob the Air Force of its opportunity to demonstrate what could be done with unrestrained air power. The theory of nuclear deterrence had grown out of the perception of the colossal nature of the Soviet threat, leading the Air Force to argue that the only really effective strategy for dealing with the Soviets was to make them understand that the destruction of their homeland would be the risk they would run if they encouraged, supported, or initiated limited conflicts.

Maxwell D. Taylor, after retiring as Army chief of staff in frustration over the role of massive retaliation in national strategy, wrote *The Uncertain Trumpet*. In this critique of massive retaliation, General Taylor held that the very approach to warfare adopted by the United States increased the possibility of conflict at the lower end of the spectrum because the United States lacked a conventional capability and, therefore, would be overly cautious about risking nuclear war over matters of little importance.[75] Henry A. Kissinger, in *Nuclear Weapons and Foreign Policy,* wrote, "The prerequisite of victory in a limited war is to determine under what circumstances one side might be willing to run greater risks for winning than its opponent will accept to avoid losing."[76] By graduated actions the enemy could design his provocations so that they would not seem to be worth the risk of total war, the only kind of war the doctrine of massive retaliation could accommodate.

The whole concept of limited war presented the military, especially the Air Force, with difficulties. In a great nuclear conflict, designated targets would be overwhelmed with bombs and warheads. There would be very little ambiguity in launching the entire force in salvos. Political objectives probably would be reduced to one: the total surrender of the enemy or whatever was left of the enemy. The strategy's elegance was its simplicity. The relationship between political objectives and targeting requirements involved purely military considerations. The distinguishing feature of limited warfare, however, was that political considerations were preeminent. In limited warfare, where purely military solutions were inappropriate, strategy entailed more than deciding on what weapon to put against which target.

The defense intellectuals, Bernard Brodie and Henry Kissinger in particular, warned of the incongruities between a doctrine of massive retaliation and fighting a limited war. Additionally, indications abounded that subversion, aggression by proxy, and revolutions would be the normal state of affairs in the decades ahead. Even the world view that cast the Soviet Union and the People's Republic of China in the roles of instigators of insurrection and manipulators of localized aggression led to the conclusion that limited wars would happen with some regularity. Air Vice-Marshal Sir John C. Slessor of the Royal Air Force, in the May 1954 edition of *Air Force Magazine*, stated, "We can take it as a foregone conclusion that our opponents, having decided that it will be too costly to overwhelm us by direct assault, will take every opportunity to turn or undermine our defenses by other means." He warned of a difficult era of "termite warfare—subversion, infiltration, and the exploitation of rebellion." [77] According to Slessor, the proper role for atomic air power would be as a "big stick" to prevent limited wars from spreading or developing into larger conflicts.

Preparing to fight a series of wars in places as different and remote as the hills of Korea, the jungles of South America, the sands of the Middle East, or the jungles and rice paddies of Southeast Asia could be very expensive. The role of the Army and the Navy would have to be expanded and, presumably, their share of the budget increased, even if the overall budget stayed relatively small. Another question was, What kind of Air Force would be needed to fight a limited war? Certainly it would have to contain more fighters and light bombers. The Tactical Air Command would have to be enlarged, diverting funds from the purchase and maintenance of bombers and tankers for the Strategic Air Command. John F. Loosbrook, an editor of *Air Force Magazine*, in 1956 wrote, "The argument that local wars can best be won with conventional means (i.e., non-nuclear weapons and surface forces) is a convenient one for those services and individuals who even now are faced with ever shrinking roles and missions."[78] The Air Force, instead of changing its mission or modifying its force structure to accommodate limited wars, tried to fit limited warfare into its approach for fighting general wars. According to the rubric, if strategic deterrence prevented the Soviet Union and the People's Republic of China from starting a general war, it would also keep them from inciting situations that might expand into nuclear conflict. Strategic forces, then, were *all* that were needed to keep the lid on the world.

The Air Force position was that if the United States could fight and win the big war, it could always win any little war. Thus, a separate body of doctrine or specifically designed strategy for little wars was unnecessary. Even the weapons that would be used in a big war could be used in a lesser conflict. "Today's nuclear weapons," wrote Loosbrook, "coupled with our determination to use them if needed, can take the profit out of aggressive war, big or little." [79] Nuclear weapons were, for the Air Force, the paramount means for fighting wars and the possibility of their use in any conflict was not to be discounted.[80]

During the 1950s the Air Force accepted the idea that when it went to war it would use the maximum firepower available. As the

30

decade progressed, Air Force thinking shifted away from the eloquent arguments about strategic bombing that had marked the struggle for independence. As weapons and aircraft became more complex, thinking became increasingly technologically oriented. Strategy devolved into weaponeering—deciding which bomb should be used against which target. Nuclear weapons were a panacea for every form of warfare, even limited wars. The Greek civil war, the Korean War, and the Vietminh victory in Indochina might never have happened, at least according to Gen Thomas D. White, Air Force chief of staff, if "the U.S. had established belief in [its] determination to use nuclear strength."[81]

The Strategic Air Command, especially from 1948 through 1957 when General LeMay was its commander in chief, dominated the Air Force. In January 1957, LeMay suggested reorganizing all offensive elements of the Air Force into an air offensive command under a single commander. "'SAC and TAC are bedfellows,'" said LeMay, "'they must deter together.'"[82] In 1957, when the number of tactical fighter wings in the Air Force dropped from 55 to 45, the secretary of the Air Force suggested that the Army should develop and use surface-to-air missiles to defend its troops.[83] Keeping enemy planes off the backs of the Army slipped beyond the scope of Air Force missions.

The Air Defense Command (ADC) ranked below TAC in the SAC-dominated Air Force of the 1950s. The Air Force leadership assumed that since the bomber would always get through, the possibility of an effective air defense was remote; hence, air defense was somewhat heretical. Nuclear bombs made defense against aerial attack even more futile. A 1955 Air Force estimate held that a good air defense system, one able to inflict 90 percent losses on an attacking force of 400 bombers, would cost $42 billion over a four-year period. Furthermore, if 90-percent attrition was the best that could be attained, then at least 40 enemy aircraft would get through to drop their atomic or hydrogen bombs on military installations and cities in the United States, causing a catastrophe without parallel.[84] When the Soviets displayed Tu-95 turboprop and Mya-4 four-engine intercontinental jet bombers over Moscow

31

B-52. The air-refueling, Boeing-built B-52 could attack targets anywhere in the world. This aircraft provided the backbone of the United States' nuclear striking power from the late 1950s through the 1980s.

during the 1955 May Day celebration, the Air Force responded not by strengthening and extending its air defenses but by opening a second plant to boost B-52 production by 35 percent.[85]

Another indication of ADC's low status within the Air Force hierarchy was that the last requirement for an airplane specifically built as an interceptor was placed with Convair in September 1956 when the Air Force ordered the F-106.[86] The follow-on to the F-106, the XF-108, an interceptor conceived to fly at three times the speed of sound and at altitudes above 70,000 feet, was cancelled in 1959 when budget reductions forced a choice between continuing the development of the XF-108 and the XB-70.[87]

The Tactical Air Command was only slightly better off; it came to resemble a "junior SAC." When Gen Otto P. Weyland took over TAC in 1954, he wanted to make it the equal of SAC.[88] Given the parameters of Air Force doctrine, the way to gain a measure of equality was to imitate the premier command's nuclear mission. In 1950 the Air Force had permitted TAC to modify nine twin-engine B-45 jet bombers and seven F-84E single-seat fighters to carry atomic bombs.[89] The swept-wing version of the latter, the F-84F, was modified to deliver a Mark-7 atomic weapon using the low-altitude bombing system maneuver.[90] By the mid-1950s the focus of support for Army troops in combat was on the delivery of small nuclear weapons.[91] When the Air Force designed a plane to replace the F-84, it chose the Republic F-105, a single-engine jet fighter-bomber that could deliver a tactical nuclear bomb at the end of a low-altitude, high-speed approach. It had both an internal bomb bay and a 20-mm, forward-firing Gatling gun, thus epitomizing the term *fighter-bomber*. In 1958, when it went into large-scale production, the F-105s began replacing F-84s, B-57s, and, eventually, the F-100s. The F-105 was destined to carry the brunt of the war to North Vietnam between 1965 and 1968.[92]

On 8 July 1955 the Tactical Air Command activated the Nineteenth Air Force at Foster AFB, Texas. The Nineteenth Air Force was responsible for what would be called the composite air strike force (CASF), the Air Force's instrument for fighting limited wars. The purpose of the CASF was to deliver as much firepower to a "hot spot" as possible, and to do so quickly.[93] The concept was

F-105 Thunderchief. After acquiring the F-105 in the late 1950s, the Tactical Air Command became a "junior Strategic Air Command," capable of delivering tactical nuclear weapons. The F-105 was designed for carrying a small atomic bomb. In Vietnam, however, F-105 crews conducted strictly conventional bombing missions and carried the brunt of the attack to North Vietnam during Rolling Thunder. The F-105 was not particularly well suited for such missions.

tested as early as 1952 when the 20th Fighter-Bomber Wing flew F-84Cs, the first fighter-bombers specifically modified to carry atomic weapons, to bases in the Pacific. In July of the same year, 68 F-84s from the 31st Fighter Escort Wing at Turner AFB, Georgia, flew 11,000 miles to Yokota AB, Japan, making seven stops along the way and using aerial refueling over the Pacific. These deployments ratified the concept by confirming the intercontinental range and potential nuclear delivery capability of tactical aircraft.[94] Borrowing doctrine from SAC, TAC pointed to the deterrent effect of the CASF. According to Brig Gen Henry P. Viccellio, "Rebellious groups may be less inclined to start shooting when they observed that jet-fighter, fighter-bomber, bomber, and reconnaissance aircraft can be overhead in a matter of hours. . . . Thus the known existence of the CASF may in itself deter local wars."[95]

The way the Air Force reacted to events in Lebanon and in the Formosa Strait in 1958 seemed to confirm the efficacy and the utility of the CASF. Responding to a coup by pro-Egyptian officers in Iraq, the Maronite Christian leader of Lebanon, President Camille Chamoun, asked the United States for military assistance to prevent a possible armed uprising by Moslems in Beirut or an invasion from Syria or Iraq. Eisenhower's reaction was strong: "We're going to send in everything we've got, and this thing will be over in forty-eight hours if we do."[96] The first Marine units landed on 15 July; by 8 August 14,357 American soldiers were in Lebanon.[97]

The Air Force's part of "everything we've got" was a combined air strike force consisting of about 100 aircraft, including F-100s, B-57s, RF-101s, RB-66s, C-130 transports, and KB-50 tankers. These were in place at the US air base in Adana, Turkey, by 17 July.[98] Within a month the situation in Lebanon stabilized and on 21 August the United States began withdrawing troops. The last Americans were out by 25 October.

Meanwhile, in late August, Chinese forces on the mainland began shelling Nationalist Chinese emplacements on the tiny islands of Quemoy and Matsu. The Peking government called for the liberation of Taiwan just as the American forces were moving into Lebanon. Responding to the emerging threat in the Formosa Strait while engaged in a major operation in the Middle East strained American military capabilities. Nevertheless, Eisenhower reinforced the Seventh Fleet patrolling off Formosa, sent Sidewinder air-to-air missiles to the Nationalist Chinese air force, and deployed a combined air strike force to Taiwan. To underscore the American commitment, the Air Force dispatched a squadron of its newest and hottest fighter, the F-104. In air-to-air action over the strait, US and Nationalist pilots shot down 33 Communist Chinese planes. The Nationalist Chinese air force suffered only eight losses. The Sidewinders scored four kills.[99] On 6 October, Peking announced it would suspend shelling for a week. The suspension lengthened into two additional weeks; firing then resumed on odd-numbered days, but at greatly reduced intensity. The crisis petered out.[100]

Following the conclusion of the crises in Lebanon and the Formosa Strait, it seemed American military power, determinedly displayed, could alter and shape events. According to Gen Thomas S. Power, commander in chief of the Strategic Air Command, it was not the Army or the Marines, or even the CASF that had resolved these situations, rather it was strategic air power that had reached beyond the immediate problem areas to "contain the Soviets." In Power's mind, "'the reason we could prevent those actions from expanding is that we had the Strategic Air Command backing these forces up.'"[101] According to Power, it was air power that had defused the situations in Lebanon and forced the Communist Chinese to back down. Beyond that, the potential power of SAC had cowed the great outside instigator in Moscow. As it turned out, it was not even necessary to deploy a lot of aircraft. The dispatching of two relatively small aerial fleets had done the job in two widely separated areas of the world. No wonder then, that by the late summer of 1964, when the first B-57 jet bombers were sent to Vietnam, they initially were flown unarmed over the Mekong Delta to *scare* the Vietcong.[102] The hubris that bloomed and flowered from these incidents enforced the idea that air power, even the threat of air power, could bend almost any enemy or potential enemy to our will. This attitude was an important ingredient in setting up the Air Force for what the Fates had in store for it in Southeast Asia.

In a more balanced appraisal of the deployment to Lebanon, Col Albert P. Sights, Jr., in a 1965 article, made the point that the employment of the CASF with its nuclear capability was entirely consistent with Air Force views at the time. Conventional capabilities were lacking. He quoted a TAC staff officer at Adana who said, "'Only a few of the F-100 pilots had strafed; none had shot rockets or delivered conventional bombs.' The B-57 crews were not much better qualified"; they too were regarded as incapable of delivering conventional bombs effectively.[103] "On the other hand, all CASF units were" trained to drop nuclear weapons.[104]

Dependence on nuclear weapons was the warp and woof of Air Force doctrine and translated neatly into strategy and tactics. In an address to the Air War College in December 1957, Maj Gen James H. Walsh acknowledged that in limited war the objective was to destroy the enemy's military forces and that did not necessarily require atomic bombs. "But," he added, "we have come to respect the decisiveness and effectiveness inherent in nuclear firepower."[105]

The assumption that limited wars could not remain limited was based on the presupposition that insurgencies, civil wars, and revolutions were the work of those outside instigators, Moscow and Peking. This view clearly reflected cold war thinking. However, on the tactical level, the assumption was that what would work in a general war would be effective against any enemy, any time, any place. Nuclear weapons, according to Dale O. Smith, promoted "military efficiency in any conceivable military task. The so-called tactical use of airpower, while the objective is to destroy a specific surface force, can be greatly enhanced by free selection of any weapon from the spectrum."[106]

By 1960 Laos had emerged as a likely battleground between East and West. As the Air Force, along with the rest of the

F-105s in joint maneuvers. A flight of F-105s streak over an Army tank during maneuvers in 1959. The Army had to adapt to the possibilities of fighting on the nuclear battlefield during the fifties.

American military establishment, began to turn its attention to Southeast Asia, the ideas, concepts, and doctrines of the preceding generation that had shaped the Air Force were all too evident in its approach. According to Gen Frederic Smith, because Southeast Asia contained so few targets suitable for ordinary nuclear attack—bridges, rail marshalling yards, factories, and highways—targeting would have to focus on "situation control" or denying the enemy access to certain areas and bombing the enemy with nuclear weapons wherever they congregated. Gen Frederic Smith described eight types of targets suitable for situation control: rain forests, valley routes, mangrove forests, bamboo forests, karsts, mountain defiles, close-contact siege or redoubt, and beach or amphibious landings.[107] He asserted that "nuclear weapons used against such targets will usually produce the double effect of (1) disrupting enemy assembly, movement, or battle activities; and (2) clearing away jungle or forest concealment, thus ensuring increased effectiveness."[108]

Dependence on nuclear weapons to fight both total and limited wars negated the need for deep thought on the subject of strategy. From the late 1950s and into the 1960s Air Force thinking and writing became increasingly insipid. As Professor Robert F. Futrell indicated in *Ideas, Concepts, Doctrine: A History of Basic Thinking in the United States Air Force, 1907–1964*, many officers assumed that since the first AFM 1-2 series manuals had been completed in 1953 and 1954 all the thinking and writing necessary for doctrinal development and strategic thought had already been accomplished.[109] Since the theories of air power were grounded in prophecies that had no real basis in historical fact, questioning doctrines and the strategies built on those theories tended toward heresy. The doctrine that dominated the Air Force of the 1950s favored strategic bombing and was, by its very tenets, definitive. Therefore, doctrine was seen as immutable, inflexible, and so basically sound as to demand no further justification, evolution, or revision. Coinciding with the decline in strategic thinking was a growing fascination with technology centered around understanding and using the tools of the trade: nuclear weapons and the increasingly sophisticated aircraft designed to deliver them. The fascination with aircraft, their numbers, and their capabilities was evident in the Senate air power hearings in 1956. Strategy and doctrine were hardly discussed, and the kind of Air Force the United States needed to meet the challenge posed by the Soviet air force was addressed almost entirely in types and capabilities of airplanes.

Related to this trend was a decline in the vitality of Air Force writing, traceable to Secretary of Defense Louis Johnson's decree in 1949 requiring all information emanating from the Pentagon to be screened not only for security but also for *policy and propriety*. When there is a basic supposition that there is a single source of truth, then censorship to stop the airing of heretical ideas can be enforced. Within that kind of atmosphere, Air Force writing stagnated. Early editions of the *Air University Quarterly Review* contained articles rich in ideas, many of them flawed, to be sure, but still vibrant. General officers and colonels proposed new ideas, argued with policy, and articulated their own thoughts on doctrine, strategy, and institutional issues. By the mid-1950s, however, that flow had pretty much ceased. Articles by general officers appearing in *Air Force Magazine, Air University Quarterly Review*, and other publications, rarely, if ever, dealt with substantive issues in a provocative or innovative way; instead their writings were little more than public-relations pitches saying, "It's a great Air Force."

As the tools of the trade became more complex, Air Force officers concentrated on mastering the use and employment of the machines and weapons they had. The technological orientation elicited a managerial mind-set, one required to manage the complex aircraft and intricate maintenance networks they demanded. Managers began to rise more rapidly in the ranks than their warrior counterparts, in part because the skills of the warrior were less needed with nuclear weapons—as evidenced by the lack of strafing and bombing capability in the pilots who deployed to Lebanon in 1958.

- - - - - - - - -

The fact that limited wars are, indeed, very different from conventional wars was ignored during and then forgotten after Korea. The sophistication needed to fight a limited war—the understanding of the relationships between culture, politics, climate, geography, and ideology—ceased to be a part of the repertoire of Air Force officers, particularly so in the leadership. That limited wars are fought for special political objectives which define the relationship between force employment and goals had no place in a service bent on fighting and winning budget battles and acquiring a follow-on bomber to replace the B-52.

In 1961, at the time Soviet Premier Nikita S. Khrushchev was reorienting Soviet policy to support wars of national liberation, Air Force Chief of Staff Curtis E. LeMay, while acknowledging the

Kennedy administration's emphasis on reorientation of the military to meet the challenges of wars of national liberation, stated, "'I think that your strategic forces must come first. . . . I worry about the trend established by this year's budget. . . . You cannot fight a limited war except under the umbrella of strategic superiority.'"[110]

Notes

1. Gen Curtis E. LeMay, address to the Air Force Association, 21 September 1961.

2. Bernard Brodie, *Strategy in the Missile Age* (Princeton, N.J.: Princeton University Press, 1985), 131.

3. Col Dale O. Smith, "Operational Concepts for Modern War," *Air University Quarterly Review* 2, no. 2 (Fall 1948): 13–14.

4. Russell F. Weigley, *The American Way of War: A History of United States Military Strategy and Policy* (New York: Macmillan, 1973), 224.

5. Quoted in James L. Cate, "Development of Air Doctrine: 1917–41," *Air University Quarterly Review* 1, no. 3 (Winter 1947): 16–17.

6. Brodie, 77, 107.

7. Robert F. Futrell, *Ideas, Concepts, Doctrine: A History of Basic Thinking in the United States Air Force, 1907–1964* (Maxwell AFB, Ala.: Air University, 1974), 12.

8. Weigley, 241.

9. Ibid., 356–58.

10. John Schlight, "The Impact of the Orient on Air Power," in *The American Military in the Far East*, proceedings of the Ninth Military History Symposium (USAF Academy, Colo.: USAF Academy, 1980), 161.

11. Col Dennis M. Drew, *Rolling Thunder 1965: Anatomy of a Failure*, CADRE Paper (Maxwell AFB, Ala.: Air University Press, October 1986), 19–20, AU-ARI-CP-86-3.

12. Lt Col Frank R. Pancake, "The Strategic Striking Force," *Air University Quarterly Review* 2, no. 2 (Fall 1948): 48.

13. James William Gibson, *The Perfect War: Technowar in Vietnam* (Boston: Atlantic Monthly Press, 1986), 68. Gibson describes the role of "the Other" as that of a mirrorlike reflection of America's own industrial might which acts as a foil to US initiatives and foreign policies in the cold war era.

14. Herbert Molloy Mason, Jr., *The United States Air Force: A Turbulent History* (New York: Mason/Charter, 1976), 216.

15. Quoted in Futrell, *Ideas*, 109.

16. Senate Committee on the Armed Services, *Air Power Hearings*, testimony of Gen Otto P. Weyland, 8 May 1956, 462 (hereinafter Symington hearings).

17. Col Dale O. Smith and Maj Gen John DeF. Barker, "Air Power Indivisible," *Air University Quarterly Review* 4, no. 2 (Fall 1950): 12.

18. Ibid.

19. Giulio Douhet, *The Command of the Air*, trans. Dino Ferrari, reprinted by the Office of Air Force History (Washington, D.C.: Office of Air Force History, 1983), 55.

20. Col Dale O. Smith, "Operational Concepts for Modern War," *Air University Quarterly Review* 2, no. 2 (Fall 1948): 9.

21. Ibid., 10–11.

22. Harry R. Borowski, *A Hollow Threat: Strategic Air Power and Containment before Korea* (Westport, Conn.: Greenwood Press, 1982), 106.

23. Futrell, *Ideas*, 125.

24. "Carrier Off—Sullivan Quits," *Aviation Week*, 2 May 1949, 7.

25. "Mr. Johnson's News Policy Bogs Down," *Aviation Week*, 2 May 1949, 58. In subsequent years the precedent established by this policy would have a suffocating effect on writing in the services, especially in the Air Force. Censors in the Air Force security and policy review process routinely exceeded their authority by denying publication to any article that did not reflect and support service policy; their actions effectively stifled criticism.

26. Futrell, *Ideas*, 126.

27. James H. Straubel, "The Case against the Flat-Top," *Air Force Magazine*, February 1949, 46.

28. See *Air Force Magazine*, March 1949, 15.

29. Futrell, *Ideas*, 129–32.

30. Ibid., 126.

31. Quoted in Futrell, *Ideas*, 147.

32. Testimony of Lt Gen James M. Gavin, Symington hearings, 22 May 1956, 741.

33. Air Force Bulletin no. 1, subject: Functions of the Armed Forces and the Joint Chiefs of Staff, 21 May 1948.

34. Quoted from Charles W. Dickens, in "A Survey of Air-Ground Doctrine," *Tactical Air Command*, historical survey 34 (Langley AFB, Va.: Office of Information Services, 1958), 14, K417.041-34, US Air Force Historical Research Center (USAFHRC), Maxwell AFB, Ala.

35. Gen Hoyt S. Vandenberg, "The Truth about Our Air Power," *Saturday Evening Post*, 13 February 1951, 104.

36. Capt Donald A. Bishop, "The Korean War, 1950–1953," *Warfare and Society*, vol. 2 (USAF Academy, Colo.: USAF Academy, 1981), 30–20.

37. Ibid.

38. Ibid.

39. M. J. Armitage and R. A. Mason, *Air Power in the Nuclear Age* (Urbana, Ill.: University of Illinois Press, 1983), 25–26.

40. Ibid., 38.

41. D. Smith and Barker, 12–13.

42. Gen Frederic H. Smith, Jr., "Nuclear Weapons and Limited War," *Air University Quarterly Review* 12, no. 1 (Spring 1960): 10.

43. *The Effects of Atomic Weapons* (Washington, D.C.: Government Printing Office, 1950), 152.

44. F. Smith, "Nuclear Weapons," 25.

45. Ibid., 16.

46. Quoted in Armitage and Mason, 44.

47. Robert F. Futrell, *The United States Air Force in Korea, 1950–1953* (New York: Duell, Sloan, and Pearce, 1961), 644. (Futrell's summation of the FEAF Report.)

48. Gen William W. Momyer, *Airpower in Three Wars* (Washington, D.C.: Government Printing Office, 1976), 6.

49. Maxwell Taylor, *The Uncertain Trumpet* (New York: Harper and Brothers, 1959), 24–25.

50. Robert F. Futrell, *United States Air Force in Southeast Asia: The Advisory Years to 1965* (Washington, D.C.: Office of Air Force History, 1981), 70.

51. Herbert S. Parmet, *Eisenhower and the American Crusades* (New York: Macmillan, 1972), 361.

52. Radford, quoted in Futrell, *Ideas*, 215.

53. Ibid., 214.

54. Futrell, *Advisory Years*, 25.

55. *The Pentagon Papers*, Senator Gravel edition (Boston: Beacon Press, 1971), 97.

56. Bernard B. Fall, *Hell in a Very Small Place: The Siege at Dien Bien Phu* (New York: Harper and Row, 1967), 455.

57. Michael Carver, "Conventional Warfare in the Nuclear Age," in *Makers of Modern Strategy from Machiavelli to the Nuclear Age*, ed. Peter Paret (Princeton, N.J.: Princeton University Press, 1986), 783–84.

58. Charles Christienne and Pierre Lissarrague, *Historie de l'Aviation Militaire Française* (Paris: Charles-Lavauzelle, 1980), 454.

59. Ibid., 461.

60. "The Korean War Speaks to the Indo-Chinese War: A Quarterly Review Staff Study," *Air University Quarterly Review* 7, no. 1 (Spring 1954): 60.

61. Ibid.

62. "Some Reflections on the 'New Look,'" *Air Force Magazine*, April 1954, 27.

63. Futrell, *Korea*, 664.

64. Edgar S. Furniss, Jr., *American Military Policy: Strategic Aspects of World Political Geography* (New York: Rinehart, 1957), 401–3.

65. F. A. Godfrey, "Crisis in Korea," in *War in Peace*, ed. Sir Robert Thompson (London: Orbis, 1981), 61.

66. Futrell, *Ideas*, 211.

67. Ibid., 205–9.

68. "Secretary Dulles' Address, January 12, 1954," reprinted in *Current History*, May 1954, 308.

69. Thomas K. Finletter, *Power and Policy: U.S. Foreign Policy and Military Power in the Hydrogen Age* (New York: Harcourt, Brace, 1954), 54–55.

70. Brodie, 249–51.

71. Futrell, *Ideas*, 218–19.

72. Ibid.

73. Air Force Manual (AFM) 1-2, *United States Air Force Basic Doctrine*, 1 April 1954, 1–36.

74. AFM 1-2, 1 March 1953, 11.

75. Taylor, 102, 136.

76. Henry A. Kissinger, *Nuclear Weapons and Foreign Policy* (New York: Harper and Brothers, 1957), 169.

77. Sir John C. Slessor, "Has the H-Bomb Abolished Total War?" *Air Force Magazine*, May 1954, 26.

78. John F. Loosbrook, "What Kind of War?" *Air Force Magazine*, November 1956, 49.

79. Ibid., 44.

80. Momyer, 248–49.

81. Gen Thomas D. White, "USAF Doctrine and National Policy," *Air Force Magazine*, January 1958, 50–51.

82. LeMay, quoted in Futrell, *Ideas*, 221.

83. Ibid., 264.

84. Ibid., 271.

85. Ibid., 256.

86. Marcelle Size Knaack, *Encyclopedia of U.S. Air Force Aircraft and Missile Systems* (Washington, D.C.: Office of Air Force History, 1978), 209.

87. Ibid., 331.

88. David MacIsaac, "Voices from the Central Blue: The Air Power Theorists," in Paret, 644.

89. Futrell, *Ideas*, 156.

90. Kevin Keaveny, *Republic F-84F (Swept-Wing Variants)* (Arlington, Tex.: Aerofax, 1987), 4. The maneuver involved a high-speed, low-altitude approach. At a known point, the aircraft would be pulled into a steep climb and shortly thereafter, the bomb would be released. The aircraft would continue into the upper portion of the loop, roll out at the top and head in the opposite direction as fast as possible. The bomb would continue climbing, following a ballistic trajectory depending on weight, velocity, and other factors. Accuracy was a matter of perspective.

91. Tactical Air Command Manual 55-3, *Joint Air Operations*, 1 September 1957, 73–76.

92. Knaack, 191–93.

93. Futrell, *Ideas*, 226–27.

94. Col Albert P. Sights, Jr., "Lessons of Lebanon: A Study in Air Strategy," *Air University Review* 16, no. 5 (July–August 1965): 42.

95. Brig Gen Henry P. Viccellio, "Composite Air Strike Force," *Air University Quarterly Review* 9, no. 1 (Winter 1956–1957): 34.

96. Parmet, 532.

97. Ibid., 533.

98. Otto P. Weyland, "Air Power in Limited War," *Ordnance*, July–August 1959, 42.

99. Futrell, *Ideas*, 306.

100. Parmet, 531–35; and Weyland, 42.

101. Quoted in Futrell, *Ideas*, 307.

102. Lou Drendel, *Air War over Southeast Asia: A Pictorial Record*, vol. 1, *1962–1966* (Carrollton, Tex.: Squadron Signal Publications, 1982), 12.

103. Sights, 42.

104. Ibid.

105. Maj Gen James H. Walsh, "The Influence of Nuclear Weapons on the Determination of Military Objectives," Air War College address, 18 December 1957, Air University Library, Maxwell AFB, Ala.

106. Brig Gen Dale O. Smith, "Airpower in Limited War," *Air Force Magazine*, May 1955, 43.

107. F. Smith, "Nuclear Weapons," 13–14.

108. Ibid.

109. Futrell, *Ideas*, 6.

110. Quoted in ibid., 344.

Chapter 2

Situations of a Lesser Magnitude

Speaking at George Washington University's winter commencement in February 1962, Secretary of the Air Force Eugene M. Zuckert declared that the Air Force not only was prepared to meet Soviet aggression but also was ready to "respond to situations of a lesser magnitude." In his appraisal of the USAF's preparedness for potential cold war clashes, Zuckert claimed that the Air Force had adapted to the "full range of conflict" and was ready to parry Soviet-inspired thrusts with forces "in step with the swift march of science and technology."[1] The Air Force had introduced the Titan and Minuteman intercontinental ballistic missiles to answer the threat posed by the Soviet Union's nuclear rocket forces. Like its sister services in the Pentagon, the Air Force was responding to initiatives imposed by Secretary of Defense Robert S. McNamara's quest to impose efficiency throughout the military establishment. On Capitol Hill the branches of the armed forces still fought intense interservice budget battles—particularly the Army over its growing role in unconventional warfare. These skirmishes threatened the Air Force's previously dominant hold on the budget.

The Kennedy Administration, the Cold War, and the Air Force

The cold war was chilly indeed when John F. Kennedy took the oath of office on 20 January 1961. The previous May, the Soviets had shot down a U-2 spy plane over Sverdlovsk, a steel production center right in the middle of the Ural mountains. During the summer of 1960, Soviet aircraft had flown resupply missions in the Congo for pro-Soviet forces. In October the Soviet Union had

Secretary of the Air Force Eugene M. Zuckert. In 1961 Secretary of Defense Robert S. McNamara warned Zuckert that reforming the Air Force and reorienting it away from massive retaliation would be a difficult job.

established diplomatic relations with the neutralist government in Laos and had used some of the same aircraft that had been busy in the Congo in summer to begin flying supplies to anti-American and pro-Communist forces in Laos. Closer to home, Fidel Castro had declared himself a Marxist-Leninist and had cozied up to the Soviets. American foreign policy decisions of the early 1960s would be colored by the same perceptions of the "outside instigator"—that Moscow-Peking cabal—that many in government believed to be behind virtually every challenge America faced abroad.

For the Kennedy administration, its first year was a time of testing by that outside instigator. An editorial in *Newsweek* stated, "The greatest single problem that faces John Kennedy—and the key to most other problems—is how to meet the aggressive power of the communist bloc."[2] In 1961 crises came in quick succession. Foremost among them was the thorough defeat of US-backed Cuban exiles during the invasion at the Bay of Pigs. In early June, Kennedy met Nikita Khrushchev in Vienna for a summit. The talks ranged over many issues, including wars of national liberation that, according to Kennedy, were dangerous because they risked escalation that might involve the major powers directly.[3] Three issues dominated the talks: the nuclear test ban, the status of Berlin, and the civil war in Laos. According to Kennedy administration insider Theodore C. Sorensen, the talks on Berlin were the most difficult because, "if Khrushchev meant what he said on Berlin, the prospects for nuclear war were very real—for Kennedy meant what he said."[4] Kennedy left Vienna feeling that he had six months to prepare the nation for nuclear war.

Had that war happened in late 1961 or early 1962, the Air Force, then at the apex of its power, was prepared to use its nuclear bombs and missiles to annihilate the Soviet Union. The Strategic Air Command (SAC) counted 1,500 jet bombers in its inventory. Thor and Jupiter medium range ballistic missiles (MRBM) and a handful of Atlases—a first-generation intercontinental ballistic missile (ICBM), along with the first squadron of Titan I ICBMs—were aimed at the USSR, China, and eastern Europe. The expanse of SAC was indicated by the fact that in 1962 it held an estimated 90 percent of the free world's total nuclear striking power and fueled that capability by consuming 20 percent of the defense budget.[5]

However, the hold that the Air Force had maintained on the defense budgets of the previous decade was slipping. At the end of the Eisenhower administration and the beginning of the Kennedy administration, a transition from reliance on over-whelming nuclear superiority to a policy of flexible response was under way. The final defense budget submitted by the outgoing Republicans in 1960 had eliminated all funding for procurement of manned bombers in 1962.[6] Furthermore, the incoming Democrats seemed intent on shaking the defense establishment out of its 1950s "New Look" mold. According to Secretary Zuckert, the policy changes they had in mind would have the greatest impact on the Air Force. He felt that these changes would be particularly difficult for the officers in the Air Force establishment because "their thinking was pretty inflexible."[7] Even though the Kennedy administration would spend lavishly indeed on strategic systems, that spending shifted from bombers to missiles; the Kennedy defense budget included an expansion of the Navy's Polaris-missile-firing submarine force—McNamara was an avowed foe of the XB-70 program.[8]

XB-70. Gen Curtis E. LeMay was committed to buying the XB-70 as the follow-on bomber to replace the B-52.

The Kennedy administration's shift from massive retaliation to flexible response came at the expense of the Air Force. Because the Air Force had been receiving the largest share of the budget, the shift seemed even harsher. Air Force thinking, based firmly in theories of massive retaliation, was too rigid to acquiesce easily to change.[9] The Air Force of the early sixties was still firmly wedded to SAC as the cornerstone of national defense. From the Air Force's perspective, SAC was the ultimate sanction that made possible the effective functioning of the rest of the commands, indeed of the other services. Within the Air Force, the issue of general war versus limited war focused on the level of sufficiency in nuclear deterrence. The ability to fight a limited war was irrelevant because nuclear superiority not only was the great arbiter but also was the absolute prerequisite of conducting a limited war. Many Air Force leaders were convinced that overwhelming nuclear striking power would deter even limited war.

The Air Force point of view was not endorsed by the other services, nor was it supported by the new administration. Within the Joint Chiefs of Staff (JCS), the Army and the Navy took the position that limited war was more likely to occur than general war and that, while the United States was ready to fight a general war, it was not well prepared for small-scale conflicts.[10] McNamara's 1963 budget, which added additional Minuteman missiles and Navy Polaris submarines but did not include further B-52 procurement, was not welcomed by the bomber pilots who ran the Air Force and the Air Staff. Nor did they like the idea of expanding the Army by two divisions and procuring enough helicopters to support those divisions. The introduction of attack helicopters into the Army left the Air Force in a quandary. If it did not want to lose the close air support mission, the Air Force was going to have to expand the Tactical Air Command (TAC) and retrain its aircrews so that they could perform the conventional as well as the nuclear mission. Any expansion of TAC and redirecting of its "junior SAC" orientation might well come at the expense of SAC. Whether the Air Staff liked it or not, McNamara's budget included additional tactical fighters to support the enlarged Army.[11]

Led by its chief of staff, Gen Thomas D. White, the Air Force argued against the provisions of the budget that called for a shift to missiles at the expense of bombers. The Air Force position was that missiles did not yet have the reliability of bombers and, until they did, the administration would be foolhardy to stop bomber production and reduce the number of existing bombers in order to buy additional missiles. Specifically, General White was opposed to phasing out of the medium-range B-47, which he considered to be more reliable than missiles, even though he admitted it was becoming obsolete. He also argued that B-52 production lines should be kept open until missile reliability improved.[12]

For the Air Force of 1961, dominated as it was by bomber pilots, the XB-70 was the only airplane that could replace the B-52. And the XB-70 would not be ready before the end of the decade. The Air Force position on manned bombers reflected the dominant role the Air Force's top bomber pilots as generals, especially Gen Curtis E. LeMay, played in determining institutional doctrine and strategy. Indeed LeMay's concept of bombing was prosaic and did not seem to have evolved from where it was during World War II. To him the B-70 was a "trisonic" B-17. According to Zuckert, "LeMay thought of the B-70 as going over enemy lines and dropping bombs as he had dropped them on Germany and Japan."[13] When Sen Stuart Symington found out the B-70 was not designed to carry Skybolt air-to-ground missiles, an item also under development by the Air Force, he told Zuckert, "If it won't carry Skybolt, it won't carry me."[14]

Additionally, McNamara insisted that the Air Force and the Navy share as much aviation hardware as possible. One of the first challenges LeMay faced as chief of staff was to talk McNamara out of forcing the Air Force to buy the Douglas A-4D Skyhawk, a light, single-engine fighter-bomber. McNamara favored this aircraft as a common tactical fighter for both the Air Force and the Navy because it cost one-third of the price of the F-105 and the Navy's F-4H Phantom. When the Air Force agreed to purchase F-4s rather than additional F-105s, McNamara relented and agreed to the common procurement of Phantoms rather than Skyhawks.[15]

President John F. Kennedy with Gen Curtis E. LeMay. President Kennedy and General LeMay watch a firepower demonstration at Eglin AFB, Florida. LeMay was never enthusiastic about President Kennedy's shift in defense policy away from reliance on massive retaliation to flexible response.

The controversy over A-4s was, however, peripheral to the debate that broiled around the selection and development of the next generation of tactical fighters.

The Air Force argued that its requirements for a tactical fighter differed considerably from those of the Navy. An ideal tactical fighter, according to the Air Force, was one that could fly at the speed of sound, fight its way through enemy defenses, and then deliver a hefty bomb load. The Navy, on the other hand, needed a plane optimized for endurance so that it could range far from the fleet to protect it from enemy bombers. From the Navy's perspective, top speed could be sacrificed for increased range. In

F-4 Phantom. Secretary Robert S. McNamara forced the Air Force to adopt the Navy's F-4 Phantom II as the primary fighter, supplanting the F-105. Phantoms remained the Air Force's first-line air superiority aircraft from the mid-1960s through the early 1980s.

addition, all Navy planes needed heavy landing gear to withstand jarring carrier landings and a high thrust-to-weight ratio that would allow for recovering from botched deck approaches. This aircraft had to be able to attack enemy shipping as well as coastal installations. Targets further inland tended not to concern the Navy. The admirals and generals were convinced that it was impossible to build one airplane that could do all the things each service wanted done. Despite arguments from each of the services, McNamara, driven as he was to foist efficiency on the Pentagon, insisted on the development of a fighter to be used by the Air Force and the Navy. The aircraft that McNamara advocated was the tactical fighter experimental—the TFX. As it turned out, the General Dynamics F-111 that resulted from this initiative would remain a controversial aircraft. Except for a token purchase foisted off on the Marines, the Navy refused to buy it.

In addition, major differences in style, honest disagreements, and misunderstandings exacerbated relations between the Air Force and the administration. General LeMay, who became Air Force chief of staff in June 1961, was a bomber pilot. Like other chiefs who had preceded him, LeMay had helped win independence for the Air Force by championing the efficacy of strategic bombing. In his mind that mission and the Air Force were one. This mind-set did not lend itself to flexibility. This rigidity of thought by the Air Force did not bode well, especially for problems brewing in Laos and Vietnam where the outside instigator was seemingly at work supporting civil war and inciting rebellion.

The Laotian Factor

President Kennedy had been in office only 10 days when *Newsweek*'s Ernest K. Lindley wrote, "Many difficult problems press upon him. Some require early action. One may demand an almost immediate and dangerous choice. That is Laos."[16] This complicated foreign policy problem became Kennedy's first foreign policy crisis. Its resolution helped define the way the United States approached what was, in 1961, a less pressing problem in Vietnam.

Three factions in Laos were locked in a civil war. Because Laos shared common borders with China, North Vietnam, Burma, Thailand, and Cambodia, the revolution there assumed strategic significance. The three factions competing for power in Laos included a pro-American military and right-wing faction headed by Phoui Sananikone, Phoumi Nosavan, and Prince Somsanith; a nonaligned group led by Prince Souvanna Phouma; and the pro-Communist Pathet Lao under Prince Souphanouvong.

When it had gained its independence from France in 1954, Laos had been a constitutional monarchy based on a coalition between prominent Laotian families, all of which were represented in the warring factions. In 1958 the nonaligned coalition government collapsed over the issue of how to integrate Pathet Lao troops into the Royal Laotian Army (*Forces Armée Royal*) and what should be the division of power among the various political groups.[17] In the turmoil that followed, the Vientiane government came under the control of the right-wing headed by Phoui Sananikone. Open

fighting with the Pathet Lao broke out and American aid, in the form of military equipment and advisors, flowed to the Royal Laotian Army (RLA).

In August 1960, while most members of the government were in the royal capital of Luang Prabang attending the elaborate funeral for King Sisavang Vong, a paratroop battalion commander named Capt Kong Le led a coup d'état in the administrative capital of Vientiane. His declared aims were an end to the civil war, removal of American advisors, and a return to neutralism. Kong Le invited Prince Souvanna Phouma to reestablish a truly neutralist government.

Meanwhile, Gen Phoumi Nosavan, along with most of the high-ranking officers in the Laotian military, had declared the formation of a Committee Against the Coup d'état and established themselves in Savannakhét where they were raising a force to march on Vientiane. Aid from the United States was funnelled to the generals through Thailand's military dictator, Marshal Sarit Thanarat. In November, Phoumi's troops began moving northward up Route 13 toward Vientiane.

At this point what should have remained a struggle for power between rival Laotian families took on a wider significance with international implications. North Vietnam had decided to take control of the infant insurgency in South Vietnam and lend guidance to its growth. Accordingly, in May 1959, North Vietnamese troops established the 559th Transportation Battalion in the area of Tchepone in eastern Savannakhét Province. This unit began widening roads and setting up the apparatus that would move men and supplies from North Vietnam into the South. Simultaneously, North Vietnamese aid to the Pathet Lao increased dramatically. North Vietnamese regulars joined the Pathet Lao in attacks on Royal Laotian Army garrisons in Sam Neua and Phong Saly provinces in northeastern Laos.[18] In October 1960 the Vientiane government, now headed by neutralist Prince Souvanna Phouma, broadened the implications of what was happening in Laos when it invited the Soviet Union to establish its first embassy in Laos and, in turn, received promises of Soviet financial and military aid.[19]

Soviet interest in Southeast Asia prior to 1960 had been limited to occasional contacts with a handful of revolutionary leaders, the most prominent being Ho Chi Minh.[20] While Soviet acceptance of Souvanna's invitation was probably an attempt to preempt the extension of Chinese influence in the region, the State Department gave it a more ominous interpretation. Although the outlines of the Sino-Soviet rift were only barely discernible to the cold warriors at Foggy Bottom, they dubbed the evolving relationship between Laos and the Soviet Union as a coordinated Moscow-Peking-Hanoi effort "to obtain control over Laos through a combination of diplomatic maneuver, political subversion and guerrilla warfare."[21]

The situation in Laos intensified in December when General Phoumi's forces laid siege to Vientiane and Soviet planes began airlifting arms to Kong Le's troops. On 11 December, Ilyushin-14 (Il-14) twin-engine transports began ferrying American-made 105-mm howitzers, M-1 rifles, and ammunition—all from stocks captured in Korea and given to Hanoi by the Chinese—to Wattay Airport.[22] After a bloody artillery duel, Kong Le's troops withdrew from Vientiane. The airlift, however, continued with Il-14s dropping supplies to Kong Le's forces as they retreated northward to the Plain of Jars. Kong Le, meanwhile, had allied himself with the Pathet Lao. Before long the Kong Le neutralists, along with their Pathet Lao and Vietnamese allies, were overrunning Royal Laotian Army garrisons throughout northeastern Laos.

Before the coup, Kong Le's battalion had been part of the Royal Laotian Army. It was probably the best unit in an army that John Kenneth Galbraith had aptly dubbed as "clearly inferior to a battalion of conscientious objectors from World War I."[23] That Kong Le's paratroopers were the best unit in the 17,000-man royal army was, in no small part, due to his leadership. On the other hand, the Pathet Lao were not substantially better than the government's army even though the upland peasants from which its soldiers were drawn were somewhat heartier than the lowland Lao and Thai soldiers who made up the Royal Laotian Army.

The Pathet Lao's major advantage was in its North Vietnamese support. The Vietnamese were "ten feet tall" in the eyes of the Laotians. The Laotians, who considered France a major military power, were truly impressed by the Vietminh victory over the French forces. The Vietnamese capitalized on this perception by using their forces as "shock troops" to demoralize RLA units or to bail out the Pathet Lao whenever a government unit gained the upper hand.[24] The effect was that the Royal Laotian Army went from debacle to debacle.

As the military situation deteriorated in the winter of 1961, the United States increased its assistance to Phoumi, furnishing AT-6 Harvard trainers fitted with guns and rocket racks. In addition, President Kennedy sent US Army Special Forces units code-named White Star to advise the Laotian army.[25] On 23 March 1961 the president announced at a press conference that Soviet transports had flown more than 1,000 resupply missions to Laos since December 1960. To underscore his determination to blunt such forays by the Communist bloc, Kennedy ordered the Seventh Fleet into the South China Sea and put troops at bases in Okinawa on alert for possible deployment to Southeast Asia.[26]

The fighting in Laos occurred at a relatively low level of conflict and was essentially conventional in nature. The Pathet Lao were organized as light infantry and were not particularly adept at guerrilla warfare. The government forces preferred to use artillery whenever it was available. However, the fighting was, for the most part, marked by small unit actions, ambushes, and Pathet Lao-Vietnamese attacks on Royal Laotian Army outposts and garrisons. Seemingly, American forces would do well in this kind of war.

However, the United States would have faced several difficult problems had troops been committed there. Laos existed as part of the international agreements drawn up at Geneva in 1954; its neutrality was a matter of consensus as well as convenience. Moreover, the civil war was almost secondary to the squabble between rival families. Those factors aside, the location was bad; Laos was halfway around the world from the United States. Further complicating any major deployment of American forces, Laos had no seaports, only a few roads that could be depicted as anything other than substandard, and no railroads. Much of the country consisted of the rugged mountains of the Annam Cordillera; in eastern Laos these mountains were covered with thick jungle. American air power would have found few targets. And even though this conflict was taking place at a relatively low level of intensity, the United States would have been hard-pressed to intervene. Because of the emphasis on nuclear war, the United States did not have enough conventional equipment and ammunition to fight a protracted war. President Kennedy was reportedly shocked when told that the commitment of 10,000 troops to Laos would deplete the Army's strategic reserve.[27]

For its part, the Air Force was not anxious to get involved in the fighting in Laos. Advisors on the scene were already chafing at restrictions placed on the use of the AT-6s. The American pilots were forbidden to use napalm and could not fire on Soviet transports hauling supplies to the Pathet Lao and neutralist forces.[28] General White expressed reservations about placing any kind of force in Laos. To him the logistical problems were overwhelming and were particularly complicated since the Air Force would have to rely on sophisticated fighter planes like the F-100 and F-105. White advocated either "going all out or just forgetting the whole thing."[29]

Nevertheless, in the spring of 1961, the plan for intervention in Laos was put into motion. The United States established a Marine helicopter repair depot at the old Japanese air base at Udorn in northern Thailand, initially deploying 16 choppers and the necessary support personnel. The JCS put Task Force 116 on alert in Okinawa and, on 26 April, sent out a general advisory to major commands all over the world. It specifically alerted the commander in chief, Pacific Command (CINCPAC), to be prepared to undertake air strikes against targets in North Vietnam and southern China.[30]

The execution of the plan did not proceed beyond the deployment of the Marine units to Udorn. If it had, Air Force C-130s would have airlifted two regiments of the Third Marine Division along with Air Group 16 (15,000–20,000 men), the Second Airborne Battle Group of the 503d Infantry Combat Team (1,900 men), and the 1st Special Forces Group (300 troops) to various spots in Thailand and Laos. The plan was to seize Mahaxay, a town 60 miles or so north of Savannakhét and to take Tchepone. These towns were to be the strongpoints for a line between the Vietnam-Laos border on the east and the Thai border to the vicinity of Thakhek on the west. South of this line, US forces would have protected the Laotian panhandle along Route 9 running from Tchepone to Seno and Savannakhét.[31]

The deployment did not take place. By late April, Kennedy had accepted the idea of a coalition government in Laos. In May negotiations between the Pathet Lao, the neutralists, and the rightists had begun at the village of Ban Namone. Meanwhile, delegates from 14 nations were meeting in Geneva to form a coalition government that would be acceptable to all parties. A year later, on 23 July 1962, the diplomats in Geneva agreed to the "Protocol to the Declaration on the Neutrality of Laos." It reinstituted the International Commission for Supervision and Control (ICSC) and reestablished the neutralist coalition. The Geneva agreement specified that all foreign advisors were to be withdrawn from Laos. The Laotian princes meeting at Ban Namone concluded their own agreement providing for a coalition government.[32] These two pacts notwithstanding, the civil war did not cease, nor did US involvement come to a complete halt.

Although the US Military Assistance Advisory Group (MAAG) in Laos closed down and its 666 military advisors were processed out of the country at ICSC checkpoints, many of them did not travel far.[33] They were absorbed into the Joint United States Military Assistance Advisory Group (JUSMAAG) in Bangkok to "carry out, within Thailand, certain necessary assistance functions for Laos." [34] The covert American war in Laos was under way.

For all its complexity, the war in Laos elicited the most conventional kinds of military responses from the United States. Tactically, the war was fought for the most part using light infantry and, when available, artillery. The Royal Laotian forces enjoyed light tactical air support while the Pathet Lao and Kong Le forces received substantial amounts of supplies by the Soviet airlift from Hanoi. Although the war in Laos was not the classical attrition warfare conducted in the West, neither was it a people's war. It was a situation of a lesser kind. It was a civil war with, as in many civil wars, outside participants. The revolutionary aspect of the civil war was almost subsidiary to the fact that it was also a squabble between rival families.

The US reaction was far from small scale. The plan to employ Task Force 116 was devised for fighting a conventional war of attrition. Furthermore, the JCS advisory instructing CINCPAC to prepare for air strikes against North Vietnam and China was indicative of the tendency to look beyond the situation at hand in search of culprits elsewhere. Indeed, there was evidence of involvement by the outside instigator(s). In addition to regular flights by Soviet planes to resupply the Pathet Lao and Kong Le's troops, US Air Force RF-101s flying from Tan Son Nhut Air Base in South Vietnam had photographed Il-14s landing at the small airfield outside Tchepone as well as dropping supplies to the North Vietnamese units in the vicinity of the village.[35]

In the minds of the American military, the war in Laos called for a conventional response. Given the nature of the fighting there, this approach on the part of the US military was probably correct. As the Laotian emergency receded, the United States was already entering the war in Vietnam. The way it had approached the situation in Laos, and supposedly resolved it, colored the way the United States approached Vietnam.

In at the Beginning

Even before the July 1962 agreements at Geneva, the United States was shifting its attention to South Vietnam, where the regime of President Ngo Dinh Diem was under pressure from the newly established national liberation front. Despite the growth of the Vietcong in 1960 and 1961, the situation in Vietnam looked hopeful. Diem was clearly America's man. The United States had incorporated all the applicable lessons of the Korean War in training and equipping his army. And because it had the 10 to 1 ratio believed necessary for success over a guerrilla force, the South Vietnamese army's chances for defeating the Vietcong seemed very good.

In contrast, the Vietnamese air force (VNAF) was small and ill-prepared, and it was clearly inferior to the army in the pecking order of Saigon's military establishment. The French had built a small Vietnamese air force consisting of two squadrons of Morane-5 Saulnier MS-502 Criquet liaison planes and one squadron of Dassault MD-315 Flamant light combat assault aircraft. A few obsolete F8F Bearcats remained from the French Indochina War. The VNAF was not an auspicious force, and the highest rank one could attain in it was colonel.[36]

As of the late 1950s, the United States had not paid much attention to the Vietnamese air force. American military assistance, administered by the US Army-dominated Military Assistance Advisory Group, was oriented toward ground forces. Furthermore, the US Air Force was not particularly interested in any third-rate air forces that, according to international agreements, could not acquire or fly jets. Growth of the South Vietnamese air force beyond equipment originally programmed for the French in Indochina was not even moderate. Thus, the VNAF had received little in the way of hardware beyond a few more F8F Bearcats, C-47 transports, and L-19 observation planes as well as a handful of H-19 helicopters already designated in military assistance programs for the French back in 1954.[37]

The US advisors had organized and trained the Vietnamese armed forces to repel a Korea-style invasion across the demilitarized zone (DMZ). Ironically, in November 1954, Gen Tran Van Don and other leading Vietnamese generals suggested that the MAAG organize their new army into light, mobile groups suitable for antiguerrilla warfare. The US advisors did not follow this "advice" for three reasons.

First, basic US strategy in the 1950s had not dealt with the degree to which indigenous military forces should be expected to defend against limited attacks or insurrections. Second, as a result of experiences gained in the Greek civil war and in Korea, the US military was not prepared to structure forces other than for conventional warfare. Third, the US military assumed that forces competent to repel external aggression would likewise be sufficient to defend against any internal threat. In other words, if one's armed forces could win the large war, the small ones would take care of themselves. Before 1961 the term *counterinsurgency* did not even exist.[38]

Thus, in 1960 and early 1961 US advisors considered the South Vietnamese air force to be sufficient for its part in the job of fighting the Vietcong. Lt Gen Lionel McGarr, the US Army general who succeeded Gen John "Iron Mike" O'Daniel at JUSMAAG, reported that the newly acquired AD-6s could deliver the firepower that was needed. The problem, however, was that the Vietnamese air force and army did not know how to coordinate their forces in combat. In April 1961 General McGarr told the Vietnam Task Force, headed by Deputy Secretary of Defense Roswell L. Gilpatric, that

> the terrific firepower of the AD-6—mobile, accurate, "massive" fire support—is not being capitalized upon. This stems from faulty organization, with consequently faulty decision-making power of the RVNAF (Republic of Vietnam Armed Forces). . . . The VNAF has the capability of greatly assisting ground anti-guerrilla action by the ARVN. It can bomb, strafe, reconnoiter (both visual and photographic [sic]), carry troops, and effectively deliver CW (chemical warfare, i.e., gas) non-lethal munitions against any type target in Vietnam. You must educate your advisors to the full and proper use of this asset.[39]

Was it merely a matter of education after all? In February, President Kennedy asked the Joint Chiefs of Staff to examine ways to improve the military's counterinsurgency capabilities. The answer they gave him was unsatisfactory. They reported that "everything was in great shape."[40] The president, not to be put off so easily, reopened the issue.

Kennedy got the Joint Chiefs' attention on his second try. He certainly seems to have gotten through to General LeMay, now Air Force vice chief of staff. According to Zuckert, "I remember LeMay coming in and talking to me about it quite enthusiastically." He felt that LeMay's enthusiasm for counterinsurgency was partially colored by his desire to keep the Army from gaining an advantage over the Air Force in this new arena of operations.[41] That notwithstanding, LeMay became the motivating spirit behind the establishment of the Air Force's counterinsurgency capability. In April 1961, Headquarters Air Force directed the Tactical Air Command to organize and equip a unit to train in World War II-type airplanes and to prepare a limited number of these planes for transfer to friendly foreign governments.[42]

Joint Chiefs of Staff. In February 1961 President John F. Kennedy told the Joint Chiefs to reorient their individual services away from reliance on massive retaliation toward a policy of flexible response centered on counterguerrilla warfare.

The 4400th Combat Crew Training Squadron (CCTS) was organized at Hurlburt Field, Florida, on 14 April 1961. It had a large and somewhat ambiguous mandate: to prepare an elite group of aviators to conduct unconventional operations in old airplanes; to develop and test appropriate tactics, munitions, and delivery techniques; and to train officers and enlisted men to be teachers and trainers in countries that needed to develop their own counterguerrilla capability.[43] In short, these air commandos were to be the Air Force's counterpart to the Army Special Forces.

Training included techniques for night operations; landings at and takeoffs from short, sod airfields; low-level navigation; and the delivery of napalm. The air commandos practiced air-to-ground gunnery and rocketry—skills that had become somewhat of a lost art for TAC in the 1950s, a period when the focus was on tactics for delivering small nuclear bombs.[44] The training was intense and seemingly devised to prepare the men for difficult assignments under unusual and "spooky" circumstances.

The volunteers who made it through the rigorous psychological and physical testing assumed they were being primed and then prepared for highly classified, covert operations. They figured they would be flying under radar coverage into places like China, Cuba, or North Vietnam to bomb bridges and tunnels or insert agents and saboteurs. "No one bothered to tell us this wasn't an insurgency operation. It would be *counterinsurgency* or maybe the Air Force didn't know the difference" (emphasis added).[45]

Initially, the air commandos acquired eight T-28Bs from the Navy and eight B-26s from Air Force Reserve units, along with 16 SC-47s. Additional aircraft were to be made available as soon as possible. By July 1961 the 4400th CCTS was fully manned at 125 commissioned officers and 235 enlisted personnel.[46] On 11 October, President Kennedy ordered them to Vietnam.

Ambiguity abounded in their mission to South Vietnam. The first deployment of T-28s was delayed while the planes and their crews waited in the Philippines for AIM-9B Sidewinder heat-seeking missiles. Adm Harry D. Felt, CINCPAC, urged that the air commandos be sent on without their air-to-air missiles.[47] Since the Vietcong had no air force, the only use for these air-to-air missiles would have been to shoot down resupply flights originating in Hanoi or possibly Phnom Penh.

Under the code name Farm Gate, the air commandos of the 4400th CCTS arrived in Vietnam in early December. Ostensibly their mission was to train pilots, crew members, and support personnel for the VNAF, in short, doing those things that General McGarr, in his briefing to Gilpatric and the Vietnam Task Force, said should be done. They were also to fly close air support missions for the Army of the Republic of Vietnam (ARVN). The relationship between fighting and training within the mission of the air commandos was never clearly defined nor understood. Were they in Vietnam to train or to fight, or was training a cover

T-28

B-26

A-1 Skyraider

In November 1961 President Kennedy ordered the 4400th Combat Crew Training Squadron to deploy from Eglin AFB, Florida, to Bien Hoa AB, Vietnam. The air commandos of Operation Farm Gate flew T-28 trainers with souped-up engines and reinforced weapon points for carrying bombs, rockets, and machine guns. They also flew B-26s of World War II vintage and A-1 Skyraiders acquired from the Navy. These old, slow propeller-driven planes proved to be effective counterinsurgency platforms.

for fighting? Requests from US Army advisors for air cover were to be answered with real strike missions. Inquiries from the press were to be answered with, "No USAF pilot has ever flown in tactical missions except in the role of tactical instructor." [48]

The air commandos, at least, believed they were in Vietnam first to fight and then to train their South Vietnamese students. According to Col Benjamin H. King, the detachment commander, that was what LeMay told him. [49] But restrictions on when and how they could engage in combat were many and detailed. They always had to have a Vietnamese student on board. Legitimate training did take place and, indeed, during a three-year period the air commandos trained enough South Vietnamese pilots in the A-1E to man a couple of Skyraider squadrons. For the most part, however, training was nothing but a ruse.[50] It provided a cover so that when a plane was shot down there would be a large Caucasian body and a smaller Vietnamese body in the wreckage and the claim that the aircraft went down on a routine training mission would be plausible.

As far as the air commandos were concerned, training was not a priority. They called their Vietnamese backseaters "sandbags" and complained when they threw up in the cockpit.[51] Colonel King discussed the issue with the ranking Air Force officer in Vietnam, Brig Gen Rollen H. Anthis, commander of the 2d Advanced Echelon (ADVON). The two seemed at odds over whether the mission was training or only a cover for combat.[52] The confusion in Vietnam reflected the uncertainty in Washington, where the State Department and the Department of Defense did not appear to agree on how air power would be used.

Other rules inhibited the air commandos. On one of their first missions, Farm Gate T-28s strayed over Cambodia and bombed a village. The protests from Phnom Penh resulted in prohibitions on flying within five miles of the border during the daylight and 10 miles at night.[53] When, in the spring of 1962, F-102s were sent to Vietnam to intercept aircraft making clandestine flights from either Cambodia or North Vietnam, the rules stated that if an American plane—be it an F-102 or T-28—shot down one of these aircraft, credit would be given to any feasible South Vietnamese pilot who might have been in the area. If none were available to take the credit, the story would be that the unidentified aircraft crashed accidently.[54] Given the heroic aura that surrounded air-to-air combat, this rule was not popular with American pilots. From the beginning the myriad rules and scarcity of combat combined to retard morale.

At War with the Army

In contrast to the Air Force's uncertainty as to the way to fight the Vietcong, the Army demonstrated comparative unanimity about what it was doing in Vietnam. Vietnam offered the Army an opportunity to regain its position vis-à-vis the other services by co-opting the counterinsurgency mission, not that the Army was all that interested in antiguerrilla warfare per se. However, as a phrase popular around the Pentagon and in Vietnam so aptly stated, "It's not much of a war, but it's the only war we've got."

The fact was that the Kennedy administration was emphasizing counterinsurgency, and, because that was the reality, the Army wanted to have primary responsibility for that mission much as the Air Force had responsibility for strategic warfare. When the Air Force established its air commando program, the Army regarded that move as a challenge to its turf. Likewise, the Air Force felt its prerogatives were being violated when the Army enlarged and improved its aviation capabilities. While the Air Force of the 1950s was not overly interested in supporting ground forces, it certainly did not want the Army to take over that mission. When, in August 1961, the Army announced plans to increase the size of its Special Forces, the Air Force decided to double the size of the 4400th CCTS.[55]

Pentagon rivalries were transplanted to Saigon where Army officers worked to exclude the Air Force from decision-making positions in the MAAG and, later, from those in the Military Assistance Command, Vietnam (MACV). In December 1962 the MAAG contained eight Army generals and only three Air Force generals. The USAF director of plans said,

> It may be improper to say we are at war with the Army. However, we believe that if the Army efforts are successful, they may have a long term adverse effect in the U.S. military posture that could be more important than the battle presently being waged with the Viet Cong.[56]

Despite the efforts of the junior officers serving as advisors and flying in support of the ARVN, the rivalry at the headquarters devolved to the battlefield. One of the major effects of the interservice rivalry was a reduced effectiveness of the tactical air control system. A MACV directive of August 1962 designated the Air Force component commander as the authority for coordinating Vietnamese and American air activities, but the Air Force did not feel that the Army accepted or abided by the provisions of the directive.[57] Beginning in mid-1962 the 2d ADVON began keeping a running log of potential and actual incidents caused by the lack of proper coordination and the absence of cooperation.

From the Air Force's perspective, the Army was to blame whenever coordination broke down or was absent. The Air Force log included examples of incidents where Army helicopters and Air Force T-28s strafed or bombed the same area at the same time without notifying one another. Air Force T-28s would be dispatched to escort Army helicopters ferrying ARVN troops into battle only to find that the mission had been scrubbed. On one occasion, in November 1963, Army Huey helicopter gunships opened fire on an ARVN unit. Vietnamese staff officers at the ARVN 7th Division's command post could not get the US Army advisor to call off the helicopters because, according to the Air Force log, he was too busy trying to secure additional helicopter gunships to join the Hueys in clobbering the friendly troops below. Finally, after the extra chopper gunships had been dispatched to the scene, the Army advisor finally listened to the Vietnamese officer and called off the gunships, thereby averting further loss of life.[58] Thus did squabbling go beyond the childish to the tragic.

Contention again raised its head when the Air Force undertook to send search and rescue (SAR) helicopters to Vietnam. The Army, opposed as it was to any expansion in the Air Force's involvement in Vietnam, was particularly anxious to retain its virtual monopoly on helicopter operations. Despite Air Force protestations that the recovery of downed aircrew members involved more than hovering and dropping down a rope, the Army insisted it could handle the mission as a part of its regular helicopter activities. After several lives were lost during botched rescue attempts, the Air Force finally convinced the Army that a dedicated and trained rescue force was needed in Vietnam. Still, the first Air Force SAR helicopters did not reach Vietnam until March 1964.[59]

An October 1962 message from Headquarters Thirteenth Air Force indicated that the tension between the Army and the Air Force was intensifying with the growing commitment of soldiers and airmen to Vietnam.

> USAF interests are suffering in SEA. The trend toward an Army dominated COIN [counterinsurgency] effort is clear. . . . Their case will cost the USAF in roles and missions and will cost U.S. lives in future actions. Army people are, in effect, being trained to consider our tactics ineffective and our capability limited, while being oversold on Army organic air.[60]

The controversy over roles and missions in Vietnam already had reached back to Washington.

In April 1962 LeMay and several staff officers visited Vietnam on a five-day inspection tour. LeMay was not pleased by what he saw. In his opinion, air power and air resources were not being used correctly by the Americans or their Vietnamese ally. During his visit LeMay talked with Ngo Dinh Diem as well as with Gen Paul Harkins, the MACV commander. What Diem had to say pleased LeMay. Diem wanted a larger Air Force presence in Vietnam, and he wanted airfields improved so that jets could be deployed there. He also wanted to implement a crop destruction program as a part of the Ranch Hand defoliation project that had begun in early January. Conversely, LeMay was displeased by Harkins's reluctance to add an Air Force lieutenant general to his staff as a deputy. Later, Harkins accused LeMay of "preferring charges" against him when he returned to Washington. No record exists of LeMay's bringing formal charges against Harkins, and General LeMay denied ever doing such a thing. In fact, upon returning to Washington, LeMay ordered a C-123 transport be modified as a command aircraft for the personal use of the MACV commander.[61]

The squabbling between the Army and the Air Force abated in 1964 and then dropped off precipitously the following year. There were three good reasons for this decline in the war of words. First, with the escalation of the fighting, both the Army and the Air Force realized each would be playing a more or less traditional role in the expanding war. The Army's presence grew considerably in the spring and summer of 1965. And, with the arrival of large numbers of troops, the Army realized its helicopters and twin-engine transports could not satisfy its transportation and logistical support needs. Second, in March 1965 the United States initiated Rolling Thunder. The bombing of North Vietnam allowed the Air Force to bomb the kinds of targets its doctrine sanctioned: petroleum storage facilities, railroad marshalling yards, roads, bridges, and industries, as limited as those were. Even though the Air Force was far from satisfied with the constraints imposed on it, the campaign was more to its liking than counterinsurgency or close air support. Third, in June 1964 Gen William C. Westmoreland replaced Harkins as the MACV commander. At about the same time, Maj Gen Joseph H. Moore replaced Anthis as commander of the 2d Air Division (successor to the 2d ADVON). Moore and Westmoreland had been boyhood friends and classmates in high school in Spartanburg, South Carolina. Their friendship was a starting point for building a more congenial relationship between the Army and the Air Force in Vietnam. Before long, Moore was calling Westmoreland the "biggest booster of tactical air support in Vietnam."[62]

Despite the squabbling, the Air Force and the Army had helped the VNAF and the ARVN stave off defeat to gain an advantage over the Vietcong in 1962 and early 1963. In letters home, Air Force Capt Edwin G. Shank, Jr., observed that Farm Gate pilots, Army chopper pilots, and the ground advisors generally worked together to ameliorate the impact of infighting at higher levels. More important, perhaps, was the infusion of equipment and the differences that improved training made in the performance of both the Vietnamese army and air force. Farm Gate's air commandos were not the only ones in Vietnam in the early 1960s. Under the code name Mule Train, other Air Force crews were flying the ARVN into and out of battle and hauling supplies around Vietnam in old C-47 and somewhat newer C-123 transports.

In early 1962 the VNAF had a total of 225 trained pilots to fill 271 cockpit and staff positions requiring flying officers. Various remedies were considered, including using American or third-country pilots in VNAF aircraft. A partial solution to the native pilot shortage was to dispatch members of the Air Force pilot's augmentation group, the "Dirty Thirty" as they became known, to supplement VNAF slots. Most of the Americans flew as copilots in C-47s, thus somewhat alleviating the pilot shortage problem.[63] At the same time, a squadron of C-123 Providers arrived as a part of Mule Train. A second squadron reached Vietnam in June. The interservice infighting that affected Farm Gate operations seemed to have had less impact on transport units, perhaps because the increasing commitment of American forces translated into additional transportation requirements for the Army. The Vietnamese national campaign plan for 1963, for instance, forecasted an airlift requirement of 4.4 million ton-miles a month, roughly twice what it had been in 1962.[64] The estimates for 1964 and beyond were considerably higher and the Army may have realized it needed the Air Force after all.

Meanwhile, Ranch Hand had begun in early 1962, and it continued for nearly a decade. This innovative operation reflected the Air Force's fascination with technology. At the beginning of the war, the leadership had seen the use of herbicides as an efficient and effective way to remove dense jungle underbrush along roads, waterways, and railroads to reduce the chances for ambush and thus save lives. Likewise, defoliating the triple-layered jungle canopy facilitated spotting enemy encampments and supply caches from the air so that the US and South Vietnamese air forces could attack those bases. In addition, hand-spraying of defoliants to clear underbrush from areas adjacent to military encampments and fortified villages provided clear fields of fire and, thereby, denied the Vietcong the concealment they could use to effect surprise attacks. President Kennedy, on 30 November 1961, accepted a joint recommendation from the Departments of State and Defense advocating an aggressive defoliation program. This decision committed the Air Force to a course of action that led to the extensive use of herbicides in both defoliation and crop destruction.[65]

In 1962 there was hardly a hint that defoliation operations would become controversial. A few in the State Department expressed mild reservations, but some individuals were cautious about all uses of air power in Southeast Asia. Secretary Zuckert, too, harbored some reservations, but he kept them to himself.[66] Otherwise, defoliation was approached as a panacea, a technological solution to what was a human and political problem.

Questions of national security policy, global strategy, and interservice rivalries aside, Vietnam was about people at war. Tactics, as in any war, were the stuff of everyday combat. Because the Air Force of the 1950s did not emphasize skills like air-to-ground rocketry, gunnery, and close-support bombing, the Farm Gate crews had to learn these techniques for themselves. Napalm, for instance, ignited in the upper branches of the jungle canopy, doing little or no harm to the intended target below. Likewise, bombs often exploded in limbs and branches high above the jungle floor. One remedy was to drop a first load of napalm to burn a hole in the canopy and then come back on a second run to attack the exposed target.[67] Another technique devised in Vietnam was to put chunks of charcoal in the napalm mixture. The ignited charcoal briquets then spread the fire to the surrounding brush or grass-roofed structures.[68]

Innovation and adaptation of tactics were essential because the Vietcong (VC) were adept at using the terrain to their advantage. Most were from rural Vietnam. Many fought in units that remained near villages where they had grown up. As time went on, the Vietcong gained a reputation that might well have been out of proportion to their actual abilities. For instance, whenever the VC decided not to engage in combat and seemingly evaporated into the jungle, Americans marveled at "the illusive enemy." Conversely, whenever the ARVN did the same thing, they were often dubbed "the cowardly South Vietnamese." As an example of the Vietcong's prowess, at least in the eyes of their American enemy, a letter from the commander, Detachment 2A, 4400th

73

CCTS, to the commander, 2d ADVON, speculated that the Vietcong sometimes concealed themselves *and* their small boats just beneath the water's surface—supposedly filling their boats with water and sinking them—whenever an aircraft appeared. Presumably they breathed through reeds poking above the water. The American went on to claim that one way of dealing with this method of hiding was to drop either a 500-pound bomb into the water nearby to kill them with the concussion or to put a napalm burst over the surface, thus burning up the oxygen and leaving the submerged VC a choice between suffocation or surfacing to die by incineration. The Farm Gate commander admitted, however, that "the effectiveness of this method is not well documented." [69]

The Air Force in Vietnam went "on the offensive" to develop new techniques and tactics to take the initiative away from the Vietcong. An example of such innovation came in response to the frequent ambushes that had closed down the rail line from Saigon north to Quang Tri. This railroad was important for moving supplies between the northern and southern parts of the Republic of Vietnam and it was vital to the economy as well. The Vietnamese tried putting armored cars and flatbed cars fitted out with sandbags and machine guns in the trains so that they looked like something out of the Mexican Revolution. Vietcong ambushes, however, continued to take a toll. Sometimes the VC would blow up the tracks and then attack the troops as they defended a derailed train. Or they felled trees to block the track and then dispatched the ARVN troops in the armored railcars and on the sandbagged flatbeds.

To keep the trains moving, the Air Force began "riding shotgun in the sky." The shotgun force usually consisted of nothing more than one or two light observation planes scouting ahead of the train. If the observer spotted anything suspicious in the underbrush or jungle ahead, he radioed the train to stop while armed troops disembarked and moved ahead to check out the area. The airborne observer might also call on T-28s or B-26s to respond with machine-gun fire, napalm, or cluster bombs. High explosive bombs would not be used because they might destroy the track, accomplishing what the VC intended all along. After aerial escorts were implemented, no further rail convoys were attacked while the planes were overhead.[70]

The deployment of Air Force units in late 1961 and early 1962 coincided with the first uses of helicopters and armored personnel carriers by the ARVN to gain mobility and firepower. At first the Vietcong were caught by surprise and did not know how to deal with these machines. But by the end of 1962, they were adjusting to the new situation. In July the ARVN seized a VC training center in Kien Phong Province. On the blackboards in one of the huts they found diagrams depicting how to shoot down helicopters.[71]

The Vietcong, like the North Vietnamese later in the war, turned America's strength in air power to its own advantage in the propaganda arena. One method employed early in the conflict that the Vietminh had used effectively against the French was to occupy a village long enough for aircraft to be called in. Before the planes arrived the VC moved back into the jungle out of harm's way. Usually the air strikes would occur anyway, causing needless deaths among villagers, thereby providing grist for the VC propaganda mill and turning the people against the Saigon government and its American ally.[72]

The infusion of aid and the work of the additional American advisors paid dividends in increased combat proficiency by both the ARVN and VNAF. The introduction of armored personnel carriers, howitzers, and helicopters and the availability of aerial firepower changed the way the ARVN fought. American commanders generally believed the South Vietnamese armed forces had improved, but had they? As the ARVN and the VNAF became richer in firepower and mobility, they also became increasingly dependent on those things. And the Americans continued to mold the Vietnamese armed forces into the images of their individual services.

In 1962 General Harkins exuded confidence. He claimed, "This past year has seen the Vietnamese take the initiative away from the Viet Cong. I think the coming year will bring greater efforts and I have all the confidence that the Vietnamese Armed Forces will

75

attain even greater success."[73] According to the general, about 30,000 Vietcong were killed in 1962. The Air Force claimed a third of that number fell to Vietnamese and American air power.[74]

The numbers game was under way. The Air Force and the Army had their set of numbers, usually quite optimistic ones, while the State Department and the CIA issued numbers that reflected their skepticism. According to the CIA, the figure 30,000 Vietcong casualties (including an estimated 21,000 killed in action) was misleading. The agency's analysts wondered how the VC, numbering only 17,600 in January, could have lost more than 100 percent of their force and still have numbered an estimated 24,000 in December. One agency analyst remarked, "This suggests either that casualty figures are exaggerated or that the Viet Cong have a remarkable replacement capability . . . or both!"[75]

Whether progress was real in 1963 or just a matter of perspective, Harkins insisted that field operations had been unaffected by the political turmoil that boiled in the wake of Buddhist unrest which exploded into demonstrations and riots in the summer of 1963. According to Harkins, since military efforts were devised for the "people in the countryside," the turmoil in the cities had little direct impact on how the ARVN prosecuted its war against the VC.[76]

Despite the turmoil and the riots in Saigon, Hue, and Da Nang, the perception was that the military situation was still good in 1963. A memorandum sent to the president after Gen Maxwell D. Taylor and Secretary McNamara visited Vietnam in September echoed Harkins's optimism. Their suggestion to withdraw 1,000 American military personnel by the end of the year, while in part a message to Diem that it was time to get his political house in order, was also indicative of the optimism that led them to believe that the South Vietnamese army and air force would be self-sufficient by the end of 1965.[77] The light already had begun to flicker at the end of the tunnel.

Official Air Force pronouncements notwithstanding, all was not well with the airmen serving in Vietnam. Captain Shank's letters, published by his wife in *Life* magazine following his death in

March 1964, offer valuable insight into the way the Farm Gate crews viewed the war. Optimism was not pervasive, complaints were numerous, and morale was low.[78] The crews fretted about the constantly changing rules of engagement. They complained that these rules were often unintelligible. In many cases the rules of engagement were influenced by local South Vietnamese politics that were beyond the interest or comprehension of most Americans. The rules of engagement were only a part of a larger, and usually inefficient, tactical air control system manned by inexperienced personnel and outfitted with unreliable equipment.

Further complicating the process of getting the bombs to the target was the role played by the Vietnamese forward air controller (FAC). Vietnamese FACs irritated the Americans because they were not, like their American counterparts, trained fighter pilots with a concomitant knowledge of what fighter-bombers could and could not do. The VNAF forward air controllers were merely observers. Their target-marking procedures were serendipitous at best. When the Vietnamese FACs ran out of or could not get smoke rockets or grenades, they flew over a target to "mark" it with the shadow of the plane. At the instant their shadow passed over the enemy position, they would tell the strike pilots to "fire."[79]

Additionally, the air commandos questioned the reliability of their aircraft: the T-28s and B-26s were showing their age. Problems developed with the wing spars of both the T-28s and B-26s. In several cases, the wings fell off after sharp pullouts or simply broke off in flight due to structural fatigue. Neither of these planes had been designed to operate from unimproved fields, and a major cause of wing fatigue in the B-26s was taxiing the aircraft with 750-pound bombs attached to specially designed racks slung beneath the wings. Moreover, the B-26 had been designed in the late 1930s as a medium-altitude, "horizontal" bomber, not a dive-bomber, and steep pullouts often spelled disaster. Likewise, T-28s (training aircraft modified especially for the air commandos) had begun losing their wings at an increased rate in 1963 and 1964.[80] Air power may, in official Air Force doctrine, be flexible, but aircraft are not always so.

As if problems with rules of engagement, the cumbersome tactical air control system, and disintegrating aircraft were not enough, the Farm Gate, Ranch Hand, and Mule Train crews (along with their supporting casts) had to live with the hardships of fighting a war in a different and primitive environment. Food service at Tan Son Nhut, the largest airfield in South Vietnam, was poor. Ice for drinks was often contaminated with dirt, sawdust, and insects. Rat feces were found in the bread purchased under contract from Vietnamese bakers. In the days before the commissary service built its many well-stocked exchanges throughout Vietnam and Thailand, items like toothpaste, aftershave lotion, and deodorant were often hard to come by, particularly at isolated spots like Pleiku or, in the early sixties, Bien Hoa.[81]

These problems indicate that, despite the importance attached to Vietnam by the Kennedy and Johnson administrations, the Air Force did not plan to be there for an extended period. Since its doctrinal departure point was that small wars could be won easily as long as it was ready to win the big wars, the Air Force had to believe that once air power was properly employed, this war could be won quickly. The Air Force, winging its way into Southeast Asia on a doctrine devised for bombing Nazi Germany, was not alone in its nostalgia for fighting World War II nor in its determination to envisage the enemy's capabilities as mirroring its own.

In a memorandum sent to President Kennedy, the Joint Chiefs of Staff recommended that the military role in Vietnam be expanded regardless of the risk of North Vietnamese or Chinese intervention. "Any war in the Southeast Asian Mainland will be a peninsula and island-type campaign—a mode of warfare in which all elements of the Armed Forces of the United States have gained a wealth of experience and in which we have excelled both in World War II and Korea."[82] General Anthis, the first Air Force commander in Vietnam, made the analogy with World War II, when, in 1967, he reflected on the importance of air power to the struggle in Southeast Asia.

Southeast Asia is not a tiny corner of the world. That portion of it directly or indirectly involved in the conflict—North and South Vietnam, and a portion of Laos—contains 207,000 square miles of territory. This is only slightly less than the 219,000 square miles in which U.S. forces fought from Normandy to Berlin—northern France, Belgium, the Netherlands, Denmark, Luxembourg, England and West Germany. The distance from Omaha Beach to Berlin is 675 miles—slightly less than the 706 miles from Saigon to Hanoi. Anzio Beach to Innsbruck north of the Brenner Pass in the Alps is 490 miles—slightly more than the 409 miles from Saigon to Hue. Zone D, the jungle fortress used by the Viet Cong, is about 500 square miles in area, roughly equal to half the area of Luxembourg. These geographical comparisons make self-evident the need for air power in Southeast Asia.[83]

Walt W. Rostow was a leading supporter of the movement within the administration to bomb North Vietnam. Rostow believed bombing North Vietnam would have similar results to the bombing of Germany and Japan.[84] He backed LeMay and the JCS when they urged Kennedy to expand the war to the North through bombing. As a member of the State Department Planning Council, Rostow argued for a policy of retaliatory strikes against North Vietnam calculated to match the intensity of Hanoi's support for the Vietcong.[85]

This impulse to fight the war at a level above the counter-insurgency effort prevailed throughout the Air Force. The crews in Vietnam believed that the war could be prosecuted more effectively if higher performance aircraft were used. They felt not only that T-28s and B-26s were unsafe to fly and increasingly vulnerable to improving Vietcong antiaircraft capabilities but also that those planes lacked the weapons delivery capability of jets like the F-100 and B-57.[86] Lt Col Charles E. Trumbo, Jr., the 2d Air Division's director of plans in 1963, expressed a commonly held opinion when he stated, "A squadron of F-100s over here could puncture the balloon of the skeptics."[87] At a higher level, a JCS team headed by Lt Gen David A. Burchinal and Maj Gen William W. Momyer argued, in a report issued after a visit to Southeast Asia, that "without augmentation of United States tactical aviation units, it could not be possible for the Vietnamese Air Force to meet its daily sortie demands (in 1963)."[88] At the highest level of the

Air Force, General LeMay pushed for an extension of the war to the North, feeling as he did that, "we ought to get in with both feet and get the chore over with, and do the things that are necessary to be done." [89]

There is reason to speculate that at the time of his assassination, President Kennedy, too, was considering a new direction for US policy in Vietnam. In September, during a television interview with Walter Cronkite, the president had stated candidly, "In the final analysis, it is their war. They (the South Vietnamese) are the ones who have to win it or lose it." [90] Kennedy might have reassessed his administration's policy on Vietnam had he lived. Kennedy-philes would like to believe that a major change of direction was in the wind. Those less entranced with "Camelot" are not as willing to be convinced that things would have been otherwise if history had taken a different course. [91]

After Lyndon Johnson became president he had some difficult decisions to make on Vietnam. His choices were limited and not all that appealing: Do we cut our losses, withdraw, and, in all

F-100. While the sentiment that "a squadron of F-100s over here could puncture the balloon of the skeptics" was typical of many Air Force leaders in the early 1960s, in reality jets like the F-100 did not prove to be as suited for close air support as A-1s and T-28s.

probability, watch South Vietnam fall to the Communists? Or do we persevere with the Saigon generals who had recently murdered Diem and who, in the months ahead, probably would engage in a series of palace coups as they jockeyed for power? Given that Johnson did not want to be saddled with the loss of Vietnam as President Harry Truman had been with losing China to the Communists, the room for maneuver in decision making appeared limited. Johnson decided to increase the scope and the intensity of the American commitment.[92]

During the first few months in office, Johnson stepped up clandestine operations against North Vietnam. Air Force EC-130s from the 6091st Reconnaissance Squadron began flying missions to intercept communications emanating from military installations in North Vietnam.[93] Simultaneously, in that summer of 1964, Navy vessels plowed along the coast of North Vietnam mapping radar sites. A thorough index of radar and communications facilities would be needed when American planes began bombing.

The war inside South Vietnam was also changing. Optimistic reports from MACV notwithstanding, the Vietcong made substantial progress during the turmoil that surrounded the political situation in Saigon. The North Vietnamese were rearming the Vietcong with standardized weaponry from socialist-bloc countries. By 1964 the AK-47 assault rifle had become the common weapon of the VC, and North Vietnamese regulars were fighting inside South Vietnam, not only as members of Vietcong guerrilla units but also in their own regiments. At the end of 1964, the advantage that the ARVN had won in 1962 had all but disappeared.[94]

On 4 August, North Vietnamese torpedo boats attacked two US destroyers in the Gulf of Tonkin. President Johnson ordered air attacks on the North Vietnamese boat bases and their supporting fuel storage facilities in reprisal. Simultaneously, six F-102 jet interceptors from Clark Air Base (AB) in the Philippines and six other F-102s from Naha AB, Okinawa, deployed to Tan Son Nhut. Additionally, eight F-100s from Clark flew to Da Nang and 36 B-57s from the 8th and 13th Bomber Squadrons were ordered to

Bien Hoa. Within a week, F-100s, F-105s, and KB-50 tankers had been dispatched to Thailand.[95]

- - - - - - - - -

The gathering of this air armada marked a watershed in the Vietnam War that was welcomed by the Air Force. While the Air Force had been uncomfortable with the counterinsurgency role assigned to it in Vietnam, it was also not focusing its attention entirely on the war in those early years. Vietnam was, even in 1964, still very much a situation of a lesser magnitude as far as the Air Force was concerned. Furthermore, the efforts of Farm Gate, Mule Train, and Ranch Hand crews had seemingly been rewarded. The ARVN and the VNAF, with aid and advice from the United States, had staved off defeat by the Vietcong in 1962 and, at least temporarily, gained the upper hand. The Air Force had made a place for itself in Vietnam and, perhaps most importantly, the Army had not usurped or co-opted the air power role in counter-insurgency operations.

Even though the war was clearly escalating and the Vietcong had grown in strength and become bolder on the battlefield, there was no reason to lose faith in old concepts or doctrines. That the outside instigator was at work providing arms and men to support the revolution in South Vietnam was not surprising. Given the tenets of cold war thinking, that was what the Hanoi-Moscow-Peking axis was supposed to be doing. Furthermore, when the transition from counterinsurgency to conventional warfare was complete, the Air Force would be allowed to use air power in the doctrinally hallowed ways it was supposed to be used by going to the source in Hanoi to bomb airfields, oil refineries, factories, railroad marshalling yards, bridges, and highways. Nothing had happened yet to shake the faith that if prepared to fight and win the big war, there was nothing to fear from these situations of a lesser magnitude.

Notes

1. Secretary of the Air Force Eugene M. Zuckert, commencement address, George Washington University, 22 February 1962, 3b, President's Office Files, John F. Kennedy Library, Boston, Mass.

2. "Global Crises Stacked Up for Mr. Kennedy," *Newsweek*, 23 January 1961, 25.

3. Theodore C. Sorensen, *Kennedy* (New York: Harper and Row, 1965), 548.

4. Ibid., 549.

5. See "Strategic Air Command," *Air Force Magazine*, September 1962, 93–94. In 1962 SAC's inventory included 600 B-52s, 900 B-47s, and a few supersonic B-58s. There were several squadrons of Atlas missiles and two operational squadrons of Titan I silo-based intercontinental ballistic missiles. The first crews designated for Minuteman silos were undergoing training in 1962. See also *Strategy and Money: The Defense Budget for Fiscal Year 1961* (Maxwell AFB, Ala.: USAF Historical Liaison Office, 1962), 36–38. During the 1950s the Air Force never received less than 39 percent of the total defense budget; in 1960 it garnered 48 percent of the available dollars. About half that sum went to the Strategic Air Command. Indeed, SAC's budget equalled that of the entire US Army.

6. "Bombers Away," *Newsweek*, 23 January 1961, 13.

7. Secretary of the Air Force Eugene M. Zuckert, interview with Lawrence E. McQuade, 18 April 1964, 15, Kennedy Library.

8. Ibid.

9. Ibid.

10. *Strategy and Money*, 39–40.

11. Robert F. Futrell, *Ideas, Concepts, Doctrine: A History of Basic Thinking in the United States Air Force, 1907–1964* (Maxwell AFB, Ala.: Air University, 1971), 341.

12. Ibid., 336.

13. Zuckert interview, 114.

14. Ibid.

15. Futrell, *Ideas*, 343.

16. Ernest K. Lindley, "The First Acid Test," *Newsweek*, 30 January 1961, 27.

17. Arthur J. Dommen, *Laos: Keystone of Indochina* (Boulder, Colo.: Westview Press, 1985), 59–62.

18. Ibid., 63.

19. M. L. Manich, *History of Laos* (Bangkok: Chalermnit Press, 1967), 332–33.

20. Peter Berton and Alvin Z. Rubinstein's *Soviet Works on Southeast Asia: A Bibliography of Non-Periodical Literature, 1946–1965* (Los Angeles:

University of Southern California Press, 1967) does not list a single work in Russian on Laos prior to 1960.

21. "Department Statement of January 7," *State Department Bulletin* 44, no. 1126 (23 January 1961): 115.

22. See Arthur J. Dommen, *Conflict in Laos: The Politics of Neutralization* (New York: Praeger Publishers, 1971), 167; and "Soviet Guns Sent into Laos by Air," *New York Times*, 12 December 1960, 1.

23. John Kenneth Galbraith, *Ambassador's Journal* (Boston: Houghton Mifflin, 1969), 107.

24. Message, 270348Z January 1962, commander in chief, Pacific Command (CINCPAC), to Joint Chiefs of Staff (JCS), National Security Files, Kennedy Library.

25. Dommen, *Laos*, 70.

26. See text of President Kennedy's 23 March press conference, *New York Times*, 24 March 1961, 1 and 7; and Arthur M. Schlesinger, Jr., *A Thousand Days* (Greenwich, Conn.: Doubleday, 1967), 311–12.

27. Dommen, *Conflict*, 189.

28. Ibid.

29. Zuckert interview, 23.

30. *The Pentagon Papers*, Senator Gravel edition, vol. 2 (Boston: Beacon Press, 1975), 42.

31. Dommen, *Conflict*, 189.

32. "Protocol to the Declaration on the Neutrality of Laos," 23 July 1962, in *The Vietnam War and International Law*, ed. Richard A. Falk (Princeton, N.J.: Princeton University Press, 1968), 568–73.

33. Dommen, *Conflict*, 239.

34. Memorandum for Maj Gen C. V. Clifton, military assistant to the president, subject: MAAG Laos, 3 September 1962, National Security Files, Laos, Kennedy Library.

35. History, 2d Advanced Echelon (ADVON), 15 November 1961– 8 October 1962, daily historical log, Pipe Stem Detachment, 18 October– 9 November 1961, vol. 2, supporting documents, K750.01-3, Air Force Historical Research Center (USAFHRC), Maxwell AFB, Ala.

36. Robert F. Futrell, *The United States Air Force in Southeast Asia: The Advisory Years to 1965* (Washington, D.C.: Office of Air Force History, 1981), 36.

37. Ibid., 49–50.

38. According to former South Vietnamese minister of national defense Gen Tran Van Don, he and other leading Vietnamese army officers tried to convince Gen John O'Daniel that the Vietnamese should use the Vietminh model of light infantry formations for organizational purposes. O'Daniel refused because it would be easier to provide logistical support if the Vietnamese army was structured comparably to US divisions. See Tran Van Don, *Our Endless War:*

Inside Vietnam (San Rafael, Calif.: Presidio Press, 1978), 148–50; and *Pentagon Papers* (Gravel) 2:433.

39. Memorandum for MAAG advisors, from Lt Gen Lionel C. McGarr, 24 April 1961, National Security Files, Vietnam, Kennedy Library.

40. Zuckert interview, 68.

41. Ibid., 62–63.

42. Charles H. Hildreth, *USAF Counter-Insurgency Doctrines and Capabilities: 1961–62* (Washington, D.C.: Office of Air Force History, 1962), 8–9.

43. Ibid., 9.

44. Allan R. Scholin, "Air Commandos: USAF's Contribution to Counterinsurgency," *Air Force and Space Digest,* August 1962, 41.

45. J. Grainger interview with Lt Col M. M. Doyle, commander, 1st Air Commando Group, 16 February 1963, Bien Hoa, Vietnam, in History, 2d ADVON, supporting documents, vol. 12, 6, USAFHRC.

46. Hildreth, 8–9.

47. Futrell, *Advisory Years,* 81. At this time North Vietnam had no jet aircraft in its air force. The Farm Gate area of operation was too far south to be menaced by Chinese air force MiGs. Thus, the only possible use for these missiles would have been to shoot down resupply flights from Hanoi or Phnom Penh to Tchepone or to shoot down planes thought to be flying from Phnom Penh to drop supplies to the Vietcong operating in the jungles west and northwest of Saigon.

48. See message, 260116Z December 1962, JCS to CINCPAC (National Security Files, Laos), and letter, CINCPAC to JCS, 1 March 1962 (National Security Files, Vietnam), Kennedy Library.

49. Quoted in Futrell, *Advisory Years,* 82.

50. Futrell, *Advisory Years,* 127.

51. Lt Gen Joseph H. Moore, Jr., interview with author, 9 November 1986, Maxwell AFB, Ala.

52. Futrell, *Advisory Years,* 127; message, 290138Z March 1962, CINCPAC to JCS, National Security Files, Vietnam, Kennedy Library.

53. Message, #968, Saigon to secretary of state (SECSTATE), subject: Farm Gate ROE and Procedures, 26 January 1963, National Security Files, Vietnam, Kennedy Library.

54. Ibid.

55. Hildreth, 15.

56. Futrell, *Advisory Years,* 148.

57. Military Assistance Command, Vietnam (MACV), Directive, Air Operations Center, 18 August 1962, tab A, 1.

58. See Discussion of MACV Directives Relating to Control and Coordination of Air, 18 August 1962–November 1963; and letter, 7th Division ALO, 13 November 1963, pt. 2, tab 20, UH-1B Controversial File, K526.549-1, USAFHRC.

59. Earl H. Tilford, Jr., *United States Air Force Search and Rescue in Southeast Asia* (Washington, D.C.: Office of Air Force History, 1980), 42–46.

60. Message, 240807Z October 1962, Thirteenth Air Force to Pacific Air Forces, Office of Air Force History, SAR File, Bolling AFB, Washington, D.C.

61. See Thomas M. Coffey, *Iron Eagle: The Turbulent Life of General Curtis LeMay* (New York: Crown Publishers, 1986), 383–85; and Futrell, *Advisory Years*, 102.

62. Moore interview; and Futrell, *Advisory Years*, 236.

63. Ray L. Bowers, *Tactical Airlift*, The United States Air Force in Southeast Asia (Washington, D.C.: Office of Air Force History, 1983), 72–73.

64. Ibid., 114.

65. William A. Buckingham, Jr., *Operation Ranch Hand: The Air Force and Herbicides in Southeast Asia, 1961–1971* (Washington, D.C.: Office of Air Force History, 1982), 21–22.

66. Zuckert interview, 73.

67. See letter, commander, Detachment 2A (Det 2A), to commander, 2d ADVON, subject: Monthly Report on the Development of Tactics and Techniques, 20 September 1962, 1, K526.54-2, USAFHRC; and Scholin, 41.

68. Response by DPS, Shank file, 1963–1964, vol. 2, K526.701-1, USAFHRC.

69. Letter, commander, Det 2, to commander, 2d ADVON.

70. Maj Gen Rollen H. Anthis, "Air Power: The Paradox in Vietnam," *Air Force Magazine*, April 1967, 36.

71. Message, 250044Z August 1962, CINCPAC, Camp H. S. Smith, to JCS, National Security File, Vietnam, Kennedy Library. A good example of how fast the Vietcong adjusted is illustrated by their performance during the Battle of Ap Bac in January 1963. About 200 VC soldiers defeated a force of more than 2,000 ARVN who were supported by helicopters and armored personnel carriers as well as T-28 and B-26 strikes. The VC shot down five choppers (one third of the force) and destroyed all three M-113 armored personnel carriers used in the attack. See Dave Richard Palmer, *Summons of the Trumpet: U.S.-Vietnam in Perspective* (San Rafael, Calif.: Presidio Press, 1978), 31–35.

72. Amb Frederick E. Nolting, Jr., feared that this might be happening in early 1963 as indicated in his "eyes only" message to the secretary of state. (American ambassador [AMEMB], Saigon, to SECSTATE, Eyes Only, subject: Performance of U.S. Mission, 23 January 1963, 1, National Security Files, Vietnam, Kennedy Library.) The Vietminh had used a similar method against the French, turning the population against them by tricking the French into bombing villages that might contain significant ambiguity of feeling. Typically, the Vietminh would dig in along a tree line near a hamlet and then open fire on the French troops or circling aircraft. Like the Americans after them, the French would dispatch planes that would bomb the village rather than the tree line, thus missing the enemy force while alienating the population in the process. See Andrew F. Krepinevich, Jr., *The Army and Vietnam* (Baltimore:

Johns Hopkins University Press, 1986), 76; and David Halberstam, *The Making of a Quagmire* (New York: Random House, 1964), 86.

73. Message, 100830Z January 1963, commander, US Military Assistance Command, Vietnam (COMUSMACV), to JCS, for General Taylor from General Harkins, National Security Files, Vietnam, Kennedy Library.

74. Futrell, *Advisory Years*, 134.

75. Current intelligence memorandum, subject: Current Status of the War in South Vietnam, 11 January 1963, National Security Files, Vietnam, Kennedy Library.

76. Message, AMEMB Saigon (Nolting) to SECSTATE, 1–4.

77. Memorandum for the president, subject: Report of McNamara-Taylor Mission to South Vietnam, 2 (National Security Files, Vietnam, Kennedy Library); and William J. Rust, *Kennedy in Vietnam* (New York: Charles Scribner's Sons, 1985), 140–41.

78. The Air Force public affairs office classified the letters, perhaps to prevent further publication, and provided classified responses to internal Air Force inquiries to each of Shank's many assertions. The interplay between reality and policy indicates that, indeed, Washington was a long way from Soc Trang and Bien Hoa.

79. History, 2d ADVON, 103.

80. See Futrell, *Advisory Years*, 181; and the Shank file, letter DPS, to Maj Gen E. B. LeBailley, director of information, subject: Letters from Captain Shank (date obscured), atch 6, USAFHRC.

81. Letter, Maj A. H. Hudson, veterinary officer, to commander, 4th Medical Detachment (VFI), US Army Support Group, Vietnam, subject: Sanitary Quality of Bread and Ice Received on Local Contract cited in interview, Capt John Hargraven with Maj Thomas J. Hickman and Joseph W. Grainger, 13 February 1963, Saigon, interview 470, USAF Oral Histories Program, USAFHRC.

82. Memorandum from the Joint Chiefs of Staff to Secretary of Defense McNamara, 13 January 1962, in *The Pentagon Papers*, ed. Gerald Gold, Allan M. Siegal, and Samuel Abt, *New York Times* edition (New York: Quadrangle Books, 1971), 159.

83. Rollen H. Anthis, "Air Power," *Air Force Magazine*, 1967, 34–35.

84. Townsend Hoopes, *The Limits of Intervention* (New York: David McKay, 1969), 21–22.

85. Futrell, *Advisory Years*, 80, 261.

86. Letter, Captain Shank to his wife, 29 February 1964, Shank file, USAFHRC.

87. Lt Col Charles E. Trumbo, Jr., director of plans, 2d Air Division, with Joseph W. Grainger, 13 July 1963, Tan Son Nhut AB, Vietnam, interview 271, USAF Oral History Program, USAFHRC.

88. Report of Visit by Joint Chiefs of Staff Team to South Vietnam, January 1963, 6, National Security Files, Vietnam, Kennedy Library.

89. Quoted in Coffey, 428.

90. Quoted in Sorensen, 659.

91. President's Office Files, 21 October 1963, Kennedy Library.

92. Herbert Y. Schandler, *Lyndon Johnson and Vietnam: The Unmaking of a President* (Princeton, N.J.: Princeton University Press, 1977), 6–7.

93. Futrell, *Advisory Years*, 228.

94. Palmer, 49.

95. Futrell, *Advisory Years*, 229.

Chapter 3

Rolling Thunder and the Diffusion of Heat

American bombs had been falling on North Vietnam for two years by the summer of 1967. Controversy over the aerial campaign dubbed Rolling Thunder raged both inside the Johnson administration and, increasingly, throughout the land. Secretary of the Air Force Harold Brown, in a somewhat ambiguous and confusing memorandum to Secretary of Defense Robert S. McNamara, likened a proposal for constricting the flow of supplies moving through the southern part of North Vietnam by concentrating the bombing in the panhandle south of the 20th parallel to transport or diffusion problems in the physical world (e.g., the diffusion of heat). Brown (a physicist) continued, "It is demonstrable that interferences close to the source have a greater effect, not a lesser effect, than the same interferences close to the output."[1] By stating the problem of aerial interdiction in terms of limiting output, Brown was communicating in managerial parlance presumably comprehensible to McNamara, the former Ford Motor Company president turned "generalissimo." The memorandum put warfare within the context of physics and industrial output. Such was the conceptualization and comprehension of warfare among many of those—both civilian and military—who advised the president.

From 1965 through 1968 the Air Force—along with the air forces of the Navy, the Marine Corps, and South Vietnam—undertook the longest bombing campaign ever conducted by the US Air Force.[2] After a million sorties were flown and more than three quarters of a million tons of bombs dropped, Rolling Thunder ended. In all but a few quarters of the American military, Rolling Thunder is generally held to have failed. The bombing did not coerce North Vietnam into refraining from support of the southern insurgency. The reasons for its lack of success are many, and blame cannot be placed conveniently on anyone or on any single group. Many factors—political, doctrinal, cultural, tactical, and environmental—resulted in the failure of Rolling Thunder. Above all it was a failure of strategy in that it was a conventional aerial campaign aimed at one country as a remedy for an unconventional war occurring in another.

The objective here is to examine how the Air Force approached the bombing of North Vietnam and to ask how and why it conducted its aerial operations as it did. This analysis also shows that Air Force leaders were unable to devise military alternatives applicable to the limited objectives decided upon by their civilian leaders. Rolling Thunder took place in what historians may well designate as one of the most difficult eras in American history since the Civil War. It was part of that era—no less nor more confused, perhaps, in its substance and execution than many efforts going on simultaneously in Vietnam. As we examine Rolling Thunder, keep in mind that history defines the parameters for action for any group at any particular time. If laying blame is dangerous, drawing neatly contrived "lessons learned" can be just as perilous. However, to excuse or, worse, conveniently forget is deadly.

The Dark before the Storm

From 1961, when Air Force units were first sent to Vietnam, airmen had longed to unleash the full potential of air power. Air commandos were frustrated at fighting the war "on the cheap." On the Air Staff the leadership of the Air Force watched apprehensively as the Army assumed the dominant role in what admittedly was not much of a war but, in fact, was "the only war we've got." Failure heightened frustration.

At the end of 1963 the Republic of Vietnam was no more stable than it had been at the end of 1961, when American advisors were dispatched in considerable numbers. The year 1964 was one of transition from counterinsurgency, with which the institutional Air Force was uncomfortable, to more conventional warfare. The

Vietcong (VC), who still carried the brunt of the fighting for the other side, were moving from guerrilla warfare to large-scale fighting. Hanoi, which had been sending regular People's Army of Vietnam (PAVN) units into South Vietnam for almost a year, seemingly sensed that the end was near for the Saigon regime and that increased support from the North might enable the Vietcong to defeat the Saigon regime by the spring of 1965.[3]

According to US government sources, 12,500 North Vietnamese troops and Vietcong cadre sent North for training had made the journey down the Ho Chi Minh Trail and into South Vietnam during 1964.[4] A National Security Council (NSC) working group concluded in late November that

> the DRV [Democratic Republic of Vietnam] contribution is substantial. The DRV manages the VC insurgency. It gives it guidance and direction [and] provides the VC [with] senior officers, key cadre, military specialists, and certain key military and communications equipment. . . . The DRV contribution may now be growing.[5]

For political reasons it was convenient that North Vietnam and China be identified clearly as the outside instigators. The American public was primed to see China as the éminence grise behind its enemies.[6] Fear of China and Chinese expansion presented a viable rationale for increasing America's commitment to South Vietnam, and North Vietnam was a logical target for military action.

The US had planned for a possible war with China and the Joint Chiefs of Staff as early as 1961 had recommended sending troops to South Vietnam to deter aggression from North Vietnam and, beyond that, China. Nevertheless, no one wanted a war with China—not the president or the Congress nor even the most hawkish generals and admirals. Besides, the preponderance of evidence pointed to North Vietnam as the outside instigator, a likely and potentially more lucrative candidate for attack. China, however, had warned that the United States should not go too far. Because there were plenty of people around who remembered the consequences of ignoring China's warnings during the march to the Yalu River in the Korean War, the US leadership took the admonition seriously. Hence, the fear of Chinese intervention precluded serious consideration of any invasion of North Vietnam. Bombing offered an appealing alternative because the US could adjust its intensity. Through judicious selection of targets and the weight of the attacks themselves, the US could turn the pressure up or down and accelerate or slow the intensity. If necessary, the US might stop the bombing abruptly. Bombing appealed to Lyndon Johnson because he "could keep control of the war in [his] own hands. If China reacted to our slow escalation . . . we'd have plenty of time to ease off." [7]

In 1964 most of the civilians surrounding the president shared the Joint Chiefs of Staff's collective faith in the efficacy of bombing only to a slightly lesser degree. Civilian strategists within the Office of the Secretary of Defense were drawn to the coercive potential of air power. [8] Their views reflected deterrence theories developed in the mid-to-late fifties. The concept of North Vietnam as an outside instigator presented a target which seemed vulnerable to air power applied in reasonably small doses. The president's advisors and the Joint Chiefs reasoned that North Vietnam was a small country, with a tiny industrial base only just emerging from the ravages of the long war with France. Hanoi, they believed, would be reluctant to risk its economic viability to support the insurgency in the South. At the State Department, Walt Rostow argued for the kind of campaign that would signal Hanoi and Peking that America was committed to using its vast resources "to persuade them that a continuation of their present policy will risk major destruction in North Vietnam." [9]

Actually, Rostow had no more hard evidence to conclude that North Vietnam's behavior could be affected by bombing than did the Air Force leadership, which was arguing for a concerted attack to destroy Hanoi's war-making capabilities by obliterating its industries, destroying its petroleum storage facilities, and wrecking its transportation systems. Certainly, conventional military wisdom argued that if industries and fuel storage facilities along with roads, railroads, and bridges were destroyed then virtually any nation would be rendered militarily impotent. If that had happened to the United States, the Soviet Union, Poland, or

Britain, such would probably have been the case. Gen Curtis E. LeMay, Air Force chief of staff in 1964, argued from a position of faith for such an attack on North Vietnam's "vital centers." As Gen William W. Momyer later put it, "All of his experience had taught him that such a campaign would end the war."[10]

While civilian policymakers thought more in terms of affecting will and changing behavior, the Air Force wanted to conclude matters quickly by destroying war-making capability and *breaking*—not merely affecting—will. Through the summer and autumn of 1964 the Air Force pushed for the kind of bombing campaign that would accomplish those objectives. They devised a set of targets—the 94-targets list—designed to destroy North Vietnam's industries and wreck its transportation system, thereby preventing North Vietnam from supporting the insurgency in South Vietnam. In February 1965, following the attack on the air base at Pleiku, Gen John P. McConnell, LeMay's successor as Air Force chief of staff, argued for a concerted 28-day bombing campaign to destroy all the targets on the 94-targets list. Walt Rostow was taken aback by the proposed aerial blitz and communicated his concerns to Secretary McNamara, warning that "too much thought is being given to the actual damage we do in the North and not enough thought to the signal we wish to send."[11] The difference in approach was between that of the military dreamer and that of the civilian pragmatist.

Not everyone around the president was convinced that air power could play a significant role in attaining American goals in Vietnam. Under Secretary of State George Ball, for instance, opposed bombing North Vietnam from the beginning. Ball had been a codirector of the United States Strategic Bombing Survey after World War II. Because the survey found that bombing had had less impact on Japanese and German war-making capabilities than had been originally believed, Ball was not sure it would deter Hanoi from supporting the southern insurgency or force the North Vietnamese to give up the goals for which they had been fighting for more than two decades.[12]

93

Caught in the middle was Lyndon Johnson. He saw himself as the culmination of American liberalism in the twentieth century. His Great Society would complete the New Deal begun by Franklin Roosevelt 30 years before. Johnson was untuned to foreign policy and unsophisticated in his approach to problems in faraway places. He tended to think that all politicians, whether on the banks of the Pedernales or along the Mekong, were alike. He liked to wheel and deal—using sticks and carrots, offering gains for concessions—to get what he wanted. If a senator wanted a dam for the folks back home or wanted a military base kept open even when it served no useful strategic purpose, that senator had to pay a political price in return. Walt Rostow and other civilian advisors offered Johnson a bombing program wrapped around sticks and carrots. "I saw our bombs as my political resources for negotiating a peace. On the one hand, our planes and our bombs could be used as carrots for the South . . . pushing them to clean up their corrupt house . . . on the other hand . . . as sticks against the North."[13] What Lyndon Johnson may have forgotten is that normally both the carrots and the sticks are used simultaneously to influence the same individual or entity.

Johnson was acutely aware that he had to bear ultimate responsibility for determining American policy in Southeast Asia. At a news conference in June 1964, the president outlined four basic themes for that policy. First, the United States would be true to its word and would stay the course in support of South Vietnam. Second, the president linked the future of all of Southeast Asia to that of Vietnam. Third, he intoned that "our purpose is peace." Fourth, Johnson proclaimed, "This is not just a jungle war, but a struggle for freedom on every front of human activity."[14] Because peace was our objective, the president was determined to avoid a wider war with China. Beyond China, as president, Johnson had to worry about what might happen elsewhere in the world as a result of American actions in Vietnam. Secretary of State Dean Rusk had convinced him that too much pressure applied to North Vietnam might encourage the Soviets to raise the level of tensions in the Middle East or Berlin. "Our goals in Vietnam were limited, and so were our actions. I wanted to keep them that way."[15] Hence, he was distrustful of military men who seemed too anxious to bomb. He not only suspected that were they willing to risk a wider war if it would advance their own careers or their individual service's best interest but also thought their doctrine was outdated, if not dangerous.

Johnson, a southern populist, had a lower-class Southerner's view of the military. The southern military tradition in which young gentlemen attended West Point or Annapolis, or better yet the Citadel or Virginia Military Institute, to earn commissions and to pursue careers in service to the country was, for the most part, confined to the aristocracy. Lyndon Johnson came from earthier origins, where young men joined the military out of desperation, to elude the law, to escape the angry father of a dishonored girl, or to find work when they had failed at everything else.

The Air Force that Flew Rolling Thunder

The Air Force of 1965 was, in many ways, the Air Force of 1947—only bigger and faster. Its top leadership, to some extent, had stagnated. Its most senior officers had been commissioned as much as a decade before the Second World War. Some of its generals had attained their rank during World War II and had been generals for more than two decades. Many colonels had held their rank since the end of that war. The younger colonels, who had received their commissions in the final months of World War II, had spent their entire careers in an Air Force wedded to the concept of strategic bombing. Airmen like LeMay, who had been on active duty since the 1930s, implemented the doctrine of strategic bombardment during World War II. Despite the controversy surrounding assessments of its results, air power enthusiasts clung to their notions of the decisive impact of strategic bombing and advocated its use on North Vietnam.[16]

Institutionally, the Air Force was committed to flying and fighting with weapons that incorporated unparalleled technological sophistication. Individually, most of the officers were fascinated with technology that translated rather nicely into fast aircraft. The Lockheed F-104, for instance, was dubbed "the missile with a man in it." The B-58 Hustler—a four-engine, delta-wing jet bomber—could fly at speeds beyond Mach 2. The

F-104. The short range and poor maneuverability of the F-104 limited its usefulness during the Vietnam War.

B-58 Hustler. The B-58's short range and inability to penetrate Soviet air defenses at low altitudes limited its effectiveness. It did, however, typify the Air Force's fascination with speed and high technology during the 1950s and 1960s.

XB-70. Although it could fly at nearly three times the speed of sound, the XB-70's inability to penetrate air defenses at low altitudes proved to be a technological dead end. Despite objections from Gen Curtis E. LeMay, Congress relegated it to the Air Force Museum.

XB-70, the prototype for the bomber fleet that LeMay longed to build, was designed to fly at three times the speed of sound and at altitudes above 70,000 feet. Faith in technology, wedded to the doctrine that strategic bombardment would be decisive in any conflict, provided an underlying certainty that air power could accomplish virtually anything asked of it.[17]

LeMay's commitment to the efficacy of strategic bombing was unshakable. He had been a player in the Pentagon's computer war games in 1964 in which scenarios were devised to reflect as closely as possible any situation that might arise in Vietnam. Two teams, Red and Blue, were assembled. Gen Earle G. Wheeler, the chairman of the Joint Chiefs of Staff, and Marshall Green, a foreign service officer with considerable Southeast Asia experience, made up the Red (Hanoi) team. The Blue team included John T. McNaughton, William P. Bundy, and General LeMay.

As the game evolved, Hanoi countered every Blue team move. When Blue bombed, Red moved men south. Because Blue was bombing Red, it was assumed that Red would retaliate in kind. Thus, Blue deployed Hawk sites around its air bases. Instead of sending its bombers (which presumably would have been Chinese since North Vietnam possessed only a handful of MiG jet fighters) against these batteries, Red used sappers to disable the Hawk sites forcing the Blue team to deploy troops to protect the missile sites. The Red team developed as many options as the Blue team, countering every move and forcing an escalation with each step. When Blue expanded the bombing, Red moved prisoners of war and school children into its factories.

LeMay supposedly became furious. During one intermission he reportedly engaged in a heated exchange with Bundy over the political restrictions under which Blue was forced to act. LeMay said Blue was swatting flies when it should be "going after the manure pile," as he referred to Red's dikes, oil depots, and ports. He is said to exclaimed, "We should bomb them into the Stone Age." To which Bundy is supposed to have answered "Maybe they're already there."[18] The results of this war game aside, everyone involved in the decision on whether to bomb North Vietnam seemed to focus more on the political events at home.

In 1964 all parties—the military, the civilians in the Department of Defense, the analysts at the State Department, and the president—were caught in the eddy of election-year politics. The president was reluctant to engage in the dramatic escalation of a sustained bombing campaign. Ironically, the Pierce Arrow strikes, those retaliatory raids after the August 1964 incident in the Gulf of Tonkin, not only destroyed approximately a quarter of North Vietnam's oil storage at Vinh and half of its small fleet of torpedo boats but also bolstered the president's popularity. The raids demonstrated his resolve while simultaneously showing that he was a reasonable man, committed to restraint. Even though the Pierce Arrow raids had been applauded, action of a more dramatic type was considered politically and militarily risky. Nevertheless, planning for a wider commitment continued with American policy moving into covert activities under the aegis of Operations Plan 34A (OPlan 34A).

Predictably, the military favored stronger action against the North. Basic US policy, however, was limited to conducting what was essentially a campaign to persuade Hanoi that the United

States was serious. In May low-level reconnaissance flights over Laos began from bases in Thailand and from carriers in the Gulf of Tonkin. The next month, after the Air Force and Navy lost some planes to North Vietnamese antiaircraft guns on the Plain of Jars, Laotian premier Souvanna Phouma gave permission for armed escort and suppressive strikes against antiaircraft guns that opened fire.[19] A few weeks later the United States stepped up covert air operations in Laos and furnished the Royal Laotian Air Force with additional T-28s to support a government drive to retake Muong Soui, a key town on the Plain of Jars.[20]

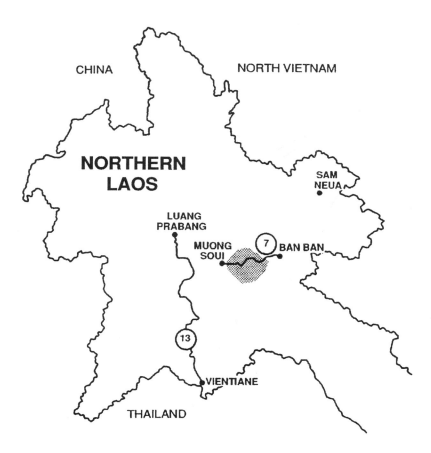

As 1964 progressed, competing strategies for bombing North Vietnam emerged. The State Department and the Office of International Security Affairs (ISA) in the Defense Department favored a graduated squeeze based on reprisal strikes. The Joint Chiefs of Staff, especially the Air Force, advocated an all-out assault on North Vietnam's military, industrial, economic, and transportation systems—a position to which the Air Force clung for the next eight years. The Navy advocated an interdiction campaign in the southern panhandle of North Vietnam, which was within range of its planes.[21]

The Air Force was the most adamant about bombing, always recommending the strongest actions against the North. As early as March 1964, when the commander in chief, Pacific (CINCPAC), developed a three-phased operations plan for bombing in Laos, eastern Cambodia, and North Vietnam, the JCS drew up its 94-targets list. The Joint Chiefs based their list of targets on the assumption that the North was an industrialized country actively engaged in furnishing massive support for the insurgency in South Vietnam and the civil war in Laos. When the administration opted for a more moderate tit-for-tat retaliatory policy in 1964 out of political expediency, the Air Force advocated provoking North Vietnam into actions to which the United States could then retaliate in force. The Air Force proposed launching a massive aerial offensive and reducing the number of ground forces called for in CINCPAC OPlan 37-64 should North Vietnam or China introduce regular forces into the fighting in Laos or South Vietnam.[22]

On 1 November 1964, election eve, word arrived at the White House that Vietcong sappers had attacked Bien Hoa Air Base, a burgeoning complex outside Saigon. Six Air Force B-57 bombers were reduced to smoldering rubble, a dozen others damaged, and five American servicemen killed.[23] The Air Force recommended B-52 raids on Phuc Yen, a MiG-capable airfield outside Hanoi.[24] President Johnson, sensitive to the political realities of election eve, decided against any immediate retaliatory action. The president, however, did ask for options for future actions focusing on bombing North Vietnam. On 11 November, Assistant Secretary

of Defense John McNaughton's team at ISA developed a draft
memorandum entitled, "Action for South Vietnam," in which he
proposed three options. Option A was to continue the present
course with reprisal actions designed to deter and to punish North
Vietnam for attacks in the South. Option B, the one favored by the
Joint Chiefs, was dubbed the "full court press" and called for
systematic attacks on the North—bombing rapidly, widely, and
intensely. Option C was labelled "progressive squeeze and talk,"
a compromise combining covert air strikes in Laos with bombing
in the North, beginning at a low level of intensity in the panhandle
and moving upward, both in latitude and violence toward the
lucrative targets in the Hanoi and Haiphong areas.[25] Option C
reflected deterrence theory in that it provided for increasing
pressure to be applied until the desired outcome was achieved. It
also provided the sense of consensus for which the president
longed.

The president decided on a modified version of option C.
Accordingly, in December covert activities in Laos increased with
the beginning of Operation Barrel Roll—armed reconnaissance
missions flown along the infiltration routes developing in the
Laotian panhandle. In the first week of Barrel Roll the US flew
two missions of four aircraft each.[26] The idea was to send a signal
to Hanoi. No one knows if anyone in Hanoi was even aware that
these missions took place.

By the end of the year the situation in South Vietnam looked
bleak. The revolving door at the presidential palace in Saigon
turned six times between the assassination of Ngo Dinh Diem and
the end of 1964. While the South Vietnamese generals and most
of their armed forces were sequestered in the major cities and
clustered around their bases on "coup alert," the Vietcong
continued to pick up strength in the countryside. In early December
the Vietcong launched a major offensive. Amb Maxwell Taylor
warned, "As our programs plod along or mark time, we sense the
mounting feeling of war weariness and hopelessness which
pervade South Vietnam, particularly in the urban areas." He
assessed Vietcong successes as resulting from "increased direction

and support of their campaign by the government of North Vietnam." Taylor said that the United States must do three things to halt the slide toward disaster. "First, establish an adequate government in South Vietnam; second, improve the conduct of the counter-insurgency campaign; and, finally, persuade . . . the DRV to stop supporting the Viet Cong."[27] As if to underline the seriousness of the situation, on 27 December two Vietcong regiments overran the government camp at Binh Gia. In the ARVN's unsuccessful attempt to recover the hamlet, nine US Army helicopters were shot down, one of the two ARVN detachments involved was wiped out, and the other ran away.[28]

Rolling Thunder Begins

In December 1964 propaganda teams from the People's Army of Vietnam fanned out across North Vietnam's countryside orchestrating "civilian-military unity days" in thousands of villages and hamlets. They presented stories and skits telling of past glories in fighting the Chinese and the French. People were organized into teams to assist in the repair of roads and railroads. Recruits for the militia forces climbed toward the two million mark—about 10 percent of the population. In villages the peasants dug bomb shelters and slit trenches.[29] North Vietnam was mobilizing for war.

If South Vietnam was not to be lost, a major change in American policy was needed. More aid, increased pressure on the North, and deployment of American combat units were all under consideration by early 1965. In February the president dispatched McGeorge Bundy to Vietnam to assess the situation. While Bundy was in Vietnam, Soviet premier Aleksey Kosygin was in Hanoi. Washington, aware of the implications of signals sent and received, suspended OPlan 34A activities. The administration hoped Kosygin might act as an agent of moderation and wanted to avoid provoking him during his visit with Ho Chi Minh. As was almost always the case, the signal sent was not received or, perhaps worse, was misinterpreted. At 2:00 A.M. on 7 February, Vietcong sappers attacked the air base at Pleiku and the US Army's Camp Holloway in the Central Highlands. The sappers damaged or destroyed a score of aircraft and killed eight Americans—the largest number in any single incident thus far in the war. From Saigon, Bundy chimed in with other advocates in Washington urging a one-shot retaliatory strike against the North.[30]

The US and South Vietnam launched Flaming Dart I the next day. It was hardly a massive blow. A handful of South Vietnamese A-1s joined six Farm Gate Skyraiders in bombing the Chap Le barracks just north of the demilitarized zone (DMZ). Twenty F-100 jets, some of which struck at antiaircraft batteries, escorted the strike aircraft.[31] Flaming Dart I was not, as Adm U. S. Grant Sharp (CINCPAC) complained, a very effective reprisal action. "First of all, as an example of what was to become an unfortunate pattern throughout the war, the civilian policy makers selected the weakest attack option available."[32] In fact, three days after attacking Pleiku, the Vietcong planted a bomb in a hotel in Qui Nhon that billeted American enlisted men. Twenty-three Americans died in the blast. The next day, in Flaming Dart II, the South Vietnamese and Americans sent 28 VNAF Skyraiders and a score of Air Force F-100s back to Chap Le while Navy planes struck Chanh Hoa, also just north of the DMZ.[33]

The retaliatory raids in February differed from the missions flown in response to the Gulf of Tonkin incident four months earlier. The Flaming Dart raids were intended to link actions in South Vietnam to reprisals against the North. The earlier bombings had been in direct response to a North Vietnamese provocation aimed at American forces outside of South Vietnam. Flaming Dart I and II were directly related to the actions of the outside instigator as manipulator of the insurgency in the South. As such, the raids were intended as a signal that the United States planned to hold the North Vietnamese responsible for Vietcong activities in South Vietnam.

After Flaming Dart II, President Johnson huddled with his principal advisors to confirm the direction set by the raids. Later he told Doris Kearns, "Suddenly I realized that doing nothing was more dangerous than doing something."[34] President Johnson had decided on a course of action: movement toward an expanded bombing of North Vietnam. It was not, however, a well-defined course devised to deliver victory in the classic military sense. The details of Rolling Thunder, as the bombing was dubbed, were vague and centered around option C, the compromise position between those who advocated restraint and those who wanted a larger program.[35] What it did provide was the flexibility and the sense of control that Johnson wanted.

The first Rolling Thunder strikes were flown on 2 March 1965. At the time no one thought the bombing would last longer than a few months. The Air Force submitted a proposal for a 28-day intensive campaign that would have struck all the targets on the JCS list. The Joint Chiefs, however, proposed a program that would do the same things, but do them over a three-month period.[36] No one—not the civilians in the Defense Department or the State Department, not the president, and certainly not the generals— believed North Vietnam could endure the bombing for more than six months.

As Rolling Thunder began, the secretary of defense was convinced that Hanoi's leaders would soon realize that the cost of supporting the insurgency would prove prohibitive. The civilians who advised him and the secretary of state were, at varying degrees, believers in the efficacy of deterrence. They were sure that there was a threshold of pain beyond which North Vietnam would not want to go and that Ho Chi Minh would offer to negotiate rather than risk the possibility of higher magnitudes of destruction. The generals and admirals, especially the Air Force generals, were convinced that the bombing would work. They reasoned that since North Vietnam had a smaller industrial base, their leaders would hold it all the dearer and, thereby, be intimidated. None of the military leaders acted as if they understood that North Vietnam was not an industrial power and that its military did not depend on a modern transportation system. No one had a monopoly on this line of thought; nor did anyone, civilian or military, understand that North Vietnam was committed to total war to accomplish its goal.

Ostensibly, Rolling Thunder had three objectives.[37] The first one was strategic persuasion. Derived from deterrence theory, strategic persuasion held that there was a level of pain that would coerce Hanoi into abandoning its support of the southern insurgency. The second objective was to raise the morale of military and political elites in South Vietnam. Because of the numerous coups, the Army of the Republic of Vietnam had been brought into the major cities and concentrated around key installations. Despite losing the war in the countryside to the Vietcong, the ARVN generals prattled about invading North Vietnam, an undertaking that might have proven disastrous. The bombing of the North was supposed to boost ARVN morale and show Saigon that the weight of American military power was wedded to their cause. The third objective was the only real tactical one of the campaign: interdiction. Rolling Thunder strikes against bridges, railroads, and roads would slow the flow of men and supplies moving south through the panhandle of North Vietnam. This goal soon dominated the campaign.

The JCS and the Pacific Command viewed the objectives differently. Admiral Sharp and Gen William C. Westmoreland (US commander in Vietnam) wrote in their joint report on the war that "the objective of the air strikes was to cause the government of North Vietnam to cease its support and direction of the insurgencies in South Vietnam and Laos."[38] This statement underscored their basic assumption that North Vietnam was the outside instigator in the South.

Adm Thomas H. Moorer, the chief of naval operations during Rolling Thunder, defined the objectives in operational terms. First, "stop the influx of war materials from outside North Vietnam, mainly from Communist China and Russia." For the admiral the outside instigator behind Hanoi resided in Moscow and Peking. Second, "destroy the war-making and war-supporting potential within North Vietnam—mainly industries and resources which support the military and supply systems." The admiral was a pilot and, as such, an advocate of air power. Moorer and Sharp were as convinced as any Air Force generals that strategic bombing would work with North Vietnam. Third, "interrupt the flow of men and materials moving along the enemy lines of communication to South Vietnam."[39] While interdiction was a part of everyone's view of Rolling Thunder, boosting the morale of the South Vietnamese was not.

In July 1965 Secretary McNamara derived five principles by which to accomplish his three goals for Rolling Thunder. Summarized, these were:

1. Emphasize the implicit threat that the bombing might get worse.

2. Minimize the loss of "face" by the DRV.

3. Optimize interdiction relative to political cost.

4. Coordinate with other influences (diplomatic) on the DRV.

5. Avoid undue risks and costs.[40]

Bombing the North

Rolling Thunder began as a campaign of *strategic* persuasion. It switched very quickly to interdiction, a *tactical* mission. Throughout the three years and nine months of concerted bombing, the focus was primarily on interdicting the flow of supplies toward the battlefields of the South.

Reflecting the aura of uncertainty and the atmosphere of compromise, the first Rolling Thunder attacks were diffuse. On the first mission a hundred Air Force jets attacked the Xom Bang ammunition depot located 35 miles north of the DMZ.[41] Almost two weeks passed before South Vietnamese planes struck a radar installation on Tiger Island, a few miles south of Xom Bang. The following day, 15 March, nearly a hundred Air Force and Navy

106

aircraft pounded an ammunition depot 100 miles southwest of Hanoi.[42]

Immediately after the Xom Bang strike, Deputy Secretary of Defense Cyrus R. Vance called a meeting of Air Force officials headed by Secretary Eugene M. Zuckert. They considered using B-52s over both North and South Vietnam as a way of avoiding ground fire. All agreed that letting the B-52s carry the brunt of the war was a way to reduce aircraft losses, but SAC and the Air Staff wanted the B-52s reserved for major targets in the North.[43] In subsequent meetings, the group, with an eye toward minimizing losses, recommended several changes in the way the US was conducting aerial operations. The Air Force leadership wanted wider authorization for the use of napalm and more latitude granted to local commanders to select alternate targets and to schedule strike times. As an indication of the extreme to which Washington had gone in controlling these early Rolling Thunder missions, one request was for local commanders to have the authority to conduct reconnaissance missions at random intervals to reduce the likelihood of telegraphing intentions. The subjects discussed indicate the early concern about controls from Washington. From the start the conduct of Rolling Thunder was controversial within the government.[44]

By the end of March the Joint Chiefs and CINCPAC were beginning to chafe at the restrictions. In mid-April, against a backdrop of increasingly strained relations, Secretary McNamara, McNaughton, William P. Bundy, Ambassador Taylor, General Wheeler, Admiral Sharp, and General Westmoreland, along with other officials and officers, met in Honolulu to discuss the future of Rolling Thunder. McNamara's report on the Honolulu conference read, in part: "With respect to the strikes against the North, (it was agreed) [they all agree] that the present tempo is about right, that sufficient increasing pressure is provided by repetition and continuation."[45] However, in his book *Strategy for Defeat*, Admiral Sharp claimed that he did not agree and, "as with most conferences that Secretary McNamara attended, the published results somehow tended to reflect [McNamara's] own views, not necessarily a consensus."[46]

Following the Honolulu conference, the bombing increased in intensity. Sortie rates climbed from 3,600 in April to 4,000 in May and 4,800 in June. Still the Air Force was not satisfied. In late June General McConnell again urged that the Air Force be allowed to strike all the targets on the list of 94, saying he considered "an intensified application of air power against key industrial and military targets in North Vietnam essential to the results desired."[47]

By the summer of 1965 President Johnson, who saw Rolling Thunder as a process of sticks and carrots, recognized that the sticks (bombs) were not working and that the carrot approach had failed as well. When Hanoi did not respond to his offer of a Mekong River development project, made in a speech at Johns Hopkins University in early April, the bombing policy veered in the direction of the hawks.[48] Although the sortie rates climbed, the restrictions remained. Strike days were specified. So were the number of sorties and targets. Attacks were usually limited to primary targets with one or two designated alternates. If the alternates were not available, as they often were not due to bad weather, unused bombs had to be dumped into the South China Sea even if other targets were clear. Reconnaissance to assess the damage inflicted had to be flown immediately after the strike and could not be escorted by armed aircraft. The concern was that the escorts would bomb an undesignated target or that while attacking an antiaircraft site they might cause collateral damage to civilian structures.[49]

There were two kinds of targets: numbered and unnumbered. Fixed targets, like the Thanh Hoa Bridge and the Thai Nguyen iron and steel complex, had designated target numbers. Unnumbered fleeting targets included trucks, trains, and boats moving along rivers and down the coast. From the beginning, the fleeting targets—those struck in armed reconnaissance missions—received more than 75 percent of the effort, in part because the system through which targets were selected, requested, and then submitted for authorization was complicated and unwieldy.

Target recommendations were made weekly from submissions devised by the targeteers and approved by the commander of 2d Air Division (Seventh Air Force after April 1965) and the commander of Naval Task Force 77 at Yankee Station, a hundred miles or so off the coast of North Vietnam. Both sets of target requests then went to Admiral Sharp in Honolulu. The CINCPAC staff coordinated the requests before sending them to the Joint Chiefs of Staff in the Pentagon, where military and civilian analysts joined with their counterparts from the Office of International Security Affairs to assess the military and political implications of each of the suggested targets. The list then went to the State Department for approval. After their cut, it was returned to the Joint Chiefs of Staff for one final look before being sent to the White House, where, in the informal atmosphere of a Tuesday luncheon hosted by the president, the list got its final review.[50] During the luncheon—usually attended by the president's press secretary, the secretary of defense, the secretary of state, and the special assistant for international security affairs, and, on occasion, General Wheeler, the chairman of the Joint Chiefs of Staff—the target list received its final pruning.[51]

During 1965 attacks were forbidden within 30 nautical miles of Hanoi and within 10 nautical miles of Haiphong. Targets within a buffer zone contiguous to the Chinese border were also off-limits. Civilian policymakers worried that striking too hard into the Hanoi "doughnut"—that restricted area at the heart of the city—might destroy North Vietnam's small industrial capacity, thereby leaving the US no prospective targets if the North did not mend its ways. From a military point of view this ban was nonsense. As far as the generals were concerned the targeting bore little resemblance to reality in that the sequence of attacks was uncoordinated and the targets were approved randomly—even illogically. A bridge might be struck on one day and a radar site the next. The targets most coveted by the Air Force, the factories (few as they were) and the power plants, were also off-limits. The airfields, which according to any rational targeting policy should be hit first in the campaign, were also off-limits. In the view of the military, Haiphong harbor

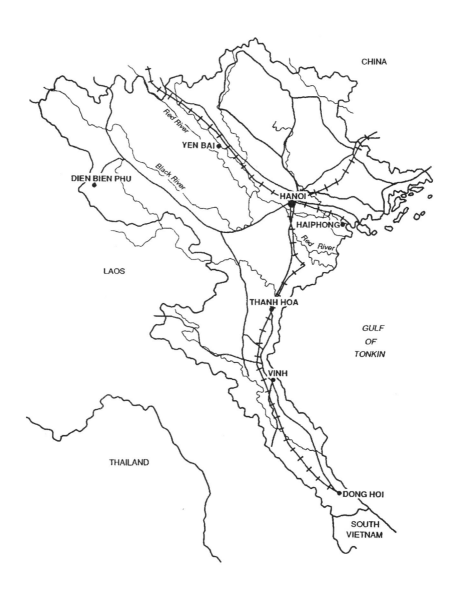

NORTH VIETNAM

was the "kingpin" of targets;[52] through it passed most of the imports from the Soviet Union and China.

Throughout Rolling Thunder, however, the military services and civilian analysts at the Defense Intelligence Agency (DIA) and the Central Intelligence Agency (CIA) debated about the nature of these imports. The experts in the CIA, along with their counterparts at DIA, argued that military supplies came overland, by rail and road, through China. THe military intelligence services tend to argue that Haiphong was the major conduit for all kinds of imports, including ammunition and weapons. The issue was never resolved, and Haiphong was not closed to shipping until President Richard M. Nixon ordered it mined in May 1972.[53]

The fear inspired by the concept of an outside instigator played a large role in preventing attacks on Haiphong. Lyndon Johnson was concerned that one misplaced bomb or miscalculated target might trigger a third world war: "Suppose one of my boys misses his mark when he's flying around Haiphong? Suppose one of his bombs falls on one of those Russian ships in the harbor?"[54]

In the summer of 1965 the focus of Rolling Thunder switched from strategic persuasion to interdiction. The shift in targets was associated with the larger decision to deploy American ground combat forces to South Vietnam. Secretary McNamara returned from a trip to Saigon on 20 July 1965 with General Westmoreland's request for 44 combat battalions. A week later President Johnson approved the request.[55]

Despite resistance from the Air Force, which still wanted to end the war in the South by bringing the North to its knees, the bombing concentrated on slowing the flow of men and supplies moving down the panhandle of North Vietnam. Almost simultaneously, a special national intelligence estimate held that extending the air attacks to military targets in Hanoi and Haiphong would neither injure the Vietcong nor "persuade the Hanoi government that the price of persisting was unacceptably high."[56] The direction was set. Although the debate would continue for the next year, the bombing of the North was subordinate to the ground war in the South.[57]

However, interdiction was not going to work any better than strategic persuasion. First, US policymakers and planners assumed that North Vietnam's transportation system was more susceptible to bombing than its very limited industrial system. Roads (such as they were) were quickly repaired. Bridges were bombed often but, in addition to being difficult to hit, were easily bypassed with dirt fords, underwater bridges, and pontoon bridges. Underwater bridges, built a foot or less beneath the surface, were impossible to spot from aircraft moving 400 knots. They were, in effect, invulnerable.

Second, the Vietcong were not absolutely dependent on North Vietnam for logistical support. They grew much of their own food and made medicines from herbs and roots. Weapons and ammunition were sometimes homemade but also were taken from dead ARVN or American troops, and sometimes purchased on the black market. The Vietcong taxed the people for money, food, and other supplies. A substantial portion of the Vietcong support came into South Vietnam from ships of socialist-bloc countries that unloaded materiel at the Cambodian port of Sihanoukville. North Vietnamese army units fighting inside South Vietnam, by comparison to American infantry units, were "light"; they did not use tanks, airplanes, and heavy artillery. Thus, PAVN units did not need a complex and sophisticated logistical support system. The one they had, though relatively primitive by American standards, was more than adequate. It was durable, redundant, easily repaired, and practically impossible to shut down.

The strategy adopted by Gen Vo Nguyen Giap was to fight on the tactical defensive, where the consumption of supplies could be regulated in accordance with the ability to receive those items. Given the nature of the Vietcong and North Vietnamese forces, they needed only 100 tons of supplies a day to sustain their operations throughout South Vietnam. While that sounds like a lot, it took fewer than 50 trucks to haul a hundred tons of supplies. By no means did all the supplies flow south by truck. Porters carried some on specially modified bicycles or carried them on their backs. Fifty-five-gallon drums were loaded with food or other goods and floated down the streams and rivers that flowed along the Ho Chi Minh Trail. Quite simply put, 100 tons of supplies a day was a trickle too small for air power to stop.[58]

Other factors led to the lack of success in bombing. The bombing was not as precise as the Air Force would have wanted. Secretary McNamara fussed about that lack of accuracy early on when he wrote, "Our primary objective, of course, was to communicate our political resolve . . . future communications of resolve, however, will carry a hollow ring unless we accomplish more military damage than we have to date." [59] Years of neglect in conventional tactics had returned to haunt the Air Force. The Air Force jets used in Vietnam were not designed to drop bombs with precise accuracy. The F-100, a relatively light fighter, could not carry a heavy bomb load, while the F-105 Thunderchief (Thud)—which could heft six 500- or 750-pound bombs under its fuselage and a pair of either types of bombs on its outboard wing pylons—had been designed to deliver a small atomic bomb. The Thud was unwieldy in the air when loaded with up to 7,500 pounds of bombs.[60]

Furthermore, the weather was rotten for nearly eight months of the year. The northeast monsoon blanketed North Vietnam from late September into early May, producing rain and fog.[61] For maximum accuracy, pilots flying the Thuds and Phantoms needed a 10,000-foot ceiling with five miles of visibility. In part they required this expanse of clear air space because of the high speed and limited maneuverability of their aircraft. Under these optimum conditions, crews used a diving technique, releasing their bombs at 6,000 feet. They could expect to put about 75 percent of their load to within 400 feet of the aiming point.[62] In bad weather, bombs often fell between 1,500 and 2,000 feet from the intended targets.[63]

Bad weather along with the heavy concentration of antiaircraft artillery detracted from the accuracy with which targets were struck. Against lightly defended targets, pilots could achieve excellent results. If the targets bristled with antiaircraft fire, the pilot's attention was understandably diverted and he tended to miss his mark. Targets in populated areas were not only the more important ones but also the more heavily defended. When collateral damage to nonmilitary structures was likely, the attacking pilots had to pass up these targets. Even so, Hanoi claimed a thousand noncombatants were being killed or seriously injured each week.[64]

Confident that its technology would carry the day in the next war, the United States had quit making conventional Mark-82 (Mk-82) 500-pound and Mark-83 (Mk-83) 750-pound bombs in the early 1960s in favor of cluster bombs, napalm, and Bullpup television-guided missiles. Consequently, by December 1965, the Air Force and Navy began running out of bombs. As the bombing intensified, the stockpile of 500-pound and 750-pound bombs dwindled quickly. In February the *Denver Post* reported that the Department of Defense had repurchased, for $21.00 apiece, more than 5,000 bombs that had been sold to the German Luftwaffe for $1.70 each. The Pentagon later admitted to repurchasing some 18,000 bombs sold to American allies.[65] There were stories of planes being sent against targets with less than optimum loads. As Admiral Sharp put it, "In some cases . . . optimum weapons necessary for achievement of maximum damage per sortie were not used when local shortages required substitution of alternate weapons for those preferred."[66]

In addition, the Air Force was determined to fight the Vietnam War, to the greatest extent possible, with the aircraft in its normal inventory: high-performance jets. Although the Air Force obtained a few Douglas A-1 Skyraiders from the Navy, along with some rebuilt T-28 trainers for use early on in Vietnam and later in Laos and Cambodia, the Air Force leadership was opposed to the large-scale acquisition of planes designed specifically for counterinsurgency or low-intensity conflict. These latter planes tended to be propeller-driven aircraft—distinctly "unsexy" and, in the opinion of General Momyer, of limited use. Momyer argued, incorrectly, that jets were, in all respects, superior to propeller planes and could perform every task required for tactical aircraft in Vietnam. His argument reflected the position of an Air Force leadership that did not want to be stuck with an inventory of slow aircraft designed for guerrilla warfare when this fracas was wrapped up, not when it would still have to plan to fight the Soviet Union. No one, of course, foresaw that the war at hand would drag on for nearly a decade.[67] In all fairness, the Air Force was not alone in its hubris.

The Bombing Escalates

After nine months under the gun, all North Vietnam had done was dig in its heels. On Christmas Eve 1965 President Johnson ordered a 30-hour cease-fire. In South Vietnam ground operations resumed the day after Christmas. The president extended the bombing suspension for another full day; he then ordered the pause continued indefinitely while diplomatic efforts to end the war proceeded.[68]

The bombing halt, which lasted 38 days, had a mixed effect. To the growing peace movement it offered hope; when the bombing resumed, that hope turned to angry frustration. To the military, particularly the Air Force, the bombing halt seemed ludicrous. Military leaders argued that the North Vietnamese were being provided time to move supplies south and to rebuild their battered transportation system and air defenses.

However, the extent to which the bombing had hampered the North Vietnamese war effort was debatable. The CIA and DIA, in their December 1965 "Appraisal of the Bombing of North Vietnam," reported that despite 55,000 sorties and the dropping of 33,000 tons of bombs, "damage has neither stopped nor curtailed movement of military supplies" and created "no evidence of serious problems due to shortages of equipment."[69] Two of six relatively small power plants had been struck and North Vietnam's oil storage capacity reduced by 20 percent. The only explosives plant and one of the few textile mills had been destroyed. Thirty highway and six railroad bridges were destroyed or seriously damaged. Bombing had caused an estimated 10-percent decrease in the capacity of North Vietnam's railroad. The minor ports at

Vinh and Thanh Hoa had been struck, but results were not apparent. Of the 91 locks in North Vietnam's dike and canal system, eight had been targeted but only one struck, with heavy damage reported. In armed reconnaissance missions, where approximately 75 percent of the effort had gone, 819 freight cars, 12 locomotives, 800 trucks, more than 100 ferry boats, and 1,000 other watercraft had been destroyed or damaged.[70]

By the end of January the "peace offensive" had failed and the air offensive resumed. Many targets were available in the southern part of the logistical system due to the accelerated movement of men and material during the bombing respite, but poor weather limited the effectiveness of the bombing.[71] Meanwhile, the Joint Chiefs and CINCPAC continued their campaign to expand the bombing. Admiral Sharp was annoyed with General Westmoreland's emphasis on close air support as a priority mission. Sharp was convinced that the Army and Marines had all the air cover they needed in South Vietnam. By extension, the admiral was peeved with McNamara and the administration because they supported Westmoreland's system of placing priority on assigning air power to South Vietnam and Laos with "North Vietnam . . . a very poor third."[72]

While the Joint Chiefs and CINCPAC argued for a reorienting northward of the bombing policy, the CIA interjected an analysis into the controversy that held that the impact of the bombing on the North had been insignificant. The Air Force, which usually chafed at any criticism of the results of its work, welcomed this appraisal because coupled with it was a recommendation for a greater bombing program aimed at the will of North Vietnam.[73] Further supporting the position propounded by Admiral Sharp and the Joint Chiefs, the Defense Intelligence Agency issued a study suggesting that more intensive bombing aimed at the North's petroleum, oil, and lubricant (POL) storage capacity would produce "local POL shortages and transportation bottlenecks until substitutes and alternatives could be found." The study also suggested that, at a minimum, bombing Haiphong's POL storage and transfer facilities would force the North Vietnamese to change the way they handled oil imports or force them to switch to importing by truck or train from China.[74]

Bombing POL targets was an attractive option because it was arguably both an interdiction and a pressure target. The Army and General Westmoreland would accept it because bombing oil storage facilities, they believed, would degrade North Vietnam's ability to move supplies toward southern battlefields. The Air Force and the Navy liked the concept because they estimated that 97 percent of North Vietnam's POL supplies were concentrated in nine remaining, unstruck storage sites, all within the Hanoi and Haiphong restricted areas. Bombing POL sites within the restricted areas might set a precedent for hitting other targets within the Hanoi "doughnut" or even for bombing and mining Haiphong harbor itself. Furthermore, bombing petroleum storage facilities fit traditional air power doctrine emanating from the Ploesti raids of World War II and the oil campaigns of 1944. Barry D. Watts, in his book *The Foundations of US Air Doctrine*, argues that in its mechanistic approach to the war, the Air Force saw North Vietnam as a correspondingly mechanized war machine, albeit one of far less capability.[75] Therefore, destroying its petroleum storage facilities would devastate its war-making capability.

The debate mounted through the spring of 1966. In April the Air Force Association added its voice to those of the generals in calling for a bombing campaign against POL storage facilities. For example, a staff writer wrote: "Air power could knock North Vietnam out of the war in a matter of days. Hitting petroleum supplies would especially hurt the North Vietnamese, since, for all their manpower, they still depend on trucks and roads to move the bulk of their supplies for their armies in the South."[76] From the generals' perspective, bombing the POL sites made good sense. North Vietnam had no oil fields. During 1965 it imported 170,000 metric tons of oil from the Soviet Union. The Joint Chiefs argued that since the North Vietnamese military consumed 60 percent of all POL coming into the country, the attacks were bound to have an effect on North Vietnam's ability to support its forces in South Vietnam and Laos. The generals noted that armed reconnaissance

117

strikes and the bombing of three major rail yards had forced the North to move supplies by trucks and motor-driven boats. Bombing POL targets would, when coupled with attacks on the railroad system, have an especially crippling effect. The JCS convinced McNamara who, in April, forwarded their recommendations to the president.

The president wavered. He wanted a consensus and did not have it. Some within the cabinet still worried that the Chinese might intervene or that a Soviet ship might be struck accidently by one of the planes bombing the oil transfer facilities.[77] Also, the peace movement at home was heating up, with polls indicating a decline in the president's popularity.[78] Finally, Sen J. William Fulbright's Senate Foreign Relations Committee held hearings throughout the spring of 1966, which seemed to legitimize the growing antiwar movement.[79] A peace initiative was under way (it did not fall through until June).

At the end of May the restrictions against attacking POL targets were relaxed slightly. Evidently, the president had decided in May that the attacks should take place soon. He was still searching for a consensus, however, and turned once more to the CIA for an evaluation of the bombing. On 8 June the CIA produced an assessment that held that while POL strikes would not stop the war effort they would have an overall adverse effect on North Vietnam's economy.[80] The report seemingly tilted the president toward bombing POL sites.

Finally, on 23 June, CINCPAC received authority to conduct the POL strikes. Initially, the missions were scheduled for first light on the following day. But, because several newspapers and all the major television networks carried stories about the forthcoming attacks, the missions were delayed until 30 June, when 116 Air Force and Navy planes bombed three POL storage sites in the heart of North Vietnam.[81] The air strike force completely destroyed a large petroleum facility outside Hanoi and heavily damaged one at Haiphong. Antiaircraft fire claimed one fighter-bomber. The US planes encountered four MiGs, shooting down one of them. The deputy commander of Seventh Air Force,

Maj Gen Gilbert L. Meyers, deemed the operations "the most significant, most important strikes of the war." [82]

The strikes against POL targets constituted the second phase of Rolling Thunder. It was to be a brief phase, lasting barely more than a month, before the focus returned to interdiction. McNamara kept a close watch on the results as analyzed by DIA. Within three weeks its analysts were reporting almost 60 percent of North Vietnam's original POL storage capacity had been destroyed. At the end of July the figure had risen to 70 percent. Overall, POL storage capacity was down from an estimated 185,000 tons to about 75,000 tons. Fifty thousand tons

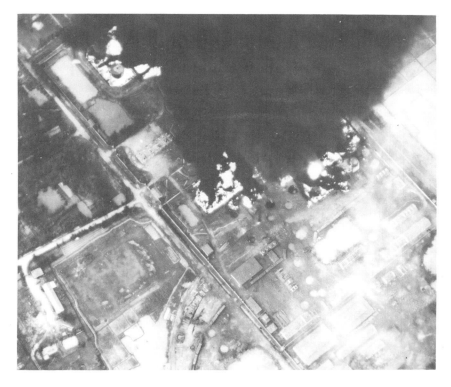

Hanoi petroleum storage site. On 30 June 1966 Air Force F-105s bombed a petroleum storage area three miles north of Hanoi. Although this after-the-fact photograph is dramatic, destruction of such petroleum storage facilities had little impact on North Vietnam's ability to prosecute the war inside South Vietnam.

were thought to be in vulnerable storage areas, two of which were located at airfields that were off-limits. The other 25,000 tons were relatively invulnerable, dispersed in 55-gallon drums throughout North Vietnam. Only an estimated 7 percent of the storage capacity at dispersal sites had been knocked out.[83]

Despite losing most of its bulk POL storage capacity, the North had plenty of petroleum in dispersed sites. North Vietnam had received oil by railroad from China and by off-loading drums from tankers anchored offshore onto lighters, which ferried the products to isolated beach transfer points.[84] The POL campaign petered out in late August when virtually all the bulk storage facilities had been destroyed and when it was evident that POL drums stored in underground dugouts and in villages throughout the country were not viable targets.

Another avenue of bombing had led to a dead end. Despite a dramatic increase in the bombing over 1965, US air power had proven unable to degrade Hanoi's ability to mount and sustain military operations. The campaign against POL storage facilities was the last escalation McNamara supported enthusiastically. The business-minded "generalissimo" had been promised results—and had been disappointed. In October 1966 McNamara travelled to Vietnam. He heard briefings that were optimistic while simultaneously asking for more latitude and increased effort. The military was caught in a paradox of its own making. On the one hand, the generals could not admit, even to themselves, that Rolling Thunder was failing. On the other, they had to ask for greater latitude to succeed. The secretary of defense, meanwhile, slipped into disillusionment. His report to the president read, in part:

> Attack sorties in North Vietnam had risen from about 4,000 per month at the end of last year to 6,000 per month in the first quarter of this year and 12,000 per month at present. Most of our 50-percent increase of deployed attack capable aircraft have been absorbed in the attacks in North Vietnam. In North Vietnam, almost 84,000 attack sorties have been flown. . . . Despite these efforts, it now appears that the North Vietnamese-Laotian road network will remain adequate to meet the requirements of the communist forces in South Vietnam—this is so even

120

if its capacity could be reduced by one-third and if combat activities were to be doubled.[85]

After the November elections the president stabilized the bombing. He decided against increasing the number of deployed squadrons or raising the number of sorties for Rolling Thunder. Even so, the bombing had been far heavier in 1966 than in the previous year, up from 55,000 to 128,000 sorties. The Joint Chiefs of Staff target list had grown to 242 targets; all but 57 had been struck. Air Force and Navy planes ranged all over North Vietnam on armed reconnaissance missions, avoiding only the Hanoi and Haiphong areas and the Chinese buffer zone.

Losses climbed with the sortie rates. In 1965, 171 planes were lost over North Vietnam. That total grew by another 318 in 1966.[86] Despite losses, the Air Force's leadership radiated sunshine about the air war. General McConnell, writing in *Air Force Magazine** in September 1966, proclaimed, "In assessing the Air Force's achievements in Southeast Asia, there is one factor that stands out: that is the impressive margin by which air power has exceeded many early estimates of its usefulness in limited conflicts."[87]

Rushing to Meet Our Thunder

North Vietnam could never have enough modern planes to take on the American air forces on equal terms. According to an estimate cited by Walt W. Rostow, the North Vietnamese air force in 1964 was tiny, with only 177 military aircraft—36 of which were MiG-15 or MiG-17 jet fighters.[88] In November 1964 Premier Pham Van Dong travelled to Moscow to request additional MiGs, surface-to-air missiles, and antiaircraft guns along with the technical assistance to build what became one of the world's best

---

* *Air Force Magazine* appeared under the title *Air Force and Space Digest* during part of the 1960s. I choose to refer to the magazine by its current title in the narrative but use the title of publication at the time in the actual citation.

air defense systems.[89] While the Soviet Union and the People's Republic of China furnished North Vietnam with their air defense weapons, it was the North's strategy that made those weapons effective.

The key to thwarting the American aerial assault lay in obviating the strengths of the US air forces in jujitsu fashion. Instead of struggling with the Americans for air superiority, the North Vietnamese opted for a lower level of strategy, one best termed *air deniability*. They used their total air defense system as an integrated entity to prevent the US Air Force, Navy, and Marine

North Vietnamese antiaircraft artillery site. During Rolling Thunder 85 percent of Air Force, Navy, and Marine Corps aircraft shot down over North Vietnam fell to smaller caliber antiaircraft guns. The North Vietnamese placed 23-mm and 37-mm guns near most potential targets and bolstered those weapons with heavy fire from automatic weapons like these 51-caliber machine guns placed in an old French fortress.

North Vietnamese surface-to-air missile site. An Air Force RF-101 photographed this typical SA-2 SAM site near Hanoi. SAMs claimed less than 100 of the 900 aircraft brought down over North Vietnam during Rolling Thunder.

Corps from doing what they wanted to do in the skies over North Vietnam. Air deniability, as a strategy, was a lower, more basic form of warfare constituting, in its essence, a people's war in the air.

Antiaircraft artillery (AAA), not surface-to-air missiles (SAM) or interceptors, provided the basis for air deniability. The North Vietnamese AAA inventory grew rapidly; by August 1966 it included 4,400 guns ranging from 23-mm to 100-mm caliber.[90] SAM sites proliferated all throughout the spring of 1965, but the missiles and the Fan Song guidance radars associated with the SA-2s were not deployed to the sites immediately. Perhaps the time differential between when the sites were built and when the missiles and radars were installed led those steeped in deterrence thinking to speculate that Hanoi was engaged in its own version of signal sending. The concept of the outside instigator was basic to the reasoning that the Chinese or Soviets had to have technicians and advisors at the sites, as indeed, they did. It seemed to follow, then, that Moscow and Peking were ultimately in charge of when and how those missiles would be used; but that was not the case.

Throughout the spring and early summer of 1965, while the Joint Chiefs repeatedly asked for permission to bomb the sites before they became operational, the secretary of defense demurred. McNamara offered his generals two reasons for disapproving the strikes. First, as long as air operations focused on attacking lines of communications south of the 20th parallel, they would not encounter the SAMs that were concentrated around Hanoi and Haiphong. Second, there was a fear that Chinese or Soviet technicians, thought to be working on the sites, might be killed.[91] Besides, the sites were not operational until the radars were deployed, and it was not until June that a Douglas EB-66 electronics warfare plane obtained evidence of Fan Song radar emissions, meaning that the radar was functioning.

About a month later, on 24 July, a SAM blew an F-4C out of the air.[92] By that time the North Vietnamese had built several sites. Once they constructed a site with launchers in place and cables laid, the North Vietnamese could make it operational overnight simply by placing missiles on launchers and hooking the radar to the vans housing the control consoles. By the end of 1965 there were more than 60 SAM sites in North Vietnam.[93] The SA-2s, along with the MiG-21s, were the most advanced elements of the North Vietnamese air defense system. In 1965 SAMs accounted for about 25 of the 171 aircraft brought down over North Vietnam, scoring a hit for every 13 missiles fired.[94] Ironically, more aircraft were lost to the antiaircraft guns installed to protect the SAMs than were lost to the missiles themselves.[95]

The SAMs posed the kind of threat that Air Force technicians could, and did, overcome quickly. While a "SAM Task Force" under Air Force Brig Gen K. S. Dempster worked on a technical solution, innovators on the scene and at TAC bases in the United States devised tactics to decrease the missile's effectiveness. The SA-2, which was nearly as large as the F-105, was not very maneuverable. The Navy's Bureau of Weapons figured out that an SA-2 needed about five seconds to compute a change in course. Pilots discovered that if they engaged in a rapid, high-speed turn or simply did a wingover (diving and reversing direction), they could throw the SAM off its course.[96] However, when heavily loaded with bombs, the F-105s and F-4s were unwieldy. Pilots found it difficult, though not impossible, to whip through those required gyrations to avoid SAMs. Crews determined it was less nerve-wracking and less physically demanding for them to fly low and fast whenever entering an area protected by SA-2s because the missiles were ineffective below 1,500 feet. The pilots could use the terrain to their advantage; the mountains and ridges blocked the radar beams tracking the invading aircraft.

Down low, however, Phantoms and Thuds were inside the effective fire envelope of even the lightest caliber antiaircraft guns. The 23-mm guns were deadly up to 3,500 feet. Even heavy machine guns and ancient Japanese and French army rifles—designed at the turn of the century and left over from the Second World War—were effective whenever they scored a hit. A single bullet in the hydraulic system of the F-105, until redundancy was added later in Rolling Thunder, made them unflyable. A bullet in the engine would shear off turbine blades, causing the engine to disintegrate in a matter of seconds. Speed was, of course, an advantage to be used to good effect. But flying at low altitude at around 600 knots, the Thuds and Phantoms gulped fuel. Fighters bound for North Vietnam usually "topped off" their tanks from KC-135 tankers orbiting over Laos or off the coast of North Vietnam. They almost always had to refuel again on their way home.[97]

Engineers soon devised both active and passive measures for thwarting the SAMs. In May 1966 AGM-45 Shrike missiles became available to the Wild Weasels (as the SAM suppression flights were called). The Shrikes locked onto the emissions from the Fan Song radar van, following them to the source. North Vietnamese operators soon learned that if they turned off the radar, the Shrikes "went ballistic" and almost always missed. A deadly game of "chicken" ensued. The Wild Weasels flew specially modified F-100s at first and then moved into twin-seat F-105s. Their mission was to protect the strike force, negating the SAM's presence by getting the Fan Song radar to go off the air or knocking it out of commission. The effective range of the Shrike was about 12 miles, a good five miles inside the effective range of the SA-2s, meaning the Wild Weasels had to get within the SAM's kill radius to do their job. The SAM was dependent on the Fan Song radar to guide it to its target, but those same emissions provided the sources to which the deadly Shrike would be streaking. Although the Weasel crew had to fly within the range of the SA-2 before it could fire a Shrike, as soon as the missile was away, the pilot could begin maneuvering to avoid the SAM coming in his direction. The radar van operator then had to decide whether to remain on the air in hopes of hitting the Weasel or to shut down to avoid the Shrike.[98] The Wild Weasel crews also attacked the SAM sites with cluster bombs, rockets, and even napalm and cannon fire. To make these direct attacks, the air crews had to fly directly over the SAM sites, which were protected with an array of antiaircraft guns. According to one former Wild Weasel pilot, SAM sites were protected by 12.7-mm, 23-mm, 37-mm, and at least one 57-mm antiaircraft guns.[99] The number of SAM sites proliferated throughout 1966, to total about 150 by the end of the year. Flying directly over these sites was a harrowing experience.

Electronic countermeasure (ECM) pods provided passive protection by warning crews when the radars were tracking, had locked onto their aircraft, and had fired. This radar-homing warning gear alerted the pilot—through a system of whistles and buzzes in his helmet and by a strobe on a display screen in the cockpit—that radar was tracking him. Initially the systems were notoriously inaccurate and to many pilots quite bothersome. As the countermeasures for dealing with the SAMs evolved, the missiles were rendered less effective. The North Vietnamese fired nine times as many missiles in 1966 as they had the previous year, but their effectiveness decreased to one hit for every 33 missiles fired.[100]

In addition to the ground-based defenses, the North Vietnamese possessed a healthy stable of interceptors. However, their MiG-15s and MiG-17s were not held in high regard by Americans at the beginning of Rolling Thunder. During the Korean War, the air forces of the United States had compiled a 15 to 1 kill ratio over MiG-15s. The difference was that in Korea, MiGs operated outside an air strategy that integrated SAMs with antiaircraft artillery. Korean MiGs engaged in "fighter sweeps," trying to take on the Americans directly, and lost. There, superior training and the marginally superior characteristics of the North American F-86 Sabre jet and the Navy's Grumman F9F Panther jets benefited our pilots.

North Vietnam used far different air-to-air tactics. In Vietnam, the MiGs made quick, hit-and-run attacks on formations of bomb-laden fighter-bombers. Usually, the MiGs made one pass and then sped away. Fighter-bombers loaded with bombs were no match for the agile MiGs. When F-105s and F-4s encountered MiGs, they either had to endure the attack or "pickle" (drop) their bombs to pursue and fight.

Thuds and Phantoms were much larger and far more powerful planes than the MiG-17s, MiG-19s, and MiG-21s they faced in Vietnam. Differences in philosophies between Soviet and American designers were evident. The F-105 was never intended as an air superiority fighter, even though it had an internally mounted gun and, occasionally, carried AIM-9B Sidewinder missiles. Until the late 1960s, F-4 Phantoms were not built with an internal gun. As discussed in the previous chapter, the F-4 was designed in the early fifties when everyone was certain high-technology missiles would bear the brunt of future aerial combat.

MiGs, even the most advanced models of the MiG-21s, were about half the size of the F-4s and F-105s. Most models were built

F-105 Thunderchief

Air Force pilots in F-105 Thunderchiefs and F-4 Phantoms flew the vast majority of the bombing missions against targets in North Vietnam during Rolling Thunder.

F-4 Phantom

with 23-mm and 30-mm guns. They were light and could turn rapidly and tightly. Their engines burned fuel more efficiently and with less smoke, making them difficult to spot. They did not, however, have the power, range, and electronics packages carried on American planes.

Also working to the advantage of the North was the fact that American fighter pilots had a tradition of aggressiveness that extolled air-to-air combat. Since the First World War, aces—pilots who shot down five enemy planes—had been glorified. Coupled with their superior training, the innate aggressiveness and a quest for glory made the American fighter pilots tenacious combat fliers. Sometimes, however, this worked against them. Often the Americans were too willing to pickle their bombs to pursue the MiGs. Under the strategy of air deniability, pickled bombs, falling harmlessly into the jungle or rice paddies below, fulfilled the goal of the North Vietnamese. Those bombs would not reach their intended targets and, on that occasion, American objectives had been thwarted, particularly if the MiGs escaped unscathed.

Despite the peripheral relevance of air-to-air combat to the objectives of Rolling Thunder, US pilots remained fascinated with proving their worth in aerial encounters throughout the war. However, the focus of the war presumably was to ensure the right of South Vietnam to endure as an independent government and the bombing of North Vietnam was part of that objective. Hence, attaining air superiority over the North was irrelevant to the ongoing battle in the South, where North Vietnam had no aerial capability. As General Momyer commented, "By the . . . Tet offensive in January of 1968, [in] the air war in the North [the US] had scored a major victory over the North Vietnamese Air Force. It was essentially a defeated air force and was withdrawn from battle." [101] He was right. But within the context of the Tet offensive and the absolute irrelevance of air superiority to the ability of the Vietcong and North Vietnamese to conduct their operations in the South, what he said was likewise irrelevant.

Nevertheless, defending oneself and one's strike aircraft were pertinent and relevant to the success of each mission. When the

Phantoms, Thuds, and Navy F-8 Crusaders tangled with MiGs, superior training and technological advantages paid off, though not by a substantial margin. The overall kill ratio, 2.3 to 1, was not as good as was achieved in Korea or the Second World War. Most of the air-to-air combat in Vietnam took place over North Vietnam or extreme eastern Laos. Thus, whenever a North Vietnamese MiG went down, if the pilot survived having his aircraft hit by a missile or cannon fire and if he survived the ejection, he was rescued by friendly compatriots and presumably lived to fight another day. In contrast, American pilots who went down in aerial combat were almost always over enemy territory.

The North Vietnamese air defense strategy made Rolling Thunder expensive, thereby adding to the controversy surrounding the bombing. The F-105 Thunderchiefs, F-8 Crusaders, and F-4 Phantoms were far more expensive than the most sophisticated MiGs, so that each US loss added to the increased cost of the war. Throughout the war, depending on when and where a US pilot was shot down, his chances for rescue from North Vietnam averaged about one in six.[102] By October 1968, while Rolling Thunder had inflicted an estimated $600 million worth of damage on North Vietnam, the cost, according to Alain C. Enthoven (a former deputy controller of the Air Force and assistant secretary of defense for systems analysis during the Johnson administration), was more than 800 dead or captured airmen and $6 billion in projected replacement costs for the 990 aircraft lost.[103]

These losses occurred despite the fact that the Air Force devised its strike packages to overcome North Vietnamese defenses. A typical strike package consisted of several diverse elements compiled to accomplish the two objectives of getting the fighter-bombers to their targets and then getting them back safe. The strike force, usually several squadrons of F-105s and F-4s, carried bombs of various sizes, but typically carried either 500- or 750-pound bombs. Because fighter-bombers loaded with bombs were vulnerable to interceptors, they were accompanied by one or more flights of F-4s armed with air-to-air missiles. This MiG combat air patrol (MiGCAP) might be as few as a single flight of four Phantoms for a smaller strike package, or could include several flights for larger efforts. Wild Weasel F-105s, carrying ALQ-87 jamming pods and armed with AGM-45 Shrike, or the more capable AGM-78 standard antiradiation missiles (ARM), flew ahead of the strike force to shut down or destroy the sites before the SAMs did any damage.

Because of the effectiveness of North Vietnamese defenses, they claimed one out of every 40 airplanes that went into the Hanoi and Haiphong areas, for example, the strike forces were accompanied by rescue helicopters and their escorts. Rescue choppers— air-refuelable Sikorsky HH-3s and the more capable HH-53s— orbited over northern Laos or the Gulf of Tonkin, ready to mount a search and rescue (SAR) operation, if needed. Because rescue helicopters were quite vulnerable to ground fire, they were escorted by Douglas A-1 Skyraiders. These planes carried an array of fragmentation bombs, rockets, and, on occasion, incapacitating gas bombs. Rescue helicopters were directed by an orbiting command post of their own, an HC-130 which doubled as a refueling aircraft, called King or Crown.[104]

Other aircraft associated with these strike forces included four-engine EC-121 Constellations that, under a variety of call signs, monitored North Vietnamese radio transmissions to warn of possible attempts at interception by MiGs. Douglas EB-66s flew ahead of the fighter-bombers to jam radars. Finally, before and usually after each strike was mounted, RF-4C reconnaissance planes and drones launched from C-130s flew over the target to get the photographs needed for assessing damage.[105]

These strike forces were a cumbersome way to attack any country. Missions had to be planned with sufficient time for coordination and assembly of the diverse elements. The aircraft themselves were complex pieces of machinery, requiring a great deal of maintenance and preparation for combat. The maintenance schedules were a vital part of the way missions were planned. Coordination of ground crews servicing the planes' engines and hydraulics, loading their bombs, and caring for their avionics systems was only one part of the process. Intelligence determined the status of enemy defense, including the location of AAA batteries and SAM sites, and estimated whether MiGs might be encountered. Mission planners coordinated all the elements of the strike package into a fragmentary order or "frag" that specified the number of aircraft, weapon loads, refueling tracks, takeoff times, and time-over-target.

This mechanistic approach to war fitted into a managerial mind-set already extant in the USAF. That mind-set dominated the way the air forces attacked North Vietnam. The *process* became an end unto itself with sortie generation as the standard by which progress was measured. The term "Dr Pepper War" accurately described the production line method by which strike packages were assembled and then dispatched. Dr Pepper advertisements touted "10, 2, and 4" as good times to enjoy the beverage. Because of the generation of strike packages, attacks on North Vietnam followed a predictable routine. Usually, there was a big effort at about 10 o'clock in the morning. A second strike would take place in the early afternoon, around two, with a smaller effort coming just before dusk.

As the air war became more mechanistic and more subject to a restrictive mind-set, ways had to be found for the managers to determine success or failure. Bomb damage assessments (BDA) were the Air Force's equivalent of the Army's body count. Aircrews often provided their own assessments of BDA and, predictably, failure did not figure greatly. Pilots were debriefed (interviewed) by intelligence specialists who prepared an operations report that was translated into a message called the OpRep-4. Pilots were asked whether they hit the target, what damage the mission had caused, and what were their impressions of enemy defenses surrounding the target. Generals were usually briefed the following morning from information compiled from OpRep-4s, meaning they got the "best" possible assessment of results. Photographic intelligence reports took longer to compile. Several days might be needed to process the film, examine it, and compile a poststrike report. Although usually more accurate, they were also less optimistic. The morning-after briefings had taken place, however, and few generals were interested in detailed reports about missions flown several days before.[106] For many reasons, bad news travelled neither fast nor far.

Switch in Strategy or in Targets?

Optimism was the watchword within the Air Force. This optimism was transmitted up the line through the generals to the Joint Chiefs, then to the secretary of defense, and, ultimately, to the president. In the mid-1960s, such optimistic reports could not hide the simple fact that the war was not going well. Consequently, in June 1966 the Department of Defense commissioned the Institute for Defense Analysis to study the air war through its Jason Division, an ad hoc, high-level group of scholars, consisting in this case of 87 scientists. These physical scientists demanded firm data and approached problems objectively. Even the most bellicose hawk could not term them "fuzzy-thinking" as they did those social scientists who were increasingly concerned with the moral implications of the bombing. The Jason scholars included men who had worked on weapons projects, including some who had been in that field since before the Second World War.

After studying the data on Rolling Thunder, they concluded that the bombing was not diminishing Hanoi's ability to conduct and support military operations in the South. Furthermore, they could not conceive of a level of bombing, short of annihilation, that might have had that impact. Their recommendations were that the bombing be stopped and that an anti-infiltration barrier be constructed running from the Gulf of Tonkin in the east, along the 17th parallel through Laos, to the Mekong River.[107]

The Jason report coincided with the discouraging estimates beginning to come out of CIA and DIA regarding the POL campaign. Secretary McNamara started having his own doubts about the bombing during the summer of 1966. At that time he travelled to Saigon, where he received another round of briefings from generals who, as always, were optimistic, yet asked for

Interdiction strike on a river bridge in North Vietnam. Bridges were among the key transportation targets struck during Rolling Thunder. Although air power managed to put many bridges out of commission, the North Vietnamese used pontoon bridges, boats, and underwater bridges to keep traffic moving south. Despite all the bombing during Rolling Thunder, infiltration into the South doubled each year between 1965 and 1968.

heavier efforts that presumably would result in victory. After his return to Washington, McNamara drafted a long memorandum for the president. In this report the secretary opposed any increase in either troop levels or bombing. McNamara noted, "The Rolling Thunder program of bombing the north has not significantly affected infiltration or crushed the morale of Hanoi . . . at the proper time we should consider terminating bombing in all of North Vietnam."[108]

The Joint Chiefs vigorously opposed McNamara's recommendations. On the same day that the secretary's memo went to the president, the Joint Chiefs, under the signature of General Wheeler, sent an "eyes only" memorandum to Johnson disputing McNamara's view of the bombing. They recommended a "sharp knock" on North Vietnam, including "attacks against *the* steel plant, the Hanoi railyards, thermal power plants, and specific targets within the Haiphong port and selected locks and dams" (emphasis added).[109]

McNamara's disenchantment with Rolling Thunder seemed to have grown in proportion to the JCS's increasingly stronger call for a wider and more vigorous campaign. The president received these opposing viewpoints while exploring yet another avenue to open negotiations. The good offices of the Soviets and Poles had come to naught. Even a letter from Pope Paul VI, sent simultaneously to President Johnson and Ho Chi Minh, failed to elicit the response Johnson hoped for.[110] When the president wrote Ho personally, the North Vietnamese leader answered that negotiations could begin only when the bombing had stopped. Ho vowed, "The Vietnamese people will never submit to force; they will never accept talks under the threat of bombs." [111] The president, however, was not convinced. He felt there was still room for increased pressure under the graduated approach he had adopted.

The Joint Chiefs, particularly the Air Force, had advocated bombing North Vietnam's industrial base from the beginning. Had the Air Force had its way North Vietnam's Thai Nguyen steel mill, its only cement plant, its single explosive plant, and most of its thermal power plants would have been destroyed by the end of the first few weeks of the campaign outlined in the original 94-targets list. It was not until March 1967, however, that these "strategic targets" were finally attacked with consistency. Later that same month, the president authorized the bombing of many of the power plants so high on the JCS list.

By the spring of 1967 the lines of delineation were clearly drawn. The Joint Chiefs were arrayed against the secretary of defense, who was supported by John T. McNaughton in the Office of International Security Affairs (ISA). Secretary of the Air Force

135

Secretary of the Air Force Harold Brown. During Rolling Thunder, Secretary Brown was in the difficult position of having to support his generals, who were increasingly opposed to the policies of the secretary of defense.

Harold Brown stood in the uncomfortable middle ground, leaning toward his generals but willing to defend administration policy. The most important faction was the president; he was struggling to maintain the equilibrium between hawks and doves. By the end of April only one thing was certain: bombing North Vietnam's

Secretary of Defense Robert S. McNamara. As Secretary, McNamara imposed a managerial approach to assess the effectiveness of Rolling Thunder. By 1967 he was convinced that bombing North Vietnam to affect the war in the South was having very little effect. In November 1967 he urged President Lyndon B. Johnson to stop Rolling Thunder and begin negotiations with Hanoi.

industries and power plants had not reduced the level of fighting in the South, nor had it nudged Hanoi to the conference table.[112]

Prompting North Vietnam to negotiate a settlement that would preserve the right of South Vietnam to exist as an independent political entity was the primary goal of the president and his civilian policymakers. From their viewpoint, though not from the perspective of the North Vietnamese, this objective was limited. In contrast, the military defeat of North Vietnam seemed to be the goal of the JCS, CINCPAC, and the generals in Vietnam. Perhaps, given that the goal of the North Vietnamese was always total victory, the generals' approach was arguably the most realistic.

Be that as it may, the limited goals entailed in American foreign policy and the military's goal of total victory were not reconcilable. The employment of air power as envisaged by the generals was, because of its aura of totality, perhaps the least viable medium for achieving limited objectives. By mid-1967 both civilian and military policymakers should have realized that nothing short of toppling the Hanoi regime was going to pressure North Vietnam into a settlement, not as long as it believed its efforts in the South might succeed. The great conundrum became how to defeat North Vietnam without defeating North Vietnam.

The military, apparently, believed it was making some progress toward its tactical goals. Airplanes hit their targets often enough and the results were measurable. A CIA report of 26 May 1967 estimated that bombing 14 of the 20 JCS-targeted electrical power plants in North Vietnam had deprived the country of 165,000 kilowatts of power-generating capability, about 87 percent of the national total.[113] General Wheeler had already stated that bombing power plants would have a deleterious effect on North Vietnam's war-making capability. Electric power was needed to make the steel for fabricating fuel storage tanks destroyed in the previous year's blitz on POL sites and to build pontoons for the floating bridges needed to replace destroyed bridges. Closing down power plants would cripple operations at North Vietnam's only cement plant—evidently back in operation after being bombed in March and nearly back to its 600,000 metric tons a year output.[114]

Perhaps, the bombing was not so much unsuccessful as it was irrelevant to the war in the South. Infiltration for 1967 as usual had doubled, going from 58,000 to 100,800.[115] The pace of the war in the South was reflected in a Military Assistance Command,

Vietnam (MACV), request in May for an additional 100,000 troops to be shipped by June, and another 100,000 to be dispatched by the following June.[116]

During his visit McNamara was briefed by the Seventh Air Force commander, General Momyer, who gave a glowing report of successes with new tactics and new weapons. According to Momyer the MiGs were on the run and the bombs were hitting their targets with 400-percent improved accuracy over the previous year. Admiral Sharp chimed in, arguing against any further limits on the bombing. If the DRV held the initiative in the South, Sharp claimed the Air Force and the Navy were on the offensive over the North. Momyer and Sharp closed their joint briefing by stating:

> We are conducting a strategic offensive. Here we hold the initiative. He is forced to react at places and times of our choosing. If we eliminate the only offensive element of our strategy, I do not see how we can expect to win.[117]

In their recommendations "to win," Momyer and Sharp made closing Haiphong harbor their first priority. Their second priority was to "destroy the six basic target systems (electricity, maritime ports, airfields, transportation, military complexes, war supporting industry)," and, finally, to keep up the attacks on the roads and trails leading south.[118]

Haiphong was, in the minds of the military, the equivalent of the industrial cities in the Soviet Urals or the German Ruhr. Because North Vietnam had no military-industrial complex, it had to rely on imports from the Soviet Union and other countries. Closing the harbor would be the equivalent of bombing an industrial country's war-making industrial complex.[119] Besides, Haiphong was about all that was left.

Yet, its destruction was also too much to ask. Walt Rostow addressed the merits of bombing the northeast railroad (which formed the other element of North Vietnam's "military-industrial complex" as a conduit for imports) and mining the harbor. He outlined three drawbacks. First, the Soviets would be forced to either sweep the mines or abdicate to the Chinese the role of

139

primary supplier of North Vietnam. Second, the Chinese might send in volunteers to protect the railroad with AAA guns and to repair bomb damage, in which case American bombs might kill Chinese troops and thus lead to a wider war. Third, the Soviets might create a crisis in Berlin or elsewhere to offset the US initiative in Vietnam.[120]

In June, after the attack on the industries and power plants had failed, the Office of International Security Affairs prepared a draft presidential memorandum which outlined three alternatives. Option A was to intensify the attacks above 20 degrees north latitude. Option B proposed reorienting the bombing to focus on the lines of communications below the 20th parallel. Option C was to increase the scope and intensity of the bombing—in essence, a combination of the previous two options. The military was split on the options. The Joint Chiefs of Staff favored option A. The Navy, because its shorter range, carrier-born fighters could range all over the panhandle of North Vietnam but were limited to bombing only the eastern half of Tonkin, favored option B. The Air Force wanted option C, which entailed considerably more bombing throughout the country.[121] It was then that Secretary Brown submitted his memorandum comparing the effect of bombing to the physical phenomena of the diffusion of heat; he was supporting option C and his generals.

On the other hand, McNamara was already viewed as a lost cause in some quarters of the military. Rostow was losing his talons as well. Even the American ambassador to South Vietnam, Ellsworth Bunker, voiced doubts about Rolling Thunder: "Aerial bombardment, . . . though extremely important, has neither interdicted infiltration nor broken the will of the North Vietnamese, and it is doubtful that it can accomplish either."[122]

The president remained uncommitted. As long as no decision had been made, the military could hope that its point of view would be accepted. So far, when the White House had made decisions, it had tended to rule in the direction of the hawks. What the Air Force did not want was to fall into the morass of interdiction—at least not an aerial interdiction campaign limited to targets below 20 degrees—more or less in direct support of Army operations in the South. Meanwhile, Rolling Thunder continued at about the same pace, and one out of 40 sorties flying into the Red River delta area did not return.

The debate over bombing was more than a palace controversy played out on message wires and through classified inter-departmental memorandums. It was also a public squabble, with the Air Force making no secret of its feelings. As in the fracas with the Navy during the B-36 controversy of the late 1940s, the Air Force Association used its magazine to carry the brunt of the public debate. Its statement of policy, adopted at the 1966 AFA convention in Dallas and published in an article in *Air Force Magazine*, was: "Airpower is doing all it's presently being called upon to do in Vietnam. But with superior technology the key to military strength, and airpower as the cutting edge, airpower is not being called upon to do enough."[123]

The Air Force had allies in the Senate as well. In July 1967, Sen John Stennis, chairman of the Senate Armed Services Committee, announced that he would hold hearings on the air war. The Armed Services Committee was the antithesis of Sen J. William Fulbright's Senate Foreign Relations Committee. If Fulbright exasperated the administration and disgusted the generals, Stennis and most of the members of his committee—which included Strom Thurmond of South Carolina, Margaret Chase Smith of Maine, and Stuart Symington of Missouri (former secretary of the Air Force)—were sympathetic to the generals and disposed to honor their opinions.

The Joint Chiefs welcomed this opportunity to take their case "to the Hill." When it seemed they were likely to end up "pouring bombs into a funnel," as they dubbed bombing focused below 20 degrees north latitude, the opportunity to go public seemed heaven-sent. The Joint Chiefs saw this as their chance to explain their version of the air war and, perhaps, bring pressure on the administration to give them the discretion they had long sought in conducting Rolling Thunder.[124]

Admiral Sharp was the first witness before the committee. He set the tone for the generals who testified over the next two weeks. The admiral assured the committee that the air war was important, in fact, indispensable, to the efforts in the South, where American forces were, thanks to the bombing up north, succeeding because they had "freed areas previously under enemy control [and] opened lines of communication denied for years."[125] Admiral Sharp called the air war against North Vietnam "a strategic offensive" and assured the committee that wars cannot be won fighting on the defensive.[126]

General Wheeler followed Admiral Sharp. He, too, told the committee that he had "come down on the side that we should undertake action against the port at Haiphong."[127] And so it went. The generals complained and the committee listened sympathetically. The generals grumbled that the targets, a list that had expanded from 94 to 359, were being doled out too slowly. General Wheeler warned that if the bombing were cut back to the 20th parallel, the losses would climb when antiaircraft guns and missiles used to protect Hanoi and Haiphong were reconcentrated in the much narrower confines of the southern panhandle.[128]

The Air Force generals claimed that thus far, Rolling Thunder had been a success, the restrictions notwithstanding. While trying to make the case for expanding the bombing, they carefully emphasized that things were going well. The former deputy commander of Seventh Air Force, retired Maj Gen Gilbert L. Meyers, testified that interdiction was working as well as it had in Korea. In a sense he was right, probably more so than he knew. The problem was that he believed aerial interdiction had been successful in Korea: "The 8th Army commanders were all enthused about our interdiction campaign in North Korea . . . and I think that official records will support that statement."[129]

Of all the military officers who paraded before the committee, General Momyer, the Air Force commander in Vietnam, probably had the best grasp of the war. His testimony revealed that he understood the nature of the conflict better than anyone on the JCS. Momyer conceded that the level of air forces in Southeast Asia

142

was sufficient, "And the reason I say that is because of the number of lines of communication you can work against, the availability of good weather, which you primarily need to work against the lines of communication and have the maximum effect."[130] He understood that interdiction in this war presented unique difficulties. Momyer outlined the classic requirements for success

Gen William W. Momyer. As commander of the Seventh Air Force during Rolling Thunder, General Momyer urged wider and more intense bombing of the North. Like most airmen he was convinced that bolder applications of air power could have been decisive.

in an interdiction campaign: vulnerable lines of communications and, above all, "some kind of formalized ground campaign in which there is a line between two opposing forces, in which you can launch an offensive that forces the enemy to consume logistics faster than he can get them down and replenish them."[131] He told the committee that Vietnam was not like Germany. Its lines of communications were more primitive, but more resilient. Furthermore, "It is not like it was in Germany when the war resources were being fabricated in the country."[132]

On the other hand, Momyer could fling open the window and let the sunshine in. When asked about the threat from MiGs he stated, "We have driven the MiGs out of the sky for all practical purposes. The MiGs are no longer a threat. If he comes up he will probably suffer the same fate that he did before, so there is no interference on the bombing mission."[133] This optimism about the defeat of the MiGs, while somewhat justified, backfired when McNamara quoted Momyer's testimony back to senators criticizing him for not authorizing attacks on Phuc Yen airfield. "I am not passing on the issue whether we should or shouldn't strike Phuc Yen. As I told you earlier, I think it is a marginal decision, but . . . the commander of the Air Force says we have driven the MiGs out of the sky, they are no longer a threat."[134]

The secretary of defense, supported by Assistant Secretary of Defense for International Security Affairs John McNaughton, began his testimony on August 25th, after most of the admirals and generals had spoken. McNamara's arguments were tightly reasoned and bolstered by figures and statistics. He held that the bombing had failed and could not succeed short of annihilating the population of North Vietnam.[135] He defended the targeting policy. To the secretary, the glass was half—or perhaps more to the point—85 percent full, not half (or 15 percent) empty because there were "only 57 targets recommended by the Joint Chiefs of Staff against which strikes have not been authorized."[136]

Secretary McNamara made his case by portraying North Vietnam as an agrarian society, one "not dependent on the continued functioning of great cities. . . . They can be fed at something approaching the standard to which they are accustomed without reliance on truck or rail transportation."[137] He pointed to the recently completed attacks on the power plants to say that while the bombing had "rendered inoperative about 85 percent of the country's central electrical generating capacity, it is important to note that the Pepco plant in Alexandria, Virginia, generates five times the power produced in all of North Vietnam's power plants before the bombing."[138]

The secretary went through each of the 57 authorized but unstruck targets to assess their individual importance, weighing that against location, potential political impact, and possible losses. He immediately dismissed five of the targets, two railroad sidings and three bridges, because they were in the Chinese buffer zone. He moved to "seven targets the Chiefs call of small value, and gentlemen, these are of small value."[139] Among them were a machine shop of 96,000 square feet and a pair of battery plants producing a total of 600 tons of batteries a year. He stated that he would not risk the life of a single pilot to bomb North Vietnam's only tire factory, which could produce only 30 tires a day. The secretary continued through the list, pointing out that nine unstruck petroleum targets contained only 6 percent of the existing POL capacity and were located in heavily defended areas of Hanoi and Haiphong. He moved to "twenty-five targets, other targets, nonpetroleum targets in heavily defended areas of Haiphong and Hanoi that are of lesser importance."[140] These included a vehicle repair depot of 48,000 square feet, comparable to, "any garage on any one of the side streets of Alexandria." There was an unstruck 94,000-square-foot warehouse in Hanoi that he likened to "the corner of the Sears and Roebuck warehouse in Washington." McNamara concluded the review thusly, "I would submit to you that I am Secretary of Defense and I am responsible for lives and I am not about to recommend the loss of American lives in relation to those targets."[141]

The secretary stopped short of advocating a halt in the bombing. He insisted that the limited objectives of the bombing were soundly conceived and pointed to the optimistic assessments of the generals who had preceded him to attest to the success of the effort. "I think from what you have heard from General Westmoreland and General Wheeler and the other chiefs, you would agree on two things. First, not one of them has presented a plan to terminate the distribution of Soviet supplies through North Vietnam and into South Vietnam. Secondly, each of them firmly believes we are winning and will continue to win."[142] In other words, the generals could not devise a strategy applicable to the war at hand—a war they claimed to be winning in any event.

Despite McNamara's arguments, the conclusions of the committee were unaffected. The final report, leaked to the press almost as soon as it was written, held, "What is needed now is the hard decision to do whatever is necessary, take the risks that have to be taken and apply the force that is required to see the job through . . . logic and prudence requires that the decision be made with the unanimous weight of professional military judgment."[143] The generals were vindicated. The secretary, and by extension, the president, had been rebuked. The president felt the pressure and veered, once again, to the hawkish position, at least for a short while.

Toward a Bombing Halt

The pressures of the autumn of 1967 were tremendous. In September, General Giap initiated the sequence of battles that set up the Tet offensive. The North Vietnamese probed in widely separated areas of South Vietnam, beginning with an attack on the Marine base at Con Thien, near the DMZ. At about the same time, Vietcong and North Vietnamese regulars struck at Loc Ninh, a district capital near Saigon. A PAVN force attacked Kontum, and the Communist-backed forces launched hundreds of quick, sharp attacks on fire bases throughout Vietnam. Intelligence indicated that North Vietnamese troops were concentrating around Tchepone, perhaps preparing for a thrust east along Route 9 and into Quang Tri Province.[144]

Lyndon Johnson, meanwhile, was deeply troubled and torn by conflicting pressures. He did not give the JCS its free hand to bomb, nor was he able to accept all of McNamara's reservations. His patience with the Joint Chiefs was wearing thin. "Bomb, bomb, bomb, that's all you know," he is said to have complained.[145] Still, as in the past, when the president veered, it was in the direction of greater force. Sortie rates climbed. By October most of the 57 targets that had not been struck by August were bombed. The chiefs were free to bomb marshalling yards, bridges, and barracks within the Hanoi and Haiphong restricted areas and along the Chinese border. He would not, however, allow them to bomb or mine the harbor at Haiphong.[146]

Controversy over the bombing increased along with its intensity. In September, McNamara asked the Jasons to take another look at the bombing to determine what, if anything, might be done to obtain better results. In their final report, the Jasons categorically rejected bombing as an effective tool. They refuted every optimistic claim made by the military. Bridges had been hit, roads temporarily cratered, and most of North Vietnam's POL storage capacity destroyed; nevertheless, the flow of men and supplies had increased substantially.[147] Admiral Sharp's assertion that "a major effect of our efforts to impede the movement of the enemy was to force Hanoi to divert the efforts of 500,000 to 600,000 civilians to full-time or part-time war related activities" was acknowledged, but the Jasons countered that since 1965 more than 720,000 able-bodied people—above those needed for the army—had been provided by normal population growth.[148] Furthermore, the Jasons held that the transportation system, far from being degraded, actually had been improved because of added redundancy. Where one road had existed previously, several had been built. Many of the bridges with felled spans had one, often more, fords or underwater bridges around them. Because of the redundancy, the North Vietnamese could move more men and supplies south in 1968 than in 1965.

The Jasons also found that the will of the North Vietnamese was strong. There were local shortages, but overall, the life-style had diminished only slightly. There were no reports of draft dodging, black-market operations, or prostitution in the North as there were in the South. The fact that North Vietnam was sending several thousand young people abroad each year to study medicine, engineering, and other subjects was an indication of some faith in the future. The Jasons's emphatic conclusion was stark in its simplicity: "We are unable to devise a bombing campaign in the North to reduce the flow of infiltrating personnel into SVN [South Vietnam]."[149]

Still, the Joint Chiefs clung to the hope that an even larger aerial campaign was in the offing. In a memorandum submitted to Secretary McNamara on 17 October, the JCS held, "NVN [North Vietnam] is paying for its aggression and has lost the initiative in the South." [150] In their addendum, the JCS prescribed guidelines for "added pressures on the enemy." First, they called for removal of all restrictions on military targets. The second priority was to mine the ports. They asked for wider use of B-52s in Laos as well as expanded covert operations there, in Cambodia, and in North Vietnam. In all, they made 10 recommendations, five of which began with the word "expand" and one of which started with "increase."

The president gave the JCS and the air commanders much of what they wanted, but not everything. There would be no mining of Haiphong. Hanoi's Gia Lam Airport, the international airport in the middle of town, remained off-limits. Still, the last months of 1967 saw the most intensive bombing of the war up to that point.

If Haiphong could not be mined, its utility could still be degraded. After supplies came into the country by rail from China and by sea through Haiphong, they converged on Hanoi. If the capital could be isolated from the rest of the country, that might serve the same purpose as mining Haiphong or closing the roads and railroads where they were most vulnerable, in the mountain passes and at the tunnels in the Chinese buffer zone.[151]

Tet and the Bombing Halt

In late January 1968 the Vietcong, with considerable support from the North Vietnamese, struck throughout South Vietnam. They attacked 36 of 44 provincial capitals and captured thousands of hamlets and villages. The scope and the intensity of the Tet offensive surprised the military in Vietnam and dismayed the American public. That dismay turned to shock at the spectacle of a Vietcong suicide squad inside the compound of the American embassy in Saigon.

The fact that an offensive of this magnitude had taken place ought to have said something about the efficacy of Rolling Thunder to hawks and doves alike. Not only did the Vietcong and their ally have enough supplies to support the offensive, they still retained the will to make enormous sacrifices.

McNamara's will was exhausted before Tet. Perhaps the Stennis hearings had drained his reservoirs. On the first of November, McNamara gave the president a memorandum entitled, Outlook if Our Present Course of Action Is Continued. The outlook was not good, according to the secretary. He acknowledged that "continued but slow progress" might be possible, but expressed real reservations as to the long-range prospects. His recommendation was to stabilize the number of troops in the South and, to prompt North Vietnam into negotiations, to stop the bombing.[152]

The president removed McNamara's name from the memorandum before circulating it for comments. General Westmoreland vehemently opposed the suggested ceiling on troops as well as any curtailment in the bombing. The president's close friend, Clark Clifford, allowed that he was "at a loss to understand the logic" behind suggesting a bombing halt as a means to entice the North Vietnamese into negotiations. Such an action would, in Clifford's opinion, "be interpreted by Hanoi as (a) evidence of our discouragement and frustration, (b) an admission of the wrongness and immorality of our bombing, and (c) the first step in our ultimate total disengagement from the conflict."[153]

On the other hand, McGeorge Bundy, Walt Rostow, and Dean Rusk were more favorably inclined to the overall thrust of the anonymous memorandum. Johnson did not have the consensus he sought and, in December, rejected his secretary of defense's suggestions. Soon thereafter, McNamara announced he was stepping down at the end of February 1968. Clark Clifford, in part because he had so strongly opposed McNamara's suggestions, was designated as his successor.

The change in direction from engagement to disengagement did not come easily. Despite the incongruity in using the bullet-scarred wall outside the American embassy as a backdrop, General Westmoreland was on television the day after the Tet offensive began, declaring it a major defeat for the enemy. As it turned out, the general was right. But this time, the American public was not buying it. McNamara's last day as secretary of defense was February 28th. His departure coincided with a request from General Westmoreland for an additional 206,000 men. Clifford's first task as secretary of defense was to head a task force examining the general's request. The task force included Secretary of State Dean Rusk; Clifford's predecessor, Robert McNamara; Under Secretary of State Nicholas Katzenbach; Secretary of Treasury Henry H. Fowler; Deputy Secretary of Defense Paul Nitze; and Director of the CIA Richard Helms as well as Walt Rostow and Maxwell Taylor.[154] The question, according to Clifford, "quickly changed from 'How could we send the troops to Westmoreland?' to 'What was the most intelligent thing to do for the country?'"[155]

Clifford's metamorphosis from hawk to dove took about a month. A lot of it had to do with what he heard—and did not hear—from the generals and admirals in the Pentagon. During his period of orientation, the briefers trotted out and mesmerized their audience with "statistics of known doubtful validity."[156] Secretary Clifford asked the generals for their plan to win in Vietnam "[and] was told that there was no plan for victory in the historic American sense." He asked them why not? The generals answered, "Because our forces were operating under three major political restrictions." They complained that they could not invade North Vietnam, mine

Haiphong, or pursue enemy forces into Laos and Cambodia. When Clifford asked how we could win under these circumstances, the generals told him that the only alternative was to continue fighting a war of attrition. When he asked for how long, there was no agreement, two years—maybe more. As Clifford later commented, "Certainly, none of us was willing to assert that he could see 'light at the end of the tunnel' or that American troops would be coming home by the end of the year."[157]

Meanwhile, the president had asked his friend Dean Acheson to assess the current situation. Based on the briefings he had received at the Pentagon, this old cold warrior reported he was unsure of what was happening in Vietnam. Acheson told Johnson, "With all due respect, Mr President, the Joint Chiefs of Staff don't know what they're talking about."[158] The president was reportedly shocked by this assertion. The president asked him to look further and report back.

All during this period of soul searching within the administration, political forces were playing upon the president in February and March. On 12 March, Sen Eugene McCarthy, an avowed peace candidate, won 42.4 percent of the vote in the New Hampshire presidential preference primary. While 7 percent less than the president, McCarthy's share of the vote was an indictment of administration policy. Worse yet, the senator's good showing in New Hampshire prompted Sen Robert Kennedy into the race for the Democratic presidential nomination. While McCarthy had little chance of wresting the nomination away from the president, Robert Kennedy posed an entirely different and far more credible threat. Lyndon Johnson did not relish losing to his most despised political adversary.

The day after Kennedy announced his candidacy, the president met with Dean Acheson. In his investigations Acheson had questioned people at the second and third levels at the Pentagon, the State Department, and the CIA. These brigadier generals, colonels, and career foreign service and intelligence officers of corresponding rank were not as sanguine as the upper leadership. Acheson concluded that the JCS was leading the president "down a garden path" and that, short of total war, victory in Vietnam was not possible. He also told the president that the country no longer supported the war.[159]

The new secretary of defense had already reported that "it has become abundantly clear that no level of bombing can prevent the North Vietnamese from supplying the necessary forces and material necessary to maintain their military operations in the South."[160] Clifford had decided against recommending any increase in bombing of the North. He did not accept the military's view that Haiphong was a significant port of entry for military supplies and that bombing or mining it would make an appreciable difference.[161]

Secretary Clifford was already at odds with his generals and with his secretary of the Air Force. On the day that Clifford's memorandum went to the president, Harold Brown sent a memorandum to Paul Nitze, at the latter's request, suggesting what was needed to meet the military situation evolving from the Tet offensive. Each of his three-point proposals included either the word intensify or *increase* with regard to bombing North Vietnam, Laos, and South Vietnam.[162]

The JCS, likewise, rowed against the tide flowing rapidly toward a bombing halt. Astonishingly, despite the evidence of Tet, they held that "the air campaign made a marked impact on the capability of North Vietnam that existed in early 1965 and the North Vietnam of today."[163] Their recommendations were to increase the weight of the bombing, and to shrink the restricted zones around Hanoi and Haiphong from 10 nautical miles to three and from three to one-and-a-half miles, respectively.

By the third week in March the president had made up his mind. The weight of opinion was against increases in troop deployment and in favor of reducing the intensity of Rolling Thunder. On the evening of 31 March 1968 the president announced that while some additional forces would be sent to Vietnam he was restricting air and naval actions against the North to an area below 20 degrees north latitude. He also announced that he would not accept his party's nomination for another term in office.[164]

The president's orders for a bombing halt north of the 20th parallel took effect immediately. On 1 April a major transshipment point at Thanh Hoa, a town just south of the 20th parallel, was bombed. Critics of the president howled that the halt was a ruse, so the president ordered a further reduction in latitude to below the 19th parallel. No targets north of that line were struck throughout the remainder of the Johnson administration.[165]

In some ways the bombing halt was a ploy. To be sure, the military still wanted an expanded aerial campaign, one that would accept a larger number of civilian casualties as part of the price of victory.[166] Such a campaign would not have to be targeted so carefully since collateral damage would be acceptable. Because the rainy season was starting over the North, that was, in fact, the only kind of large-scale bombing that could have been undertaken by fighter-bombers. The bombing that continued, however, was limited to supply dumps, transshipment points, and supply concentrations along the lines of communications below the 19th parallel.

With Rolling Thunder curtailed, the planes that had been flying to Thanh Hoa, Yen Bai, Hanoi, and Haiphong were now bombing the lines of communications west of the Annam Cordillera in Laos, where the weather was good. The bombing there was dubbed Commando Hunt, and it became the largest interdiction campaign in the history of aerial warfare.

Despite the fact that fighter-bomber wings still remained at their work elsewhere in Indochina, the longest bombing campaign in American military history was subsiding. President Johnson ended it, at least for the most part, on 1 November 1968. Officially, however, Rolling Thunder continued between 1 November 1968 and April 1972. Any attack north of 19 degrees north latitude during that period was termed a Rolling Thunder mission; however, such missions were rare and inconsequential. In April 1972 President Nixon began anew the bombing of the North, ordering planes back north of the 19th parallel in response to North Vietnam's massive invasion of the South that began on 31 March. The new campaign was called Linebacker.

153

- - - - - - - - -

In retrospect, Rolling Thunder has become a classic example of the failure to devise a strategy appropriate for the war at hand. Critics of air power are, perhaps, too hasty to point to it as an example of the failure of air power. Defenders are too quick to blame Rolling Thunder's failures on weak-willed politicians, a "misguided" press, and the antiwar movement. A few jaded hawks still claim it succeeded, or at least nearly succeeded.

Other than possibly boosting the morale of a few South Vietnamese generals, Rolling Thunder failed to achieve its principal objectives. It failed as an effort at strategic coercion. The bombing did not discourage Hanoi from supporting the Vietcong. Despite Rolling Thunder, North Vietnam provided supplies and manpower enough to stalemate the efforts of a 500,000-man American army. Nor did Rolling Thunder break the will of the North Vietnamese, prompting their leaders to seek a negotiated end to the conflict before they were ready to do so. North Vietnamese propaganda, in fact, thrived on the bombing. It was far easier to arouse the people against American aggressors overhead, than it was to elicit sacrifices against Yankee imperialists hundreds of miles to the south. As for negotiations, these did not begin until the Americans limited the bombing. On that point Ho Chi Minh was as good as his word. Semiserious talks did not begin until President Johnson announced the virtual end of Rolling Thunder on 1 November 1968.

How could one of the longest bombing campaigns in the history of aerial warfare, during which a million sorties were flown and around three quarters of a million tons of bombs dropped, fail so totally? Rolling Thunder failed for two reasons. First, in their pride, American civilian and military planners did not, probably could not, imagine that North Vietnam would endure American aerial attacks. Too many people believed too much in the efficacy and applicability of military power. Furthermore, civilian policy-makers did not understand air power enough to know that their policies might be crippling its potential effectiveness. Military leaders, for their part, were victims of a doctrine that they could not, or would not, believe had little applicability in a limited war.

Second, military leaders failed to develop and propose a strategy appropriate to the war at hand. Bombing strategic targets in the North and the unconventional war going on in the South had little direct interconnection. Furthermore, even when they realized that the constraints imposed by civilian policymakers would not be totally removed, the generals and admirals never devised a strategy applicable to the war as it was defined for them.

During the bombing and during the years since, military leaders complained about restrictions and constraints. Despite the fact that Rolling Thunder was an extensive bombing campaign, it was also restrained. While some argued that unleashing air power in 1965 would have a major impact on the North and on the course of the war in the South, those who argued the opposite view could not prove that it would not.

Despite all the evidence to the contrary, the Air Force viewed Rolling Thunder as only one of its many successes in the Vietnam War. General Momyer wrote in *Airpower in Three Wars*:

> Along with the counter-air campaign, interdiction of the major LOCs [lines of communication] in the northern routes also had been effective. All the main bridges were down, and most of the marshalling yards were blocked. A single through-line was kept open at great expense in repair crews.[167]

In its official wrap-up of the war, *Summary of the Ten Year Southeast Asia Air War, 1963–1973*, published after the 1973 withdrawal of all American forces from South Vietnam, the Air Force held:

> Despite the bombing restrictions, Rolling Thunder operations degraded the North Vietnamese industry, forcing the country from an exporting to an importing posture. North Vietnam's electrical power capability was reduced by 75-percent of its original capacity and more than 85-percent of its bulk POL was destroyed. In addition, the transportation system was seriously disrupted, restricting the enemy to nighttime shuttle operations.[168]

155

The failure of Rolling Thunder is not an indictment of the efficacy of air power. It is, however, an example of the misapplication of air power under the aegis of an inappropriately devised strategy. Blame for that can be laid on many doorsteps.

Notes

1. Memorandum, Secretary of the Air Force Harold Brown to Secretary of Defense Robert McNamara, 3 July 1967, in *The Pentagon Papers,* Senator Gravel edition, vol. 4 (Boston: Beacon Press, 1971–1972), 194.

2. Rolling Thunder began on 2 March 1965 and continued until President Johnson limited the bombing on 31 March 1968 to targets below the 20th parallel. On 1 November 1968 he further limited the bombing to support of armed reconnaissance missions. Except for "protective reaction strikes" the bombing of North Vietnam had ended, at least until Linebacker One operations began in April 1972 in response to the massive invasion of the South undertaken by North Vietnam on 31 March 1972. During the Nixon administration, there were occasional strikes above 19 degrees which were termed Rolling Thunder missions. In actuality, then, Rolling Thunder lasted much longer than is generally thought and was the longest bombing campaign ever conducted by any country in any war.

3. Dave Richard Palmer, *Summons of the Trumpet: U.S.-Vietnam in Perspective* (San Rafael, Calif.: Presidio Press, 1978), 62–64.

4. Gen William C. Westmoreland, "Report on Operations in South Vietnam, January 1964–June 1968," in Adm U. S. G. Sharp and Gen William C. Westmoreland, *Report on the War in Vietnam* (as of 30 June 1968) (Washington, D.C.: Government Printing Office, 1968), 95.

5. National Security Council, Working Group on Vietnam, "Intelligence Assessment: The Situation in Vietnam," 20 November 1964, in *Pentagon Papers* (Gravel), 3:651–55.

6. See draft memorandum, William P. Bundy, "Conditions for Action and Key Actions Surrounding Any Decisions," 5 November 1964, in ibid., 593; and George McT. Kahin, *Intervention: How America Became Involved in Vietnam* (New York: Alfred A. Knopf, 1986), 287.

7. Doris Kearns, *Lyndon Johnson and the American Dream* (New York: Harper and Row, 1976), 264.

8. Leslie H. Gelb and Richard K. Betts, *The Irony of Vietnam: The System Worked* (Washington, D.C.: Brookings Institution, 1979), 249.

9. Memorandum, W. W. Rostow to Secretary of State Dean Rusk, subject: Some Observations as We Come to the Crunch in Southeast Asia, 23 November 1964, in *Pentagon Papers* (Gravel), 3:645.

10. Gen William W. Momyer, *Airpower in Three Wars* (Washington, D.C.: Government Printing Office, 1978), 13.

11. *Pentagon Papers* (Gravel), 3:234, 342.

12. See David MacIsaac, *Strategic Bombing in World War Two: The Story of the United States Strategic Bombing Survey* (New York: Garland Publishing, 1976), 54–55; and John Morrocco, *Thunder from Above: The Air War, 1964–1968*, The Vietnam Experience (Boston: Boston Publishing, 1984), 30.

13. Kearns, 264–65.

14. "President Outlines Basic Themes of U.S. Policy in Southeast Asia," statement by President Johnson at news conference, 2 June 1964, *Department of State Bulletin*, 22 June 1964.

15. Lyndon Baines Johnson, *The Vantage Point: Perspectives of the Presidency, 1963–1969* (New York: Holt, Rinehart, and Winston, 1971), 119.

16. For a fuller explanation, see Col Dennis M. Drew, *Rolling Thunder 1965: Anatomy of a Failure*, CADRE Paper (Maxwell AFB, Ala.: Air University Press, 1986), 19–20, AU-ARI-CP-86-3.

17. See Earl H. Tilford, Jr., "Air Power in Vietnam: The Hubris of Power," in *The American War in Vietnam: Lessons, Legacies, and Implications for Future Conflicts*, ed. Lawrence E. Grinter and Peter M. Dunn (New York: Greenwood Press, 1987), 71. As discussed earlier, Air Force doctrine evolved from the 1920s and had remained basically unchanged from 1935.

18. There is some controversy as to whether or not General LeMay ever said those words. David Halberstam quotes the exchange between LeMay and Bundy in *The Best and the Brightest* (New York: Random House, 1972), 461–62. In the book *Mission with LeMay* appears the statement, "My solution to the problem would be to tell them frankly that they've got to draw in their horns and stop their aggression, or we're going to bomb them back to the Stone Age." (Curtis E. LeMay with Mackinlay Kantor, *Mission with LeMay* [Garden City, N.J.: Doubleday, 1965], 565.) Although LeMay has claimed that Kantor added the words, "bomb them back into the Stone Age," whether or not the general said them is somewhat irrelevant. He seemed to have believed them and acted accordingly.

19. See message, 071502Z June 1964, Detachment 3 (Det 3), Pacific Air Rescue Center, to Headquarters USAF; message, 071533Z June 1964, Det 3, Pacific Air Rescue Center, to Headquarters USAF, Search and Rescue (SAR) file, Office of Air Force History, Bolling AFB, Washington, D.C.; and *Pentagon Papers* (Gravel), 3:182.

20. Norman B. Hannah, *The Key to Failure: Laos and the Vietnam War* (Lanham, Md.: Madison Books, 1987), 120.

21. Gelb and Betts, 136.

22. *Pentagon Papers* (Gravel), 3:203.

23. Harry G. Summers, Jr., *The Vietnam War Almanac* (New York: Facts on File, 1985), 33.

24. *Pentagon Papers* (Gravel), 3:207.

25. Memorandum, "Action for South Vietnam," John T. McNaughton, in *Pentagon Papers* (Gravel), 3:601–2.

26. Morrocco, 30.

27. Amb Maxwell Taylor briefing, 27 November 1964, subject: The Current Situation in South Vietnam—November 1964, in *Pentagon Papers* (Gravel), 3:666–74.

28. Shelby L. Stanton, *The Rise and Fall of an American Army: U.S. Ground Forces in Vietnam, Nineteen Sixty-Five to Nineteen Seventy-Three* (Novato, Calif.: Presidio Press, 1985), 4.

29. William S. Turley, *The Second Indochina War: A Short Political and Military History, 1954–1975* (Boulder, Colo.: Westview Press, 1986), 90.

30. See *Pentagon Papers* (Gravel), 3:270–71; and Kahin, 276–77.

31. Carl Berger, ed., *The United States Air Force in Southeast Asia, 1961–1973: An Illustrated Account* (Washington, D.C.: Office of Air Force History, 1977), 69.

32. Adm U. S. Grant Sharp, *Strategy for Defeat: Vietnam in Retrospect* (San Rafael, Calif.: Presidio Press, 1978), 57.

33. *Pentagon Papers* (Gravel), 3:306.

34. Kearns, 263.

35. James Clay Thompson, *Rolling Thunder: Understanding Policy and Program Failure* (Chapel Hill: University of North Carolina Press, 1979), 28.

36. Ibid., 29.

37. See Senate Committee on the Armed Services, *Hearings before the Preparedness Investigating Subcommittee of the Committee on the Armed Services* (hereinafter *Stennis Committee Hearings*), testimony of Robert S. McNamara, 90th Cong., 1st sess., 25 August 1967, vol. 4, 275.

38. Sharp, "Report on Air and Naval Campaigns against North Vietnam," in Sharp and Westmoreland, 16.

39. *Stennis Committee Hearings*, testimony of Adm Thomas H. Moorer, 23 August 1967, 3:243.

40. Memorandum for the president, 28 July 1965, in *Pentagon Papers* (Gravel), 4:28–29.

41. Morrocco, 52.

42. Ibid., 54.

43. *Pentagon Papers* (Gravel), 3:333.

44. Ibid., 334.

45. Memorandum, secretary of defense to the president, 21 April 1965, in *Pentagon Papers* (Gravel), 3:385.

46. Sharp, *Strategy*, 80.

47. *Pentagon Papers* (Gravel), 3:385.

48. Kathleen J. Turner, *Lyndon Johnson's Dual War: Vietnam and the Press* (Chicago: University of Chicago Press, 1985), 122–25.

49. Sharp, "Campaigns against North Vietnam," 16.

50. See Raphael Littauer and Norman Uphoff, eds., Air War Study Group, Cornell University, *The Air War in Indochina* (Boston: Beacon Press, 1971), 37–38; and Morrocco, 56.

51. W. Hays Parks, "Rolling Thunder and the Law of War," *Air University Review* 33, no. 2 (January-February 1982), 13. The chairman of the Joint Chiefs of Staff, incredibly, was not invited to attend these meetings regularly until the autumn of 1967, over two years after Rolling Thunder began.

52. Littauer and Uphoff, 38.

53. See Clifford Working Group, memorandum to the president, "Significance of Bombing Campaign in North to Our Objectives in Vietnam," 6 March 1968, in *Pentagon Papers* (Gravel), 4:251–52; and Berger, 95.

54. Kearns, 270.

55. Memorandum to the president, 20 July 1965, in *Pentagon Papers* (Gravel), 4:24.

56. Special National Intelligence Estimate, 23 July 1965, in *Pentagon Papers* (Gravel), 4:24.

57. Littauer and Uphoff, 39; and Morrocco, 64.

58. See Guenter Lewy, *America in Vietnam* (New York: Oxford University Press, 1978), 391; and *Pentagon Papers* (Gravel), 3:55–57.

59. See memorandum, secretary of defense to the Joint Chiefs of Staff, 17 February 1965, in *Pentagon Papers* (Gravel), 3:332. McNamara complained after the initial Flaming Dart missions that bombing had to be more accurate to be effective. He cited the raids on the Xom Bang ammunition depot and at Quang Khe Naval Base as examples. In these raids, 267 sorties were sent against 491 structures. Only 47 were destroyed and an additional 22 damaged.

60. Interview with Col Michael Muskat, USAF, Retired, 12 February 1988; and G. I. Basel, *Pak Six* (La Mesa, Calif.: Associated Creative Writers, 1982), 19.

61. Harvey H. Smith et al., *North Vietnam: A Country Study* (Washington, D.C.: Department of the Army, 1967), 17.

62. Muskat interview.

63. Townsend Hoopes, *The Limits of Intervention* (New York: David McKay, 1966), 77.

64. Littauer and Uphoff, 48.

65. Morrocco, 121–22.

66. Sharp, "Campaigns against North Vietnam," 16.

67. See Christopher Robbins, *The Ravens* (New York: Crown, 1987), 115. According to Robbins, Amb William H. Sullivan, in Laos, was convinced that "a high performance jet flying at eight hundred knots . . . was not the most effective instrument to use against truck convoys that were moving at a snail's pace down the muddy Ho Chi Minh Trail." Consequently, he was committed to using propeller planes like the T-28 and A-1E, as well as multiengine gunships along the trail.

68. Morrocco, 116–17.

69. See *Pentagon Papers* (Gravel), 4:55–56; and Drew, 41.

70. *Pentagon Papers* (Gravel), 4:55–56.

71. Sharp, "Campaigns against North Vietnam," 24.

72. Sharp, *Strategy*, 115.

73. *Pentagon Papers* (Gravel), 4:71–72.

74. DIA Estimate of Results of POL Strikes, 31 January 1966, in *Pentagon Papers* (Gravel), 4:68.

75. See Barry D. Watts, *The Foundations of U.S. Air Doctrine: The Problem of Friction in War* (Maxwell AFB, Ala.: Air University Press, 1984), 113; James William Gibson, *The Perfect War: Technowar in Vietnam* (Boston: Atlantic Monthly Press, 1986), 335–37; and *Pentagon Papers* (Gravel), 4:74.

76. J. S. Butz, Jr., "Those Bombings in the North," *Air Force and Space Digest*, April 1966, 42.

77. Thompson, 51.

78. Turner, 145–46.

79. Johnson, *Vantage Point*, 246–49; and Thompson, 50.

80. *Pentagon Papers* (Gravel), 4:103–4.

81. See POL Execution Message, 22 June 1966, in *Pentagon Papers* (Gravel), 4:105–6; Sharp, "Campaigns Against North Vietnam," 25; and Morrocco, 128.

82. Quoted in *Pentagon Papers* (Gravel), 4:106.

83. See Gibson, 339; and *Pentagon Papers* (Gravel), 4:109–10.

84. J. S. Butz, Jr., "Airpower in Vietnam: The High Price of Restraint," *Air Force and Space Digest*, November 1966, 43.

85. Draft memorandum, "Actions Recommended for Vietnam," from Secretary of Defense Robert S. McNamara, 14 October 1966, in Neil Sheehan et al., *Pentagon Papers*, ed. Gerald Gold, Allan M. Segal, and Samuel Abt, *New York Times* edition (New York: Quadrangle Books, 1971), 556–57.

86. *Pentagon Papers* (Gravel), 4:156.

87. Gen John P. McConnell, USAF chief of staff, "USAF's Score in Limited War: Impressive," *Air Force and Space Digest*, September 1966, 52.

88. W. W. Rostow to Secretary McNamara, letter, subject: Personal, 16 November 1964, in *Pentagon Papers* (Gravel), 3:634.

89. Palmer, 74–76.

90. An unknown number of aircraft were shot down by lighter caliber weapons like the .50 caliber and Chinese or Soviet 12.7-mm heavy machine guns. Additionally, the North Vietnamese populace was armed with rifles so that they could fire away at low-flying intruders. It is not known how many planes were lost to light ground fire.

91. Momyer, 20.

92. *Illustrated History of the Conflict in Southeast Asia*, ed. Ray Bonds (New York: Crown Publishers, 1979), 88.

93. Sharp, "Campaigns against North Vietnam," 19.

94. Ibid., 26.

95. In the summer of 1965 no one knew how to deal with the SAMs. On the first Air Force strike against the missile site which brought down the F-4C on 24 July 1965, F-105s were loaded with 750-pound bombs, then downloaded and rearmed with napalm. Each flight leader reportedly had no armament other than the 20-mm cannon in his plane's nose. Four F-105s were lost in that initial strike. See Morrocco, 107–9.

96. Larry Davis, *Wild Weasel: The SAM Suppression Story* (Carrollton, Tex.: Squadron Signal Publications, 1986), 8; and Morrocco, 112.

97. Jack Broughton, *Thud Ridge* (Toronto: Bantam Books, 1985), 60–65.

98. Morrocco, 112–13.

99. Muskat interview.

100. See Sharp, "Campaigns against North Vietnam," 27; and Momyer, 136.

101. Momyer, 311.

102. Earl H. Tilford, Jr., *The United States Air Force Search and Rescue in Southeast Asia, 1961–1975* (Washington, D.C.: Office of Air Force History, 1980), 121.

103. See Alain C. Enthoven and K. Wayne Smith, *How Much Is Enough: Shaping the Defense Program, 1961–1969* (New York: Harper and Row, 1971), 304; and Lewy, 395.

104. Tilford, *Search and Rescue*, 92–95.

105. Momyer, 125–32.

106. Ariel (pseudonym for USAF Capt Morris Blachman), "The Stupidity of Intelligence," *Washington Monthly,* September 1969, 23.

107. Jasons's report, 29 August 1966, in *Pentagon Papers* (Gravel), 4:116–19.

108. Draft memorandum, Secretary of Defense Robert S. McNamara to President Lyndon B. Johnson, "Actions Recommended for Vietnam," 19 October 1966, in *Pentagon Papers* (*New York Times*), 555.

109. Memorandum, Eyes Only, JCS to the President, 14 October 1966, in *Pentagon Papers* (*New York Times*), 564–65.

110. Johnson, *Vantage Point*, 253.

111. Ho Chi Minh to Lyndon B. Johnson, letter, 10 February 1967, in *America in Vietnam: A Documentary History,* ed. William Appleman Williams et al. (Garden City, N.Y.: Anchor Books, 1985), 261.

112. See *Pentagon Papers* (Gravel), 4:138; and Morrocco, 151–52.

113. CIA Report, 20 May 1967, in *Pentagon Papers* (Gravel), 4:153.

114. Memorandum, JCS to the president, 5 May 1967, in *Pentagon Papers* (Gravel), 4:152–53.

115. Lewy, 84.

116. Thompson, 54.

117. Briefing, Momyer/Sharp to SECDEF, 19 July 1967, in *Pentagon Papers* (Gravel), 4:195–96.

118. Ibid.

119. Sharp, *Strategy*, 135.

120. Memorandum, Walt W. Rostow to Dean Rusk, 6 May 1967, in *Pentagon Papers* (*New York Times*), 587.

121. Draft presidential memorandum, 12 June 1967, in *Pentagon Papers* (Gravel), 4:190.

122. Bunker, quoted in Thompson, 56–57.

123. AFA Statement of Policy, "Airpower Can Do More in Vietnam," *Air Force and Space Digest*, May 1966, 6.

124. Thompson, 56.

125. *Stennis Committee Hearings*, testimony of Adm Ulysses S. Grant Sharp, 9 August 1967, pt. 1, 1:7.

126. Ibid., 9–10.

127. Ibid., testimony of Gen Earle G. Wheeler, 16 August 1967, 2:126.

128. Ibid., 188.

129. Ibid., testimony of Maj Gen Gilbert L. Meyers, 29 August 1967, 5:496.

130. Ibid., testimony of Lt Gen William W. Momyer, 16 August 1967, 2:132.

131. Ibid., 143.

132. Ibid.

133. Ibid., 168.

134. Ibid., testimony of Robert S. McNamara, 25 August 1967, 4:305–6.

135. Ibid., 277.

136. Ibid., 278.

137. Ibid., 279.

138. Ibid.

139. Ibid., 302.

140. Ibid.

141. Ibid.

142. Ibid., 301.

143. Senate Committee on the Armed Services, *Air War against North Vietnam, Summary Report of the Preparedness Investigating Subcommittee*, 90th Cong., 1st sess., 1967, 9–10.

144. See George C. Herring, *America's Longest War: The United States and Vietnam, 1950–1975* (New York: Alfred A. Knopf, 1979), 185–86.

145. Quoted in Lawrence J. Korb, *The Joint Chiefs of Staff: The First Twenty-Five Years* (Bloomington, Ind.: University of Indiana Press, 1976), 181.

146. See Herring, 179; and Morrocco, 158–60.

147. Jasons's report, December 1967, in *Pentagon Papers* (Gravel), 4:228.

148. See Sharp, "Campaigns against North Vietnam," 39; and Jasons's report, 227.

149. Jasons's report, 275.

150. Memorandum for the secretary of defense, 17 October 1967, subject: Increased Pressure on North Vietnam. JCSM-555-67, in *Pentagon Papers* (Gravel), 4:210–13.

151. Morrocco, 158.

152. Johnson, *Vantage Point*, 377.

153. Ibid., 375.

154. Ibid., 394.

155. Clifford quoted in Clark Dougan and Stephen Weiss, *Nineteen Sixty-Eight*, The Vietnam Experience (Boston: Boston Publishing, 1983), 76.

156. Ibid.

157. Clark M. Clifford, "A Viet Nam Reappraisal: The Personal History of One Man's View and How It Evolved," *Foreign Affairs*, July 1969, 10–11.

158. Quoted in Hoopes, 204–5.

159. Ibid., 205.

160. Draft presidential memorandum, 4 March 1968, in *Pentagon Papers* (Gravel), 4:250–52.

161. Ibid.

162. Memorandum, SECAF to Paul Nitze, 4 March 1968, in *Pentagon Papers* (Gravel), 4:260. The secretary suggested the following course of action:

1. First, actions against North Vietnam should be *intensified* by bombing all the remaining important targets and/or neutralization of the port of Haiphong [emphasis added].

2. Second, air actions should be *intensified* in the adjoining panhandle areas of Laos/NVN [emphasis added].

3. Third, a change to the basic strategy in SVN is examined in which *increased* air actions in SVN are substituted for increased ground forces [emphasis added].

163. JCS response to the Clifford memorandum, in *Pentagon Papers* (Gravel), 4:253–54.

164. Johnson, *Vantage Point*, 420.

165. See Sharp, *Strategy*, 227; and Johnson, *Vantage Point*, 494.

166. JCS response to the Clifford memorandum, cited in note 163.

167. Momyer, 311.

168. "Summary of the Ten Year Southeast Asia Air War, 1963–1973," vol. 2, suppl. Doc. III-N, 21, USAF Historical Research Center, Maxwell AFB, Ala.

Chapter 4

"However Frustrated We Are"

In his keynote address to the annual meeting of the Air Force Association on 19 March 1969, newly installed Secretary of the Air Force Robert C. Seamans, Jr., said:

> There seems to be a trend toward viewing all national questions in the context of the frustrating struggle against aggression in Vietnam. . . . But there is no doubt that, however frustrated we are with the conflict in Vietnam, the cost of failure to provide adequate forces for our security could be infinitely higher than the cost of Southeast Asia.[1]

The Vietnam War was, in fact, peripheral to the theme of the secretary's speech, entitled "Continuing Cooperation between NASA and DoD." A year had passed since President Lyndon Johnson had curtailed air strikes against North Vietnam and had stated that he would not seek reelection. Many things had happened in the meantime to frustrate large segments of society. Assassinations had claimed civil rights leader Martin Luther King in Memphis, Tennessee, on 4 April 1968 and presidential candidate Robert F. Kennedy in Los Angeles on 4 June 1968. At its Chicago convention in July, the Democratic party ripped itself apart over the issue of Vietnam, paving the way for Richard Nixon's victory in November.

Meanwhile, American troop strength in Vietnam climbed past 565,000. In part, Richard Nixon won the White House intimating that he had a secret plan to end the war. By March 1969 no one was sure what that plan might be, but it seemed certain that America would never be the same after 1968. The war was a long way from being over. The period from 1968 to 1972, even as American forces began the tortuous disengagement and withdrawal, saw the greatest bloodletting of the conflict and even larger and louder protests against the war. Air power covered the retreat

165

Secretary of the Air Force Robert C. Seamans, Jr. Seamans was secretary when President Richard M. Nixon initiated the Vietnamization program in July 1969. During Seamans's tenure, the Air Force shifted its attention from Vietnam back to the more familiar European scenarios.

and in the years from 1968 through 1971, air power was used—at times lavishly—to ensure the success of that withdrawal.

Shifting Gears in 1968

Even before Lyndon Johnson announced the curtailment in the air war over North Vietnam, Rolling Thunder had subsided due to deteriorating weather. From 1 January to 31 March 1968, the US

Air Force flew 7,581 sorties against targets above the demilitarized zone—a decrease of 5,657 from the previous quarter.[2] In the South a combined Vietcong and People's Army of Vietnam (PAVN—the North Vietnamese army) offensive during Tet—along with the siege of 5,000 US Marines and a battalion of South Vietnamese Rangers at Khe Sanh—riveted the attention of the American public to what seemed like an evolving disaster. With the curtailment in air strikes against the North, the Air Force was, to some extent, groping for direction—not unlike a kayaker shooting through a white-water rapid, heading downstream fast but unable to determine exactly where, and all the while fending off rocks and contending with dangerous eddies.

The Air Force, like the other services, fought in a strategic vacuum in 1968 and 1969. As the nation moved toward disengagement, the Air Force, with its offensive-oriented doctrines, was especially affected, and eventually disaffected. In a sense, Secretary Seamans's speech to the Air Force Association, focusing as it did on the relationship between the Department of Defense and the National Aeronautics and Space Administration, represented a spiritual disengagement from the war. Despite the fact that the war was raging in Southeast Asia, the Air Force refocused its attention on space and toward meeting the Soviet threat in Europe—in a spiritual sense returning to where it had been during the "time of atomic plenty." Back at the war, the emphasis shifted to tactics, techniques, and technological innovations, all employed under an increasingly pervasive managerial concept of warfare that evolved as a substitute for strategy.

The Tet offensive in 1968 was a watershed in the war and in American policy. It was unique in the annals of military history because the side that won the resounding tactical victory suffered an incalculable strategic reversal.[3] Despite the fact that the United States and the Republic of Vietnam inflicted an estimated 50,000 casualties on their enemies, the Tet offensive (the Communists' most resounding military defeat thus far) became, from the standpoint of the overall conflict, *the* most important victory of the war for the national liberation front and Hanoi because it had a profound psychological impact on the American public. The Tet offensive hit the United States squarely in its "center of gravity," that significant intangible described by the nineteenth-century Prussian military theorist Carl von Clausewitz as "the hub of all power and movement, on which everything depends."[4] America's center of gravity was not its army in the field, not even the territory held by that army, but public opinion, which, by 1968, was terribly divided on Vietnam. The Tet offensive slammed into that gravity center with the force of a speeding locomotive, shredding the optimistic projections of generals and the credibility of the Johnson administration. Tet 1968 came at a time when the efficacy of American air power in bombing the North was under question by many within the administration, including Secretary of Defense Robert S. McNamara, who left office at the end of February. When Gen William Westmoreland asked for an additional 206,756 men—setting a new proposed ceiling of 731,756 men in South Vietnam—as a prerequisite for avoiding defeat, President Johnson faced a major decision with awesome implications. To deny the request would signal that the administration no longer believed a military solution was possible; to fulfill it meant calling up the reserves and making a vast, new commitment. Johnson waffled, firmly denying the request for 200,000-plus additional troops but not ruling out some lesser figure.[5]

As the air war over North Vietnam diminished, the focus shifted to supporting the war in the South. The weather there was not bad, and the airmen were busy. Fighter-bombers and gunships provided support to US and Army of the Republic of Vietnam (ARVN—the South Vietnamese army) troops struggling to reclaim the cities, towns, and villages overrun by the Vietcong and PAVN forces during Tet and then hounded the enemy into the countryside. While air power was important in these roles in the post-Tet period, it was vital in preventing disaster for the garrison at Khe Sanh.

The final stage of the siege at Khe Sanh got under way on 20 January 1968, when the PAVN unleashed a mortar, artillery, and rocket attack, followed by an assault on the perimeter. This attack triggered Operation Niagara, a joint American aerial campaign in which bombs fell like water cascading over Niagara Falls. Before the siege ended on 8 March, the Air Force, Navy, and Marines had flown more than 24,000 fighter-bomber and 2,700 B-52 sorties to drop 110,000 tons of bombs.[6] While no one knows how many North Vietnamese troops were killed at Khe Sanh, a reasonable estimate is 10,000 casualties.[7]

Operations to support the Army, Marines, and ARVN during Tet and the Marines at Khe Sanh, however edifying, were not totally satisfying for an Air Force institutionally oriented toward the strategic offensive. With the more lucrative targets around Hanoi and Haiphong off-limits, the Air Force searched for an alternative strategy.

The search for direction was also going on in Washington. After Robert S. McNamara departed as secretary of defense, the generals and admirals at the Pentagon offered his replacement, Clark Clifford, the same old shibboleths about "unleashing air power" on the North to close the ports and to cut the roads and rail lines north of Hanoi leading into China despite the new secretary's admonitions that such actions were politically impossible. Clifford completed the metamorphosis from hawk to dove in less than a month.[8]

Given the lack of direction in American policy, it was fortunate that the threat in Vietnam had abated somewhat after the drubbing inflicted on the Vietcong and the North Vietnamese army during Tet. For the Americans, the ground war was going rather well in 1968. Beginning on 6 April, elements of the 1st Air Cavalry Division, the 1st Marine Division, and four ARVN battalions completed Operation Pegasus, the ground campaign to raise the siege at Khe Sanh. Subsequently, Military Assistance Command, Vietnam (MACV), pronounced that the 77-day ordeal was over.[9]

Elsewhere, American and South Vietnamese forces tallied impressive scores against the enemy. Two weeks after raising the siege at Khe Sanh, US and ARVN forces launched Operation Delaware, a multidivisional assault into the A Shau Valley—a key infiltration corridor into I Corps. Allied troops had not been in the valley since 1966, and in the interim the Vietcong and PAVN

169

regulars had used it as a base from which to stage attacks throughout the northern provinces.[10] To the south, US Army units fanned out into the jungle in what Lt Gen Julian J. Ewell termed "double teaming" the enemy with a combination of military pressure and a strong pacification effort.[11] In May, June, and July the Communists launched a second series of attacks dubbed "Mini-Tet." These spasms of violence lacked the concerted power of the earlier Tet attacks and, in most places, amounted to little more than "attacks by fire"—standoff shellings by mortars and rockets on bases and installations.[12] One of the bases hit hardest was the US Air Force installation at Pleiku where, during the early

Army mechanized infantry on patrol. Although US troops began withdrawing from Vietnam in late 1969 and early 1970, the war became bloodier as the People's Army of Vietnam began taking over the brunt of the fighting from the Vietcong. Despite advantages in firepower and mobility, US forces suffered more casualties between 1969 and 1972 than they had between 1965 and 1968.

morning hours of 29 July, a Vietcong sapper squad infiltrated to blow up a pair of C-130 transports and damage six others, along with a C-47 and an F-100 fighter.[13]

By the end of 1968 Hanoi may have suffered 100,000 casualties as a result of Tet, the allied counteroffensive, and Mini-Tet. The enemy general offensive had been defeated. While 1968 went down as an unmitigated military disaster for the Communists, for the United States it became the turning point of the Vietnam War.

Search for Tomorrow

While Washington shifted gears during the last months of the lame-duck Johnson administration, the US had no clearly defined national policy on Vietnam that was translatable into goals toward which the military could devise an appropriate strategy. The Army and Marines were reacting to enemy initiatives during Tet. Even the offensives undertaken in the wake of Tet were designed to take advantage of the weaknesses created when the Vietcong threw themselves on American bayonets. During Tet, the offensive that followed, the siege of Khe Sanh, and Mini-Tet, air power too reacted to enemy initiatives by supporting the US Army, ARVN, and Marines.

As 1968 ground along, Washington and MACV considered several options. The first was to continue the strategic defensive and tactical offensive that Westmoreland had pursued to a stalemate in 1966 and 1967, that is, to do more of the same. That option was ruled out. Another option was to defend the cities and population centers of the eastern plain, letting the Communists dominate the jungled mountains and highlands. Gen Earle G. Wheeler labelled this policy as "defeatist."[14] A third option, which evolved into Vietnamization during the early months of the Nixon administration, actually had its genesis in the latter days of the Johnson administration. The United States would assist the South Vietnamese while intensifying its pacification efforts, the ultimate purpose being the withdrawal of American forces. Bombing, restricted as it was to the southern panhandle of North Vietnam, would be more closely tied to the ground situation in the South.[15] In a larger sense, this was a cut and run strategy and air power would cover the retreat. The massive interdiction efforts and the widespread use of sensors during Operation Commando Hunt were clearly linked to the US effort to disengage from the war in Southeast Asia.

Operation Commando Hunt

During the siege at Khe Sanh, acoustic and seismic sensors were dropped into the surrounding countryside as part of an operation centered on the Niagara intelligence center at Tan Son Nhut. There analysts correlated information gathered from sensor activations with photographic interpretation reports and prisoner inter- rogations.[16] The Niagara intelligence center worked with Dutch Mill, the Air Force's newly established infiltration surveillance center located at Nakhon Phanom Royal Thai Air Force Base (RTAFB), Thailand. Sensors played a key role in locating North Vietnamese units so that they could be targeted not only by artillery from within the Khe Sanh compound and from fire support bases in the surrounding area but also by air strikes. In the predawn hours of 29 February, analysts at Dutch Mill and the Niagara intelligence center relayed information which helped artillery, radar-equipped fighters, and B-52s smash three attacks by the PAVN's highly touted 304th Division.[17]

The impact of the sensor program was not lost on the Air Force. Sensors were part of the Air Force's effort to track and analyze traffic moving along the Ho Chi Minh Trail. The trail had been first attacked back in 1964 as a part of Operation Barrel Roll. Over the years, while gunships and fighter-bombers attacked trucks on the roads in Laos, the primary focus of the air war had been on North Vietnam. Operations along the trail were secondary. After President Johnson limited the bombing of North Vietnam on 1 April 1968 and then ended that bombing, for all intents and purposes, on 1 November, the Ho Chi Minh Trail and traffic moving down it increased in importance as the weight of the aerial effort shifted to interdiction in Laos.

Operation Commando Hunt began on 15 November 1968 with Commando Hunt I. It continued until April 1972, ending with Commando Hunt VII. Each campaign in between lasted approximately six months, roughly covering the period of either a dry or wet season, as dictated by the monsoonal climate. The campaigns had two objectives: first, to reduce the enemy's logistical flow by substantially increasing the time needed to move supplies from North Vietnam into the South; second, to destroy trucks and supply caches along the roads, pathways, and streams and in the truck parks and storage bases along the trail.[18]

The genesis for Commando Hunt was in the 1966 study by the Jason Division of the Institute for Defense Analysis. This group of scholars declared that bombing North Vietnam was likely to be ineffective and suggested an electronic barrier be constructed across Laos. Secretary McNamara, always ready to turn to a technologically derived alternative, suggested that a billion-dollar program, eventually dubbed "McNamara's fence," be undertaken to cut the Ho Chi Minh Trail. While neither the administration nor the Department of Defense supported the idea completely, it became the genesis for the longest aerial interdiction campaign ever conducted.

With the decrease in the bombing of North Vietnam, there were plenty of resources available for Commando Hunt. In November 1968 bombing missions into southern Laos climbed by 300 percent, from 4,700 sorties in October to 12,800 in November.[19] This increase was partly the result of the end of the rainy season in Laos and the start of better weather, but the stepped-up bombing had only started. Before the war ended, the Air Force, along with the Navy and Marine Corps, would drop over 3 million tons of bombs on Laos, three times the tonnage directed at North Vietnam.

Commando Hunt involved attacks against three, and later four, target categories. First, there were the attacks on trucks as they moved along the roads. Early in the bombing of the Ho Chi Minh

Trail, during Operation Barrel Roll and then in Operation Steel Tiger,* propeller-driven fighter-bombers and jets were used against trucks. However, it soon became apparent that risking a multimillion-dollar plane, especially a sophisticated jet, to destroy a single truck was foolish. Jets, the airplane of choice in the Air Force of the 1960s, were not as accurate in ground attack missions as prop planes. Gunships gradually took over and then came to dominate the "war on trucks."

Second, there were the attacks on the trail itself. The Ho Chi Minh Trail was a network of roadways, pathways, and waterways which, by 1968, included over 200 miles of two-lane dirt roads along with several thousand miles of single-lane side roads, pathways, and small rivers and streams down which supplies could be moved. Up to 10,000 trucks could shuttle down the trail at any one time.[20]

Third, Commando Hunt encompassed attacks on the terrain— the mountain passes, river fords, and the jungle. Bombs slamming into hillsides often caused landslides to block roads, at least temporarily. The mountain passes leading from North Vietnam into Laos were thought to be vulnerable to this kind of attack. Bombing, and to a lesser extent chemical defoliation under the auspices of Ranch Hand, were used to strip the jungle of foliage or to eliminate the trees altogether, thus making it easier to see and attack trucks. Bombing not only destroyed river fords but also altered the course of rivers, thus hampering efforts to float supplies south in sealed, 55-gallon drums.

As Commando Hunt developed, the North Vietnamese moved larger numbers of antiaircraft guns into position along the trail. By 1970 the attack on defenses along the trail became a fourth aspect of the battle. The 23-mm and 37-mm guns presented an especially dangerous threat for slow, lumbering gunships. Fighter-bombers armed with cluster bombs and napalm, and later with highly

---

*Barrel Roll was the code name for operations over Laos in December 1964. It later applied only to air operations over northern Laos. Steel Tiger began on 3 April 1965, as the Laotian complement to Rolling Thunder. In December 1965, the Tiger Hound area of operations was established to cover bombing missions south to the Cambodian border.

accurate laser-guided bombs, were used to destroy these antiaircraft artillery (AAA) sites so that other aircraft could operate more freely.

Although Commando Hunt was an interdiction campaign, it was not of the traditional kind conducted in Europe during World War II or by the USAF in Korea. There were no easily spotted and targeted railroad marshalling yards or difficult-to-repair concrete and steel bridges to be wrecked. The trail, largely concealed beneath dense jungle canopy, consisted of dirt roads and wooden bridges which were easily repaired.

Fighter-bombers like the F-100, F-105, and F-4 were used to bomb and strafe trucks but, because trucks were relatively small and difficult for a pilot flying at better than 200 knots an hour to hit, gunships assumed a greater role in attacking vehicles. As the war progressed, so did gunship technology. Gunship versions of the C-119 and C-123 twin-engine transports as well as AC-130s carrying 20-mm and 40-mm cannons and, after 1971, 105-mm howitzers replaced the AC-47s with their 7.62-mm Gatling guns. Of all the aircraft associated with Commando Hunt, gunships gained the most prominence, and they dominated in the war on trucks.

Many other types of aircraft, of course, operated over the Ho Chi Minh Trail. In January 1966 the Air Force launched Operation Cricket, which entailed the use of single-engine, propeller-driven O-1 Bird Dogs and A-1E Skyraiders from Nakhon Phanom as forward air controllers over the northern panhandle of Laos for Steel Tiger sorties. North of that, in the Barrel Roll area, the mission was primarily one of close air support, with armed reconnaissance taking a secondary role. As part of Steel Tiger F-100s and F-105s patrolled the trail during the day, running most of the traffic into the safety of concealed truck parks to await darkness.[21]

The Strategic Air Command's B-52s had begun flying missions over Laos in late 1965, with the first on 11 December targeted against the Mu Gia Pass area. By June 1966 B-52s had flown 400 sorties over Laos, generally against terrain targets like passes or against the roads in an attempt to crater them. On occasion B-52s were used to blast supply caches, truck parks, and suspected troop concentrations.[22] The North Vietnamese reacted to the increased tempo in aerial operations by beefing up their air defenses along the roads and around truck parks. In the first months of 1966 antiaircraft guns downed 22 US aircraft in southern Laos.[23] B-52s flying above 30,000 feet were invulnerable to 23-mm and 37-mm AA guns, and speed offered some advantage to fighter-bombers even during low-altitude bomb runs. The slow and cumbersome AC-47s, however, provided perfect targets for enemy gunners. The three 7.62-mm Gatling guns on the AC-47s were ineffective at a range beyond 1,500 yards, thus when the gunships went into their firing orbits they were well within the envelope for 23-mm and 37-mm guns. By mid-1966 four AC-47s had been lost over Laos, three to guns along the trail. Consequently, they were withdrawn and—at the request of the US ambassador to Laos, William H. Sullivan—were redeployed there to defend Royal Laotian Army and progovernment guerrilla outposts on the Plain of Jars and elsewhere.[24]

Enemy defenses, more than any other single factor, drove gunship development. In February 1966 Headquarters US Air Force initiated Operation Shed Light, a program to enhance overall night reconnaissance and strike capabilities. Project Gunboat emerged as one of the Shed Light proposals.[25] It fostered the development of the AC-130 gunships, which accounted for most of the truck kills in Commando Hunt.

Sporting 20-mm Gatling guns and 40-mm Bofors cannons and equipped with low-light-level television, laser range finders, and Black Crow infrared detection systems to seek out hot spots associated with truck engines, the AC-130 bolstered the *statistical* success of Commando Hunt operations. In 1968 the Air Force claimed 7,332 trucks destroyed or damaged as compared to 3,291 the previous year.[26] Commando Hunt I, having produced results, blended into Commando Hunt II in May 1969 with the start of the annual southwest monsoon.

Commando Hunt was supported by the Igloo White sensor program that began in December 1967 under the auspices of Task Force Alpha at Nakhon Phanom RTAFB. After 1968 Igloo White was tied to Vietnamization. The sensors, combined with the gunships and other aircraft attacking the Ho Chi Minh Trail, would, hopefully, slow the flow of men and supplies to the battlefields of the South and thus buy time for the United States to turn the war over to the ARVN and to gradually withdraw American troops.

The Igloo White sensor system consisted of three principal elements: acoustical and seismic sensors sowed by aircraft along the infiltration routes; the airborne relay aircraft that received and transmitted the signals; and the all-important nerve center of the system—the infiltration surveillance center (ISC) at Nakhon Phanom—where assessment officers and trained intelligence specialists analyzed sensor data processed by computer. When the system functioned smoothly, the resulting intelligence became part of a targeting process that moved rapidly from an assessment officer manning a scope where sound and seismic data were displayed visually to another officer who then directed the airborne command post to call in strike aircraft on specific targets.[27]

Specially equipped EC-121Rs—converted four-engine Lockheed Super Constellation transports—were used as relay platforms until 1971, when modified single-engine Beechcraft Debonairs first supplemented, then replaced, the EC-121s. The Debonairs were tiny, certainly by comparison to the transoceanic airliners modified by the Air Force into the EC-121s. In fact, these planes were small in comparison to the average single-engine, privately owned aircraft. The relay aircraft, whether the large EC-121 or the petite Debonair, acted as a key link in the electronic communications process, transmitting signals to Task Force Alpha. Although larger, the EC-121 was not as capable as the single-engine Beechcraft in its relay role. Furthermore, the EC-121 put up to a dozen crewmen and technicians at risk since it could not climb above the range of higher caliber AAA, and it was too slow to escape any MiG attack that might develop out of the southern bases in the panhandle of North Vietnam. The Beechcraft, on the other hand, could be operated as a drone. Or, if flown, at most only one person was put at risk. Additionally, its comparatively small size and radar cross section made it difficult to see visually or electronically. Furthermore, it could climb higher than an EC-121 to fly beyond the range of 37-mm and 57-mm guns.[28]

The Ho Chi Minh Trail was seeded with the various kinds of sensors. Wherever possible, sensors were sown in strips, either in the jungle or along the roadsides. Once wired, the trail became an electronic battlefield where sensor information was used as a part of the targeting process. When the seismic and acoustical responses had been analyzed, and a determination made that a viable target was likely to exist at a certain place and time, the airborne command post would be instructed to direct a gunship or a flight of fighter-bombers to the target.[29] On board the F-4s, prowling the night sky with their load of cluster bombs (a weapon proven highly effective against trucks singly or in convoy), the backseater would enter the target coordinates into a small computer that determined the correct course to steer and even the point at which he should release the bombs.[30]

During the daylight hours the ISC normally passed target information to a forward air controller who queried Hillsboro—the airborne command and control center (ABCCC) C-130 on daytime orbit over southern Laos—for a fighter with the appropriate combination of weapons and then directed it to the target. In other cases, the ISC assigned the fighters to a forward air controller patrolling Laos in a spotter plane or to a forward air guide* hidden in a secluded position along the trail. At night, Moonbeam, the evening shift for ABCCC over southern Laos, directed the gunships, specially modified B-57Gs, and F-4s to their targets. Often the AC-130s served as tactical controllers, using their night sensors (low-light-level television and infrared optics) to find

---

*Forward air guides were Lao, Hmong, or Thai mercenaries in the employ of the CIA.

targets and call in air strikes. The AC-130s, AC-123s, and AC-119s often worked directly with the ISC assessment officers who tipped them to possible activity along the trail.[31]

The AC-130s became the centerpiece of the Commando Hunt campaigns, but they were not alone over the Ho Chi Minh Trail. Although less sophisticated and not as effective as the AC-130s, AC-119 and AC-123 gunships contributed to the burgeoning "truck count." Fighter-bombers also claimed substantial numbers in the truck-killing operation, with Air Force F-4s boasting 1,576 trucks destroyed and 6,130 damaged in Commando Hunt III alone.[32]

In addition to the AC-130s, other highly sophisticated aircraft worked on the Ho Chi Minh Trail. In September 1971, 11 B-57Gs were introduced to augment the truck-killing force. These were outfitted with forward-looking radar, infrared and low-light-level television, laser ranging devices, higher performance engines, additional crew armor, and an improved ejection capability. Along with F-4s and Navy A-6s, updated with Commando Bolt long-range navigation (loran) and airborne moving target indicators (AMTI), these B-57s supplemented the AC-130s in denying the cover of darkness to the North Vietnamese moving along the trail.[33]

The Commando Hunt campaigns continued in succession into a new decade, but strategy changed very little—amounting only to refinements in concepts and techniques. Enemy defenses prompted changes in gunship configuration so that by late 1971, AC-130s were using 105-mm howitzers to gain a greater standoff range.[34] Of course Commando Hunt involved more than attacking trucks. It incorporated attacks on major elements of the logistical system, including the roads, storage areas, AAA emplacements, and even features of the terrain.[35]

One tactic developed in 1969 for attacking the topography was to use standard Mk-82 500-pound and Mk-83 750-pound bombs to crater the roads or to cause landslides that would cut the roads, and then to seed those sections with gravel mines to hamper repair activities.[36] This tactic not only harassed the enemy, it also backed up traffic or channeled it onto alternate and predictable routes, thereby facilitating the targeting process in that planes could be dispatched to specific routes with some assurance of lucrative results. Among the most effective road cuts were those caused by landslides from cliffs and embankments. These were most readily obtained in the four entry corridors at the mountain passes leading from North Vietnam into Laos: Napè, Mu Gia, Ban Karai, and Ban Ravine.

During Commando Hunt V, which began on 10 October 1970, two-thirds of all attack sorties and virtually all B-52 missions were targeted against the entry corridors or other geographical features rather than at truck parks or storage areas. In Commando Hunt V, planners and intelligence officers devised interdiction boxes labelled A, B, C, and D for each of the passes. Additionally, target boxes were drawn around the major transportation hub at Tchepone. The boxes varied in shape from one mile square to a quarter of a mile in width and a mile and a half in length. During Commando Hunt V a daily average of 27 B-52 and 125 fighter-bomber sorties dumped bombs into these boxes. The role of the B-52 Arc Light strikes was to crater the road system and to cause landslides in these pass areas. Fighter-bombers contributed to that process and hampered road repair crews and truck movement through the target boxes.[37]

But was interdiction working and was it worth the expense and effort? Because of the enormous tonnage of bombs dumped into the interdiction boxes, Laos became the second most bombed country in the history of aerial warfare, right behind South Vietnam in that dubious distinction. Before the war ended a total of three million tons of bombs fell on Laos.[38] The bombing, among other things, fueled the noisiest elements at the fringe of the antiwar movement. Commando Hunt, like the bombing of northern Laos, was draped in secrecy. Even when it discovered piecemeal that there was substance to the ravings of the radical fringe, the American public only got part of the story. Many people assumed that the United States had expanded the war illegally, doing so in contravention of the 1954 and 1962 Geneva agreements on Laos.

The image of a wealthy superpower like the United States making war on tiny Laos was as ludicrous as it was unpleasant for many Americans.

Despite the enormity of the effort, the interdiction campaign did not do much to impede the flow of men and supplies to the South. Part of the problem was physical. The continuous bombing levelled some of the terrain, making flat and barren areas that had been rugged, mountainous jungle. Intense bombing like that unleashed on the interdiction boxes pulverized the earth, facilitating rather than hindering North Vietnamese efforts at repair by providing ample supplies of gravel. Most often, however, the truck drivers simply wound their way around the craters and continued southward.[39]

Most telling, perhaps, was that despite this intense bombing campaign the North Vietnamese were able to change the complexion of the war in South Vietnam. The more conventionally organized and equipped People's Army of Vietnam began playing a leading role in the fighting. To be sure it often used guerrilla tactics but it was not, like the Vietcong, a guerrilla army. In 1968 and 1969 the war was in transition from a predominantly guerrilla war with an increasingly conventional complexion to a more conventional war, albeit one with a substantial guerrilla dimension. By 1970 the war was clearly dominated by the North Vietnamese army with its more conventional forces dependent on supplies coming down the Ho Chi Minh Trail. From the level of casualties inflicted on the Americans after 1968, it is reasonable to assume that the North Vietnamese, and what was left of the Vietcong, never wanted for supplies.

Meanwhile, Vietnamization continued in South Vietnam. From a peak of 550,000 Americans in early 1969, troop figures dropped steadily. By the end of the year the number was down to 475,000. The next December it stood at 335,000. By the end of 1971, only 157,000 American soldiers were left in Vietnam, mostly in support roles.[40]

The one thing that could have derailed Vietnamization would have been a 1968 Tet-style offensive. The bombing of the Ho Chi

Minh Trail was part of the effort to prevent that from happening. How effective it was can only be estimated since Hanoi controls the documentation that would reveal the true scale of the effort and the impact of American bombing on the flow of supplies to the South. However, interdiction was not as effective as the Air Force promised it would be. Every year American forces, either alone or with their South Vietnamese ally, took drastic action on the ground inside South Vietnam or in Cambodia and Laos against large concentrations of enemy forces to prevent them from launching a major offensive. The campaign in the A Shau Valley in 1969 by US Marines, the Cambodian incursions in the spring of 1970, the ARVN invasion of Laos in February and March of 1971, and, finally, the massive invasion of South Vietnam by the North Vietnamese army in the spring of 1972 testify that Commando Hunt was not as effective as official Air Force figures led many to believe.

Productivity as Strategy

Figures were the name of the game during Commando Hunt. The compilation of statistics as indicators of progress became an end unto itself, supplanting the need for an appropriately devised strategy. And that became the crux of a larger problem for the Air Force and the war it was prosecuting.

From the beginning, American objectives in Southeast Asia had been limited. Now that the withdrawal was under way, the US had no easily definable criteria by which to assess success or failure. Still, partly because it is in their nature of to do so, Americans expected progress or at least quantifiable measures of success. Commando Hunt provided the figures that sated that appetite.

By the end of the 1960s the compilation of statistical measures of success was institutionalized. The body count had earned a certain notoriety by then. Rolling Thunder piled up volumes of numbers. Every week the Office of the Secretary of the Air Force produced a report detailing the number of sorties flown by aircraft, the number of bombs dropped by types, and even how many antiaircraft reactions were encountered and the kind of hits that occurred on each aircraft. Measures of success—failure was not addressed—were gleaned from these statistical summaries. In 1968 one Air Force document, for instance, entitled "Impact of In-Country/Out-Country Force Allocations on Interdiction Effectiveness," stated,

> In Section II the characteristics of two very different operational situations were specified: (a) a pre-offensive logistical buildup phase, and (b) an in-country offensive phase. If enemy casualties killed by air per sortie in country is taken as a measure of effectiveness for in-country operations, and enemy trucks damaged or destroyed per out-country sortie is taken as the measure of effectiveness for the interdiction program, then the in-country and out-country sortie productivity can be directly related.[41]

The word *productivity* epitomized what the war had become: an exercise in management effectiveness. According to the same document, "when interdiction sortie requirements are up, strike effectiveness is up and when sortie requirements are down, mission *productivity* is down" (emphasis added).[42] The propensity to quantify was enhanced by the demand for efficiency long before Commando Hunt accelerated the process and exacerbated the problem. In 1967, for instance, the AC-47 "Spooky count" had risen to 1,596 outposts and hamlets successfully defended and "ammunition expenditures peaked in September at 4,733,633 rounds."[43] But the driving factor for quantification in Commando Hunt was the truck count.

As Commando Hunt evolved through its various campaigns, the truck count rose steadily and was duly reported on "destroyed/ damaged" or "des/dam" slides in daily briefings at Seventh Air Force in Saigon and at Headquarters Seventh/Thirteenth Air Force at Udorn RTAFB. The des/dam numbers grew dramatically over time. The total number of trucks *estimated* destroyed rose from 9,012 in 1969 to a high of 12,368 in 1970.[44] Since this number exceeded the 6,000 or so trucks the Central Intelligence Agency (CIA) believed existed in all of North Vietnam, the Air Force was forced to reassess its criteria for determining whether a truck had, indeed, been destroyed, damaged, or merely seriously scratched.[45]

At the root of the problem was the faulty criteria for determining if a truck, indeed, had been destroyed or damaged. If a truck was peppered with 7.62-mm minigun fire or rounds from the 20-mm Gatling gun, it was counted as damaged. If, however, there was a secondary explosion caused by an ignited gas tank or ammunition cargo, the truck would be counted as destroyed. A direct hit by the 40-mm gun resulted in an automatic "truck destroyed" credited to the particular gunship. If the shell impacted within a few meters, the truck would be listed as damaged. In late 1971, under the Pave Aegis program, eight AC-130s received a computer-aimed, 105-mm howitzer and, after testing, six of these gunships were deployed to Ubon RTAFB, Thailand. They added immensely to the already impressive and substantial tally of trucks counted as destroyed or damaged simply because even near misses ran up the score.[46]

In 1971 the Seventh Air Force conducted tests on a range at Bien Hoa to see just how effective these gunships were. Results indicated that trucks hit with 40-mm rounds were quite often only superficially damaged and that near misses "hardly ever flattened tires."[47] Analysts were forced to rethink their accounting systems as well as the previous campaign's results.

The Commando Hunt V truck count had been 16,266 vehicles destroyed and 4,700 others damaged. Analysts had been unable to rectify, however, the number of trucks estimated at entering Laos (6,000 by one count) with the 20,966 trucks reported destroyed or damaged by air power! After reviewing their figures, analysts in Saigon still reported a whopping 11,000 trucks destroyed and 8,000 damaged in that one campaign alone. The controversy was never settled among analysts, the Air Force, and those who questioned the figures. The North Vietnamese provided an answer of their own when, according to a CIA report, their order for trucks from the Soviet Union and other Communist countries for 1972 amounted to no more than 6,000 vehicles.[48] What really accumulated, however, was the weight of estimates and analyses—piled higher and deeper.

Indicative of the inability of air power to significantly diminish the flow of men and supplies moving to the South was that South Vietnam was forced to invade Laos in 1971 in an effort to cut the Ho Chi Minh Trail with ground forces. Finally, the massive invasion launched by Hanoi in 1972 with PAVN regulars—backed by tanks and heavy artillery—pouring out of southern Laos, the Central Highlands of South Vietnam, and Cambodia, as well as crossing the demilitarized zone between the two Vietnams rather eloquently provided testimony to this particular failure of air power.

From 1969 to 1972 the war changed dramatically. In South Vietnam, American forces continued to withdraw while turning the war over to the South Vietnamese. The fighting had spilled over into Cambodia, first with the secret bombing and then with an invasion by American and South Vietnamese forces in search of PAVN and Vietcong base camps and staging areas. There were sporadic, perhaps spasmodic, air raids on the North. Air power played a role in all these operations but these disparate actions did not always seem to be related to each other or to a coherent strategy.

The Commando Hunt campaigns contributed mightily to the setup that eventually resulted in defeat. Undoubtedly, gunships destroyed a large number of trucks while B-52s and fighter-bombers wreaked havoc on the roads and jungles. Whatever tactical advantages were gained, however, paled beside the impact resulting from the enforcement of the managerial ethos that took over during Commando Hunt. In what came to resemble "production line warfare," success was assessed primarily on dubious statistics, the compilation of which became an end unto itself. Statistics, however, proved no substitute for strategy, and for all the *perceived* success in that numbers game, the Air Force succeeded *only* in fooling itself into believing Commando Hunt was working.

The Air War in Northern Laos

The air war over northern Laos was related to the Commando Hunt campaigns, at least strategically if not tactically. American policy in Laos was to maintain that country's neutrality and independence in accordance with the Geneva agreements of 1954 and 1962. In the strategic scheme of things, it was necessary to keep Laos as a buffer state between China, North Vietnam, and Thailand. The American bombing of the Ho Chi Minh Trail complicated these interests as did the North Vietnamese use of southeastern Laos as an infiltration corridor into South Vietnam. The neutralist government of Souvanna Phouma in Vientiane kept an official silence about the North Vietnamese along the trail as well as the American bombing despite the fact that Vientiane was under pressure from the Pathet Lao, who were allied with Hanoi and in control of large portions of northeastern and central Laos.

Because international agreements forbade the introduction of US ground forces into Laos, the war was, from the American perspective, almost exclusively an air war. There was, however, a great difference in the way air power was used over the trail and the way it was employed in northern Laos. In the north, the Air Force supported the Royal Laotian Army and Gen Vang Pao's Hmong guerrillas in their war with the Pathet Lao and PAVN regulars.

During the mid-to-late 1960s, the ground war in northern Laos followed a cyclical pattern. Each dry season, Pathet Lao forces, backed by the PAVN, advanced out of Sam Neua along Route 6 and out of Barthelemy Pass through Ban Ban toward the strategic Plain of Jars (Plaine des Jar—PDJ) and on toward the royal capital of Luang Prabang, where King Savang Vatthana lived. During the wet season, Hmong irregulars and Laotian army units counter-attacked to regain the territory forfeited during the dry season.[49] Hanoi seemed to be using northern Laos like a steam valve to relieve pressure along the Ho Chi Minh Trail. Whenever they believed Vientiane allowed the United States too much latitude in action against the trail, the PAVN and the Pathet Lao would go to

186

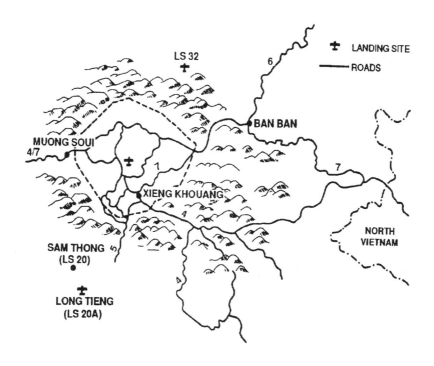

NORTHERN LAOS (Lima Sites)

the march in the north. Consequently, aircraft had to be diverted from bombing the infiltration corridor to help stem the advance of Communist forces toward the PDJ. Everyone—the Americans, the Laotians, and the Vietnamese—knew that the PAVN could run amuck all the way to Luang Prabang as well as to Vientiane anytime Hanoi so desired. That was not the point, however. In northern Laos, North Vietnam fought its own "limited war" with goals and objectives tied to the use of the Ho Chi Minh Trail and the part it played in helping Hanoi realize its ultimate, cherished, and certainly unlimited goal of uniting all of Vietnam under a single government.

Under most circumstances, given the size and population of Laos, the use of American air power, at virtually any level, in northern Laos would have seemed excessive. In this war, however, where so much aerial firepower was directed against the Ho Chi Minh Trail, the scope of Operation Barrel Roll, as the aerial campaign over northern Laos was dubbed, seemed minuscule by comparison. Only an estimated 2 percent of the aerial effort in Southeast Asia went into northern Laos.[50]

Air operations in northern Laos went back to the summer of 1964 and the highly secret reconnaissance flights over the PDJ. Along with these conventional missions, there was an even more secret unconventional operation that predated the reconnaissance flights by at least two years. Air commandos had been training Lao pilots since 1962, first to fly AT-6s and then to fly T-28s under the auspices of Project Water Pump at Udorn, Thailand. Operation Barrel Roll got under way in December 1964 with T-28s and F-105s, sent to Thailand in the wake of the Gulf of Tonkin Resolution, tossing bombs at the jungle north of Sam Neua. These aircraft flew two weekly missions of two sorties each. The missions were designed to "send a message" to Ho Chi Minh concerning the level of American resolve.[51] It is quite likely Ho never knew of the bombings, and if he did, any message Ho received from this limited application of air power may have told him things about the strength of American resolve never intended by those in Washington who had thought up this scheme.

During Rolling Thunder, Laos had to compete with North Vietnam for strike sorties. After November 1968, however, there were plenty of planes and bombs for Laos, and air operations increased accordingly. From 1962 until 1967 Vang Pao's Hmong guerrilla forces, with some support from the Royal Laotian Army, held the line against the Pathet Lao and the PAVN. Meanwhile, the United States established unmanned TACAN (tactical-aid-to-navigation) sites on mountaintops deep in Pathet Lao-PAVN-held territory near the North Vietnamese border. These sites aided crews flying from bases in Thailand to targets inside North Vietnam but were easily destroyed by the enemy. In late 1967 the Air Force built an all-weather navigation system at Lima site (LS) 85, a landing strip and Hmong stronghold at Phou Pha

Thi, 35 miles west of Sam Neua. Initial probes by the Pathet Lao and PAVN were unsuccessful, so on 12 January the Vietnamese sent two antiquated AN-2 single-engine Colt biplanes, loaded with troops firing AK-47s and throwing grenades "to bomb" LS 85. They did virtually no damage and were shot down by an Air America helicopter pilot who chased the Colts in his Huey to down them with his Uzi submachine gun.[52] On 10 March 1968, however, a PAVN regiment stormed and captured Phou Pha Thi, killing all the Americans in the process.

The fall of Phou Pha Thi signalled the beginning of a strong PAVN-Pathet Lao offensive. This time they did not stop until their troops took Muong Soui on the edge of the PDJ and made camp in the hills around Luang Prabang. Accordingly, air action over northern Laos increased sharply.[53]

Laos was divided into five military regions (MR). Air power was used to fit the needs of whatever party was at interest in the region—the Hmong, the Vientiane government, or the United States. Of the five regions, only MR II (incorporating the PDJ) and MRs III and IV (in southeastern Laos where the Ho Chi Minh Trail was located) were significant.

Most of the air operations in MR II, or Barrel Roll, focused on the Plain of Jars and the area east to the North Vietnamese border. The air war here was unique in that conventional air power was used to support unconventional ground operations. Air Force F-4s and F-105s, and on occasion B-52s, bombed PAVN and Pathet Lao positions in support of Vang Pao's Hmong guerrillas. They were joined by the not-all-that-conventional T-28s of the 56th Special Operations Wing, planes much preferred by the Hmong and Royal Laotian Army troops because of their slower speed and higher accuracy in ordnance delivery.

In Military Region III, covering northern Steel Tiger, and in Military Region IV, which incorporated Steel Tiger south to the Cambodian border, air strikes that were part of Commando Hunt were controlled by the commander, US Military Assistance Command, Vietnam (COMUSMACV), in Saigon. Air operations in the other military regions were controlled by the air operations

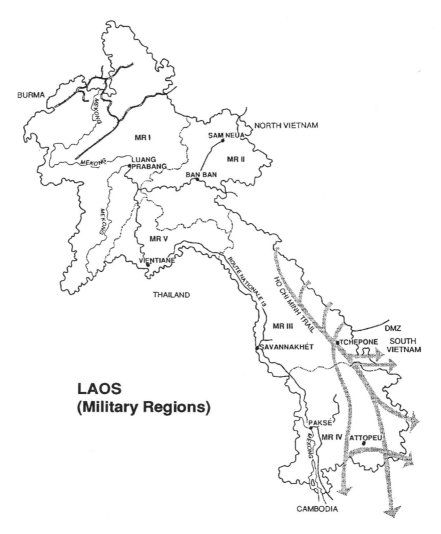

LAOS
(Military Regions)

center in Vientiane. If they were planned and flown by Americans, as was the case most of the time, then these operations came under the control of Headquarters Seventh/Thirteenth Air Force at Udorn, but with the ultimate authority residing with the American ambassador to Laos.

That ambassador was extremely powerful in that he was responsible for all US air operations in support of the Vientiane

190

government. The air attaché (AIRA), an Air Force colonel, reported directly to the ambassador and supervised all Air Force personnel in Laos. The ambassador also controlled CIA or CAS (controlled American source)* activities in Laos. It was a complex and not altogether clear system for operating in such a complicated air war.

In actuality, Air Force activities in northern Laos and in southern Laos west of the Ho Chi Minh Trail to the Mekong River were planned and coordinated by representatives of the CIA, the AIRA from Vientiane, and Air Force officers assigned to Headquarters Seventh/Thirteenth Air Force. They met regularly, either at Udorn or in Vientiane, to produce a series of working agreements delineating areas of responsibility and methods for coordination. There were plenty of disagreements and misunderstandings, particularly because the major generals who served as deputy commander, Seventh/Thirteenth Air Force resented having Air Force personnel and resources under the control of individuals other than themselves.

No matter who he was, the Air Force general at Udorn was in a difficult position. He served as the focal point for coordination of activities between the Air Force and the ambassador in Vientiane, who supervised the air attaché and controlled CIA activities. The general was also the deputy to both the Seventh Air Force and Thirteenth Air Force commanders and answered to them on operational matters. He had absolutely no authority over the air attaché in Vientiane nor over the hundreds of airmen working and flying covertly in Laos, including the Raven FACs. He certainly had no control over Laotian military officers nor the Hmong chieftains who directed the better part of the ground war. A great deal depended on the general's personality and his ability to check his ego in a situation fraught with frustrations.[54]

Air operations in northern Laos were of three types. First, air power was used more or less conventionally to support the Royal

---

*The term *CAS* became synonymous with the CIA and its operations in Southeast Asia.

Laotian Army and Vang Pao's guerrillas. Air Force F-4s and F-105s, while not the favorites of the soldiers on the ground, supported Vang Pao's troops during their annual dry season counteroffensives to recover territory lost to the Communists during the rainy season. When the seasons flipped and the enemy went over to the offensive, Air Force jets, including B-52s after February 1970, defended friendly held territory and slowed the enemy onslaught.[55]

Air power was used in its less conventional form when Air Force gunships entered the fray in 1965. When AC-119s and AC-123s began replacing AC-47s in South Vietnam, the venerable Spooky gunships started showing up in the Royal Laotian Air Force (RLAF). Gunships proved especially useful in defending Vang Pao's hilltop strongpoints from nightly attacks by Pathet Lao and PAVN sappers.

The second and third kinds of air activity in Laos were covert in nature, and even more highly classified than the quasi-conventional operations in support of the Vientiane government. Through Project 404, Air Force personnel coordinated the operational end of covert activities in Laos. Project 404 was the program under which Water Pump, the training of Lao aircrews, had functioned since 1964. The Raven FAC program also came under Project 404.[56] Ravens were Air Force forward air controllers assigned to Laos. They usually lived in Vientiane or in other towns along the Mekong, staging out of local airfields or flying from Lima sites controlled by the Hmong or Royal Laotian Army. They worked directly for the air attaché and flew their missions in tiny Cessna O-1 Bird Dogs or in single-engine T-28s assigned to fields in Vientiane, Paksé, Savannakhét, Long Tieng (LS 20 alternate), and Luang Prabang—the locations of the five air operations centers run by the Air Force in Laos. Air Force officers and CIA operatives assigned to the air operations centers supported the ambassador with intelligence, administrative services, and communications as well as actual air missions under a program called Palace Dog.

Because of the Geneva Accords of 1962, both Project 404 and Operation Palace Dog were extremely sensitive. Air Force officers in Laos worked and fought in civilian clothes. They did not carry military identification cards and, in case of capture, could only hope for a quick death—something usually denied American prisoners by the Pathet Lao. The air operations centers themselves were austere and every effort was made to avoid any kind of incident that might bring unwanted attention to the fact that American servicemen were in Laos.[57]

At times Air Force and CAS efforts blended to the point of indistinguishability. Such was the case when Air Force CH-3 and CH-53 Sikorsky helicopters based at Nakhon Phanom carried CIA-sponsored irregular forces into action along and east of the Ho Chi Minh Trail. Hmong guerrillas were not the only ones fighting deep inside North Vietnamese-occupied territory. Under Operation Prairie Fire, American Special Forces reconnaissance teams were hauled into Pathet Lao and PAVN held areas by the Air Force's 21st Special Operations Squadron.[58]

Air America, Bird and Son, and Continental Air Services— private companies under contract to the CIA—supported the Air Force with transport services. Air America gained the most notoriety as its grey choppers, silver C-7 Caribous and C-123s, and grey-mottled C-46s and C-130s moved men and supplies between provincial capitals, the Lima sites, and battle fronts. Air America's transports kept Vang Pao's guerrillas supplied with everything from pigs and White Horse scotch to ammunition and rice. On occasion, Air America choppers picked up downed Air Force crews. Sometimes Air America pilots—many of whom had several years of experience flying in Laos—acted as forward air controllers, guiding and directing air strikes in support of Hmong or Royal Laotian Army units. These "civilian" airlines played an indispensable part in the covert war and, along with Palace Dog crews and Raven FACs, worked with the more conventional Air Force units to help Vang Pao and the Royal Laotian government hold the line against formidable and, in the end, overwhelming forces.

The unconventional nature of the air war in northern Laos contrasted with the production-line kind of war being fought along the Ho Chi Minh Trail. For all the differences between the air war over northern Laos and Commando Hunt operations along the trail, the war in Laos was not an entity in itself. It was both related to and affected by what went on in South Vietnam and Cambodia.

Cambodia

Cambodia, from 1964 to 1970, had remained on the sidelines of the Vietnam War. Prince Norodom Sihanouk walked a diplomatic tightrope between forces larger than himself and Cambodia combined. The North Vietnamese and Vietcong used the border region for sanctuary, honeycombing it with base camps and supply dumps. There was little the Cambodians could do about it, even if Phnom Penh had been inclined in that direction. Sihanouk made the best of a bad situation by allowing his powerful Vietnamese neighbors to use Cambodian territory while covertly acquiescing in the American bombing of these sanctuaries.

Vietcong- and North Vietnamese-occupied areas of the Cambodian border region functioned as the southern terminus of the Ho Chi Minh Trail. Another infiltration system existed further to the south, around the Parrot's Beak region. Supplies from China and the Soviet Union, along with men and supplies from North Vietnam, sailed into Sihanoukville, where Cambodians transferred them to trucks for the trip up Friendship Highway, a road built by American aid in the 1950s.[59]

Two years prior to the 1970 American and ARVN invasion of Cambodia, Air Force planes began flying missions into the border region. One could never be absolutely sure where the border between South Vietnam and Cambodia might be. Each nation claimed territory extending a kilometer or two either way. Tactical aircraft often flew missions in support of ground units operating in the area and the pilots always reported that their bombs fell inside South Vietnam. Because the border region was so

194

ill-defined, they were not necessarily trying to deceive anyone. At worst, they were avoiding the hassles that would have resulted if they had claimed to have dropped their bombs in Cambodia. However, other missions flown into Cambodia in 1969 and 1970 involved B-52s, and the Air Force made a very definite effort to conceal the true nature of these missions.

The secret bombing of Cambodia was related to the war in Vietnam in three ways. First, the areas bombed were an integral part of the Vietcong and PAVN logistical network supporting operations in the region around Saigon. Second, North Vietnam had not shown restraint in moving men and supplies southward through its panhandle and then into Laos and down the Ho Chi Minh Trail. The assumption had been that when President Johnson curtailed the bombing of North Vietnam on 31 March 1968 and then ended that bombing on 31 October, Hanoi would reciprocate by reducing its support for the war in the South. MACV estimates, however, not only showed an increase in traffic along the Laotian corridors, but also indicated that between October 1967 and September 1968, at least ten thousand tons of arms had rolled from Sihanoukville along Friendship Highway into the border region and then on to Communist forces fighting inside South Vietnam. In 1969 the Nixon White House was convinced that the flow was continuing.[60] Third, the bombing was tied to the overall US strategy of disengagement. Nixon knew, given the mood of the country, that he could not order a resumption of bombing over the North without risking a major escalation in the antiwar movement. Bombing the Cambodian sanctuaries seemed to offer a way of sending Hanoi yet another message, and doing so without igniting passions at home.[61] Additionally, if Vietnamization was to succeed, the North Vietnamese and the Vietcong could not be allowed another offensive like Tet 1968. Such an operation would have doomed the Vietnamization policy and hampered further withdrawals of American troops.

After considerable discussions the first secret B-52 missions over Cambodia took place on 18 March 1969. The target was base area 353, a logistical storage network three miles inside Cambodia, even according to Saigon's maps. The Pentagon assigned the code name Breakfast to the bombing. In May, Nixon ordered additional strikes in roughly the same region, dubbing these Supper, Lunch, Dessert, and Snack, according to the various base areas. The whole series was called Menu, and it continued until May 1970.[62]

For the Air Force, the secret bombings of Cambodia went beyond normal clandestine operations where secrecy and deception are acceptable. These secret bombing operations involved deceiving its own officials and lying on official records. Deception to fool the enemy was one thing, but lying to Congress and key members of the government, including the chief of staff of the Air Force and the secretary of the Air Force, was something else.

The deception was revealed when a former Air Force major, Hal Knight, wrote a letter to Sen William Proxmire asking for "clarification" as to US policy on bombing Cambodia. In his letter Knight admitted he falsified reports to indicate that B-52s which had bombed Cambodia had instead dropped their loads on South Vietnam.[63]

The deception went far beyond Hal Knight's pay grade, originating in the White House. Nixon and Kissinger believed secrecy was vital to the process of disengagement, and that revelation of the bombing could hinder that process. They did not inform the secretary of the Air Force or the Air Force chief of staff when a limited number of Air Force officers were incorporated into their scheme. Col Ray B. Sitton, an Air Force officer with a background in the Strategic Air Command, worked out a system for using Arc Light strikes in South Vietnam to cover the cross-border missions. Radar bomb navigators were taken aside after the routine mission briefing and told that as they neared their drop points, they would receive a new set of coordinates from radar controllers inside South Vietnam. Poststrike reports would be filed using the regular target coordinates. Top secret, "back channel" communications systems were then used to pass the real information to a very small number of military and civilian officials.[64]

Despite Nixon's obsession with secrecy, the *New York Times* ran a sketchy article on the bombing on 2 May 1970. Even though Menu ended on 26 May, B-52 strikes into Cambodia continued in the open to support US ground forces which had entered that country on 1 May.[65] Menu lasted 14 months, during which time B-52s flew 3,630 sorties into Cambodia and dropped 100,000 tons of bombs. Undoubtedly, supplies were hit and destroyed, but the prize catch, the Central Office for South Vietnam (COSVN), escaped. Far from being an Asian Pentagon, COSVN was, in fact, only a radio transmitter and a dozen or so party cadre who could pack up and move off quickly whenever they had to do so.[66] Still, the US and ARVN ground forces had to invade Cambodia to destroy the well-entrenched logistical infrastructure that existed in the border region and which seemed to have eluded destruction by bombing.

The Cambodian incursions, as the cross-border raids were called, were what the generals had wanted all along: their chance "to take the war to the enemy" by hitting the sanctuaries. While the strikes into Cambodia were, for the American brass, a welcome departure from attrition and graduated response, still they were tied to disengagement. As it was in Laos, the role of air power in Cambodia was to cover that retreat. The irony was that as the United States withdrew its forces, the war spread and by 1970, the fighting ranged over a larger geographic area than before.

After Sihanouk was overthrown, Cambodia's little air force, consisting of a handful of transports and a few MiG-17s, began supporting the burgeoning *Forces Armée Nationale Khmer* (FANK) in operations against the Vietcong and North Vietnamese in the eastern provinces. The Chinese cut off shipments of spare parts to Phnom Penh and the MiGs were soon grounded. The 56th Special Operations Wing (SOW) at Udorn began training pilots for the Khmer air force, but in the meantime the US Air Force, along with the South Vietnamese air force, carried the burden of the air war in Cambodia, flying in support of the FANK and bombing the southern extensions of the Ho Chi Minh Trail.

The air war in Cambodia expanded along with the ground fighting. In 1970, 8 percent of the Air Force's total combat sorties went into Cambodia. The next year the figure jumped to 14 percent. Until the invading armies from North Vietnam forced a shift in sortie allocation back to South Vietnam to counter the PAVN's spring invasion in 1972, that figure remained about the same. Meanwhile, B-52s began pouring about 10 percent of their available sorties into Cambodia.[67]

The 1970 incursions into Cambodia and the bombing from 1969 to 1970 were, like Commando Hunt, linked to Vietnamization and, by extension, to America's retreat. Nearly two-thirds of South Vietnam's population lived in the Mekong Delta region and in the area just north and west of Saigon. If the Communists had launched another Tet offensive in that area while substantial numbers of Americans were still serving in Vietnam, the process of withdrawal would have been hampered by the political right at home and by President Nguyen Van Thieu in Saigon. The Cambodian bombing and the incursions had, if nothing else, prevented any large-scale action by the North that would allow the American political right or Thieu to block the continuation of the withdrawal.

Back to Laos

After the Cambodian incursions ended in the summer of 1970, President Thieu, encouraged by the ARVN's performance there, advocated an invasion of North Vietnam. The United States vetoed that idea, but there was a great deal of support, both at MACV and in Washington, for an ARVN adventure into Laos to cut the Ho Chi Minh Trail. The flow of men and supplies down the trail continued, Air Force claims as to the legions of trucks destroyed notwithstanding.

The ARVN invasion of Laos, Operation Lam Son 719, had two objectives. First, it was an effort to disrupt the accumulation of supplies detected in and around the transshipment point at Tchepone. Second, it was, at its most optimistic, an attempt to sever the trail by moving a force west, along Route 9, to Tchepone. If successful, the flow of troops and materiel into Quang Tri Province by way of Route 9 and into the Central Highlands through the A Shau Valley would be reduced if not cut off.

In January 1971 elements of the US 101st Airborne Division and the Fifth Infantry Division reoccupied Khe Sanh. The former Marine base became the embarkation point for the ARVN, which began its thrust into Laos on 8 February and headed for Tchepone some 25 miles to the west. This time, unlike in Cambodia, the ARVN was on its own. No American troops, not even advisors or forward air guides, could accompany the South Vietnamese. The Cooper-Church amendment, passed on 29 December 1970, forbade the use of Americans in Laos or Cambodia.

By the end of the first week most of the ARVN task force of over 15,000 men was in Laos. The main thrust developed along Route 9, a narrow dirt road that ran through rugged hill country which turned into jungle the closer one got to Tchepone. As the ARVN advanced it built numerous fire support bases to provide artillery support and to serve as base camps for raids into the surrounding countryside where the supply dumps and truck parks were located.

Between 11,000 and 12,000 North Vietnamese troops, about evenly divided between an estimated 12 AAA battalions and 6,000 or so logistical support troops—men who drove or maintained trucks and ran the trail system—waited for the ARVN. This initial resistance force combined with early monsoonal rains to stall the ARVN advance on 11 February; they had moved only 12 miles into Laos.

Then the North Vietnamese counterattacked. As many as five PAVN divisions—including the fabled 304th, 308th, and 320th—marched down the trail from the southern panhandle of North Vietnam and began assaulting the ARVN forces, which were strung out along Route 9 and dug in at their fire support bases. The South Vietnamese quickly went from the offensive to the defensive. In their penny-packet fire support bases, ARVN units were vulnerable to concerted attacks by the PAVN, supported as

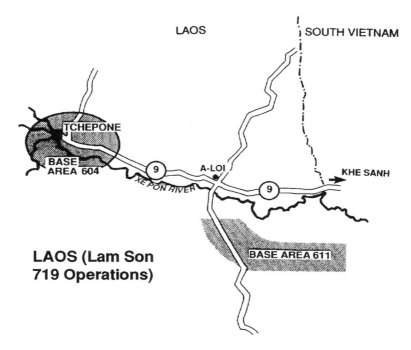

LAOS

SOUTH VIETNAM

TCHEPONE

BASE AREA 604

9

A-LOI

9

KHE SANH

XE PON RIVER

**LAOS (Lam Son
719 Operations)**

BASE AREA 611

they were by T-34 and T-54 tanks as well as by 122-mm and 130-mm artillery.[68] When the weather cleared on 6 March 1971, President Thieu, anxious to salvage some kind of face-saving token of a victory from what was degenerating into a debacle, ordered two battalions of ARVN rangers helicoptered into Tchepone. They took the abandoned village, which itself had little military significance, and began to march eastward, hoping to link up with the main force units stalled at A-loi. Only a few ever made it.[69]

The generals at MACV, the ARVN leadership, and even Henry Kissinger and Richard Nixon had been enthusiastic about Lam Son 719 because they were convinced that superior firepower, particularly air power, would be decisive. Firepower, as it turned out, was decisive, but it went in favor of the enemy. Air power, again, played an important but not a decisive role in that it prevented a defeat from turning into a disaster that might have been so complete as to encourage the North Vietnamese army to keep moving right on into Quang Tri Province.

In the early stages of Lam Son 719 the Seventh Air Force supported the ARVN from sorties normally allocated for ground support operations in I Corps in South Vietnam and from those targeted against the Ho Chi Minh Trail as a normal part of Commando Hunt. But as the operation continued, and then became increasingly precarious, sorties were redirected from support of Vang Pao in northern Laos and from Cambodia to cover the developing debacle in Laos.[70]

In Laos, the North Vietnamese were ready to take on American air power. As they did in the North, the PAVN relied on antiaircraft artillery and heavy machine guns to gain air deniability. Heavy machine guns supplemented 23-mm and 37-mm guns to cover virtually every potential landing zone (LZ). Mortar crews bracketed the LZs so that when the choppers sat down, they did so through a barrage of falling mortar rounds as well as through heavy machine gun fire. Heavier AAA blanketed the area, proving especially deadly to the Huey helicopters and threatening to American and South Vietnamese tactical aircraft.

Helicopter pilots thought Lam Son 719 was hell. Estimates as to the total number of helicopters lost varied. The 101st Airborne Division reported 84 choppers destroyed and 430 others damaged. ARVN helicopters counted, the total rose to 108 helicopters destroyed and 618 damaged.[71] The Army was sensitive to the subject of helicopter survivability and tried to minimize the impact of adverse statistics. As one Air Force colonel said, "If they can get the tail number out of the wreckage and glue a new chopper onto it, they'll never admit that the aircraft was lost."[72]

As the withdrawal turned into a rout, problems with coordination of air strikes mounted. The few ARVN English-speaking forward air guides were killed or captured, or fled their units. Before long there were no men on the ground qualified to direct air strikes. Furthermore, the PAVN tossed a new element into the war: tanks.

The occasional PT-76 encountered by the ARVN was little more than an armored car. Its relatively thin armor and small 76-mm gun made the PT-76 no match for the M-41 light tanks used by the ARVN in Lam Son 719. But in the spring of 1971, the PAVN introduced T-34 and T-54 tanks to the fighting; with their 90-mm and 100-mm guns and thick armor, they were more than a match for the M-41s. The appearance of these enemy tanks outside the perimeter of an ARVN fire support base often set off a panic among the defenders that caused them to break and run before the assault developed.

PT-76s could be destroyed by a direct hit from the 40-mm shells fired from AC-130s and AC-119s; even a near miss with a 500-pound bomb was enough to cripple these light tanks. The T-34s and T-54s, however, were not susceptible to damage from 40-mm hits and required a direct hit from a 500-pound bomb to be destroyed. The 12.7-mm machine gun mounted on the turret of the T-54s posed a significant threat to any jet lining up for a bomb run—on 22 March an F-100 was shot down as its pilot levelled off for a shallow-angle attack. Despite these odds, the Air Force reported bagging 74 tanks and damaging another 24. Army helicopters claimed six tanks.[73]

The antiaircraft guns posed such a threat that the Air Force directed 1,284 sorties against them. While cluster bombs were, as usual, the weapon of choice for suppressing heavy machine-gun fire, these usually only killed the crews but left the guns undamaged, especially the heavier 23-mm, 37-mm, and 57-mm AAA weapons. The larger guns required a direct hit by a bomb or an accurate napalm splash to put them out of commission. Laser-guided Mk-84 2,000-pound bombs were used on many AAA sites with good results. The Air Force claimed some 70 antiaircraft guns destroyed and five others damaged in 172 sorties using laser-guided bombs.[74]

One of the reasons accounting for the overwhelming success of the North Vietnamese counterattack was that the weather was poor during much of late February and early March. The bad weather diminished the utility of tactical air power, but B-52s were unimpeded by low-level clouds or by the mist that hung in the valleys even on clear days. During Lam Son 719, B-52s flew 1,358 sorties, mostly from U Tapao RTAFB, Thailand; they dropped 32,000 tons of bombs on base area 604, a large PAVN staging and supply base south of Tchepone. These giant bombers were also used to "prep" an LZ by clearing out trees and any enemy troops that might be waiting beneath prior to the insertion of friendly troops by helicopters. They were also used with good effect against troops massed around the numerous fire support bases where the ARVN units "holed up" after 11 February.[75]

At night, gunships roamed the skies over the area of operations. Their night-vision devices, coupled with the use of seismic sensors sown throughout the trail complex, helped Air Force crews detect enemy movements. Gunships were used to defend fire bases and to attack tanks; AC-119Ks using 20-mm high-explosive-incendiary, armor-piercing-incendiary (HEI/API) rounds reported knocking out 10 tanks. AC-130s firing 40-mm HEI/API ammunition accounted for 14 tanks. All the tanks reported destroyed by gunships were assumed to be PT-76s.[76]

By 24 March the last ARVN units were out of Laos and Lam Son 719 was over. Officially, ARVN casualties were listed at 5,000 killed and wounded—one-third of the force. Additionally, 137 Americans were killed and 818 wounded. At least 108 American helicopters were destroyed and another 618 damaged. Seven fixed-wing Air Force planes were shot down.[77] Official figures told only a part of the story, but even they did not agree. According to figures issued by the US Army's XXIV Corps, the ARVN lost 9,000 killed, wounded, or captured and the US casualties amounted to 253 killed and missing with 1,149 wounded.[78]

All losses aside, everyone claimed victory. President Nixon, in a television broadcast to the nation on 7 April, sanguinely stated, "Tonight I can report Vietnamization has succeeded."[79] He went on to announce that because of Lam Son 719, withdrawals of American troops could be accelerated.[80] President Thieu, reviewing what was left of his invasion force at Dong Ha, claimed that the operation in Laos was "the biggest victory ever."[81]

Meanwhile, Hanoi dubbed the "Route 9-Southern Laos Victory" (as they called it), "the heaviest defeat ever for Nixon and Company."[82] The US Army praised the role played by its helicopters and the Air Force touted the armed helicopter and fixed-wing fighter-bomber as "a natural, effective, fighting team."[83] The Air Force's Gen William Momyer declared, "Lam Son 719 was indeed a costly operation to the South Vietnamese and U.S. helicopter forces." He added that it was "costly because of weak planning that produced inadequate tactical air support."[84]

Lam Son 719 Fallout

Presidents Thieu and Nixon might have recalled Sir Winston Churchill's admonition after Dunkirk, "Wars are not won by evacuations."[85] Overly optimistic claims aside, Lam Son 719 marked a transition in the war. While the ARVN offensive had disrupted the Ho Chi Minh Trail and, perhaps, bought time for the US withdrawal (an additional 60,000 American troops left South Vietnam during the two months of Lam Son 719), it was far from devastating for the North Vietnamese.[86] While Hanoi's losses were high, they were certainly well worth the cost of defending their logistical pipeline.

After April 1971 the North Vietnamese were reasonably certain that the ARVN would not attempt another stab at the Ho Chi Minh Trail. Hence, their engineers and road construction battalions began rebuilding, consolidating, and expanding the road network. North Vietnamese troops, with support from the Pathet Lao, moved west, reducing the territory controlled by the Vientiane government. Since the fall of Attopeu (an important town on the Bolovens Plateau in southern Laos) on 30 April 1971, the Communists had been slowly extending the territory under their control west of the trail. After Lam Son 719, that process accelerated.

Other developments indicated that the war was shifting gears. In Hanoi in late December 1970 and January 1971, even as planning for Lam Son 719 got started 700 miles away in Saigon, the politburo held the 19th Plenary Session of the Lao Dong Party. The members decided that a major invasion of the South would be undertaken in 1972 to win the war.[87] Soviet freighters began unloading trucks, T-54 tanks, and long-range 130-mm guns, as well as SAM-2 and SAM-7 shoulder-fired missiles and a wealth of other equipment. Soon this arsenal would be moving along the secured and expanded logistical network in Laos.

Although Lam Son 719 did not realize the hopes it had engendered, it did mark a watershed. Vietnamization had not succeeded, but neither had it failed. Americans continued to withdraw and the character of Vietnamization changed. Just as the Soviet Union provided their client with heavier arms, so too did the United States, though not to the same degree. Heavier M-48 tanks and self-propelled 175-mm guns were transferred to the ARVN. In Saigon, MACV and the ARVN collaborated on a new *Combined Arms Doctrinal Handbook*, which stressed large-unit actions and improved coordination between air and ground elements.[88]

Frustrations Continue

Lam Son 719 had been as frustrating as it was ambiguous in its outcome. Overly optimistic claims of victory notwithstanding, it was the last major offensive ground operation the United States engaged in, even in a support role. The Air Force continued its Commando Hunt campaign, filling up the tally sheets with trucks reportedly destroyed or damaged along the Ho Chi Minh Trail as air operations over Laos and Cambodia continued.

The PAVN thrust to the west was a response to Operations Desert Rat and Silver Buckle. In these addendums to Lam Son 719, Thai mercenaries and Laotian irregulars edged toward Muong Phine, a town on the western edge of the trail, about 10 miles from Tchepone. Muong Phalane, a key town in central Military Region III, about 15 miles west of Muong Phine, changed hands several

SOUTHERN LAOS

times in early 1971 before it was captured and held by an overwhelming PAVN force in May. Further south, the PAVN took Saravane and went on to capture Paksong in the same month. The way was clear for a thrust toward the Mekong, but it did not develop. The North Vietnamese were intent upon their primary objective of winning the war in South Vietnam in 1972. By expanding the territory in Laos under its control, the North was ensuring that US-backed Laotian forces would be unable to launch anymore Desert Rats or Silver Buckles.

Meanwhile, the war in northern Laos took a turn for the worse. By February 1971 only a handful of friendly positions remained at the edge of the PDJ. Vang Pao's headquarters at Long Tieng was surrounded and sappers probed at the perimeter. South of Long Tieng, Vang Pao's irregulars moved into a blocking position between advancing PAVN forces and the flat plain north of Vientiane. Farther to the north, for the first time since 1962, the Pathet Lao were camped within sight of the royal capital of Luang Prabang.[89]

All this was happening while American forces continued their withdrawal. All F-105 units, except the Iron Hand anti-SAM aircraft, had been withdrawn in October 1970. The old and battle-worn A-1 Skyraiders were on their way into the Vietnamese air force inventory as a part of Vietnamization. Squadrons of F-4s were being withdrawn from Thailand and relocated to the United States or Europe. During the 1970–71 dry season, Air Force support for Vang Pao dropped nearly 70 percent from that of the previous year, from an average of 114 sorties a day to only 38.[90]

This reduction in effort reflected a theaterwide trend. By 1971 the total number of Air Force sorties per month stood at half the sortie peaks reached two years before. Arc Light sorties, for instance, were reduced from 1,800 per month in 1969 to 1,000 in 1971. Another measure reflecting a total drawdown in effort was the drop in tons of cargo hauled by Air Force transports from a 1967 high of 911,000 tons to 720,000 tons in 1970.[91] Air power was changing its role from the offensive-oriented strategy of Rolling Thunder to an offensive defensive, and it was not a role

Air strike in the Republic of Vietnam. While many in the Air Force tend to believe that the bombing of North Vietnam was the focal point of the air war, far more tonnage had been dropped on South Vietnam. When the United States completed its withdrawal in 1973, it had dropped some four million tons of bombs in the South. By comparison, only one million tons of ordnance had fallen on North Vietnam. The Republic of Vietnam was the most bombed country in the history of aerial warfare—a dubious distinction for an ally.

entirely understood by Air Force leaders who saw air power in its more conventional dynamics.

Proud Deep Alpha

At the end of 1971 those American ground forces still in South Vietnam were there clearly in a defensive role. Aerial reconnaissance provided ample evidence that North Vietnam had stockpiled supplies north of the DMZ and had increased the flow of men and materiel to the South. In the last three weeks of 1971, 10 US aircraft were shot down over North Vietnam and Laos, indicating a stepped-up tempo in the air war.[92]

Meanwhile, the Paris peace talks had stalled. America's chief negotiator, Henry Kissinger, believed that Hanoi had decided to win the war on the battlefield in 1972. On 17 November 1971 the North Vietnamese negotiators told the American delegation that due to the illness of their chief negotiator, Le Duc Tho, subsequent meetings would be suspended. Kissinger's reply that the American team was ready to meet with any designated substitute went unanswered.[93]

Beginning on 26 December a five-day bombing campaign was launched on targets south of the 20th parallel. Operation Proud Deep Alpha, as it was called, had two objectives. First, its tactical goal was to destroy antiaircraft batteries and SAM sites that had been menacing US reconnaissance aircraft monitoring the buildup of forces in the southern panhandle. Second, it was an effort to persuade the North Vietnamese not to go forward with what appeared to be shaping up as a large offensive in 1972.[94]

Proud Deep Alpha was the largest series of air attacks on North Vietnam since the bombing halt of 1968. American aircraft flew 1,025 sorties against POL storage facilities, supply caches, SAM sites, and truck parks.[95] Ominously, the North Vietnamese seemed undeterred. In early 1972 they began shelling ARVN outposts just south of the DMZ with long-range artillery. The shelling was a foretaste of things to come.

- - - - - - - - -

Part of the setup leading to air power's defeat in Southeast Asia was the Air Force's fascination with technology and its managerial cohort, bureaucracy. From the heyday of the Air Force's buildup in jet bombers and supersonic fighters during the 1950s, technology and the managerial imperative came together in Vietnam to inspire a form of warfare that could be appreciated only by accountants, statisticians, and managers. Because of the way the institution had developed since 1947, the Air Force had generated plenty of accountants and placed too many of them in leadership positions. Their fascination with the cold objectivity of numerical indicators made it difficult, if not impossible, for the Air Force to devise an appropriate strategy. By late 1971 the enemy in Hanoi and the air power leaders in Washington, Honolulu, and Saigon—the former who refused to lose and the latter who did not know how to win—were both defeating the Air Force, and by extension, US objectives in Indochina.

Notes

1. Secretary of the Air Force Robert C. Seamans, Jr., address to the 1969 Air Force Association Convention, 19 March 1969, Houston, Tex., "Continuing Cooperation between NASA and DoD," in *Air Force Magazine*, May 1969, 100.

2. US Military Assistance Command, Vietnam (USMACV), Year-end Review of Vietnam: 1968, 4 December 1968, 10, K717.0414-17, US Air Force Historical Research Center (USAFHRC), Maxwell AFB, Ala.

3. Dave Richard Palmer, *Summons of the Trumpet: U.S.-Vietnam in Perspective* (San Rafael, Calif.: Presidio Press, 1978), 201.

4. Michael Howard, *Clausewitz* (New York: Oxford University Press, 1983), 39.

5. See Lt Gen Phillip B. Davidson, USA, Retired, *Vietnam at War: 1946–1975* (Novato, Calif.: Presidio Press, 1987), 504; and Lyndon Baines Johnson, *The Vantage Point: Perspectives of the Presidency, 1963–1969* (New York: Holt, Rinehart, and Winston, 1971), 402–10.

6. USMACV, Year-end Review: 1968, 15.

7. Bernard C. Nalty, *Air Power and the Fight for Khe Sanh* (Washington, D.C.: Office of Air Force History, 1977), 104.

8. Clark M. Clifford, "A Vietnam Reappraisal: The Personal History of One Man's View and How It Evolved," *Foreign Affairs*, July 1969, 10.

9. John S. Brown, ed., *The Vietnam War: An Almanac* (New York: World Almanac Publications, 1985), 200.

10. Ibid., 200; USMACV, Year-end Review: 1968, 13; and Palmer, 208.

11. Lt Gen Julian J. Ewell, "Impressions of a Field Force Commander in Vietnam," 15 April 1970, 6–7, K717.131, USAFHRC.

12. Palmer, 208.

13. Col Abner M. Angst, Jr., commander, 31st Tactical Fighter Wing, end-of-tour report, 3 May 1968–8 February 1969, 32, K740.131, USAFHRC.

14. *The Pentagon Papers: The Defense Department History of United States Decisionmaking on Vietnam,* Senator Gravel edition, vol. 3 (Boston: Beacon Press, 1971–1972), 550–55.

15. Davidson, 530.

16. Nalty, 91–93.

17. Davidson, 561.

18. Commando Hunt Report, 15 November 1968–31 March 1969, iv, K740.04-1, USAFHRC.

19. John Morrocco, *Rain of Fire: Air War, 1969–1973*, The Vietnam Experience (Boston: Boston Publishing, 1986), 20.

20. Edward Doyle, Samuel Lipsman, and Terrence Maitland, *The North*, The Vietnam Experience (Boston: Boston Publishing, 1986), 46.

21. The standard work on gunship development is Lt Col Jack S. Ballard, *Development and Employment of Fixed-Wing Gunships, 1962–1972* (Washington, D.C.: Office of Air Force History, 1982). See particularly pages 20, 35, and 46–47.

22. Carl Berger, ed., *The United States Air Force in Southeast Asia, 1961–1973: An Illustrated Account* (Washington, D.C.: Office of Air Force History, 1982), 105.

23. Ibid., 108.

24. Ballard, 45. For ranges, see page 262.

25. History, Seventh Air Force, 1 July–31 December 1969, vol. 1, pt. 2, 266, K740.01-25, USAFHRC.

26. Morrocco, 46.

27. John L. Frisbee, "Igloo White," *Air Force Magazine*, June 1971, 48–53. Three kinds of sensors were used in the Igloo White system. The first was an acoustic sensor derived from the sonobuoy developed by the US Navy to detect submarines. The Air Force version used a battery-powered microphone instead of a hydrophone to detect trucks or even eavesdrop on conversations between enemy troops. There were two kinds of acoustical sensors: "spikebuoy" and "acoubuoy." Spikebuoys fell to the ground to bury themselves so that only their camouflaged antennas showed. Acoubuoys were designed to snare in a tree and hang in the dense jungle foliage where they were difficult to spot. These sensors were used to confirm the location of suspected camping areas and truck parks. The air-delivered seismic detection (ADSID) device was the most widely used sensor. It detected ground vibrations caused by trucks, bulldozers, and the occasional tank, though it could not differentiate with much accuracy between the vibrations made by a bulldozer and a tank.

28. Ibid.; and Bill Gunston, *Aircraft of the Vietnam War* (Wellingborough, Northamptonshire, England: Patrick Stephens, 1987), 78.

29. A particularly good account of the process can be found in James William Gibson, *The Perfect War: Technowar in Vietnam* (Boston: Atlantic Monthly Press, 1986), 396–97.

30. Frisbee, 52.

31. Ibid., 58.

32. In Commando Hunt III, from November 1969 to March 1970, AC-130 Surprise Package gunships averaged 7.34 trucks destroyed or damaged per sortie while other AC-130s got 4.34. AC-123s accounted for 3.12 trucks per sortie and AC-119s got only 2.27. See Seventh Air Force, Commando Hunt III Report, May 1970, in History, USMACV, annex A, VI-95, 96, Office of Air Force History, Bolling AFB, D.C.

33. *USAF Operations in Laos: 1 January 1970–30 June 1971*, Headquarters Pacific Air Forces (PACAF), Corona Harvest, 31 May 1972, 27, K717.0432.6, USAFHRC.

34. Ballard, 173.

35. *USAF Operations in Laos*, 26.

36. History, Seventh Air Force, 1 July–31 December 1969, vol. 1, pt. 1, 174.

37. *USAF Operations in Laos*, 7.

38. Raphael Littauer and Norman Uphoff, eds., *The Air War in Indochina*, rev. ed., Air War Study Group, Cornell University (Boston: Beacon Press, 1971), 281.

39. *USAF Operations in Laos*, 65.

40. Palmer, 222.

41. "Impact of In-Country/Out-Country Force Allocations on Interdiction Effectiveness," Headquarters Seventh Air Force, Directorate of Tactical Analysis, 6 September 1968, vol. 2, 1968–1969, 13, K717.0414-17, USAFHRC.

42. Ibid., iii.

43. Ballard, 88.

44. Morrocco, 40.

45. *USAF Operations in Laos*, 21–22.

46. Ballard, 173.

47. See *USAF Operations in Laos*, 76–79. Did Air Force leaders believe these figures? As a young lieutenant on the staff of the chief of intelligence at Seventh/Thirteenth Air Force, my job was to deliver the morning briefing to the commander. The truck count was part of each briefing. Figures for the "des/dam" slides came from the ABCCC reports by Moonbeam and Alleycat, the C-130s on night orbit over Steel Tiger and Barrel Roll. A joke among briefers at Udorn, shared with our counterparts in Saigon, was that a "great Laotian truck eater" was at work on the Ho Chi Minh Trail, devouring the hulks of trucks reported as destroyed or damaged. The figures became both an end unto themselves and a joke, but the general I briefed believed them. On one occasion, after I had briefed that over 300 trucks had been destroyed or damaged the previous night, the general leaned back in his chair and stated, "Gentlemen, what we have here is the end of North Vietnam as a viable fighting power."

48. Ibid., 79.

49. Littauer and Uphoff, 77–78.

50. Ibid., 79.

51. Morrocco, 27.

52. See Berger, 126; and Christopher Robbins, *The Ravens* (New York: Crown, 1987), 42–43.

53. Littauer and Uphoff, 78.

54. *USAF Operations in Laos*, 98–99.

55. The decision to use B-52s in northern Laos was a difficult one for the Nixon administration to make. For elaboration, see Henry Kissinger, *The White House Years* (Boston: Little, Brown, 1979), 452–53.

56. Robbins, 118.

57. *USAF Operations in Laos*, 97–98.

58. See Charles M. Simpson III, *Inside the Green Berets: The Story of U.S. Army Special Forces* (New York: Berkley Books, 1984), 223; Robbins, 228; and *USAF Operations in Laos*, 97.

59. William Shawcross, *Sideshow: Kissinger, Nixon, and the Destruction of Cambodia* (New York: Simon and Schuster, 1979), 64.

60. Kissinger, 241.

61. Ibid., 240.

62. See Gen John D. Ryan, USAF chief of staff, to Hon John C. Stennis, chairman, Senate Committee on the Armed Services, 26 July 1973, in *Hearings before the Committee on Armed Services*, 93d Cong., 1st sess., 121–22; and Kissinger, 247.

63. Hal Knight to Sen William Proxmire, 18 January 1973, in Senate, "Bombing in Cambodia," *Hearings before the Committee on Armed Services*, 5.

64. Morrocco, 12.

65. Kissinger, 240.

66. Truong Nhu Tang, with David Chanoff and Doan Van Toai, *Viet Cong Memoir* (New York: Vintage Books, 1985), 128.

67. See Littauer and Uphoff, 88; and Shawcross, 218–19.

68. See Davidson, 645–47; and Palmer, 242.

69. Davidson, 648–49.

70. Col J. F. Loy, Jr., et al., "Lam Son 719, 30 January–24 March 1971: The South Vietnamese Incursion into Laos," Project CHECO, Headquarters PACAF, 14 March 1971, 81, K717.0413-98, USAFHRC.

71. "101st Airborne Division (Airmobile), Final Report, Air Mobile Operations in Support of Lam Son 719, 8 February–6 April 1971," vol. 1, 1 May 1972, 151, Momyer Collection, 168.7041-152, USAFHRC.

72. Quoted in David Fulghum and Terrence Maitland, *South Vietnam on Trial: Mid 1970 to 1972*, The Vietnam Experience (Boston: Boston Publishing, 1984), 89.

73. Loy et al., 9.

74. Ibid., 110–11.

75. See ibid., 118; and "101st Airborne Division, Final Report," IV-1.

76. Loy et al., 115.

77. Ibid., 2.

78. Fulghum and Maitland, 90.

79. Max Frankel, "Laos Push Upheld," *New York Times*, 8 April 1971, 1.

80. Text of the president's 7 April speech, *New York Times*, 8 April 1971, 6.

81. "The War: Edge of an Abyss," *Time*, 12 April 1971, 24.

82. North Vietnamese Radio Hanoi, quoted in Fulghum and Maitland, 90.

83. Unnamed Air Force officer, quoted in "101st Airborne Division, Final Report," I-52.

84. Gen William W. Momyer, *Airpower in Three Wars* (Washington, D.C.: Government Printing Office, 1978), 323–24.

85. Winston S. Churchill, *The Second World War*, vol. 2, *Their Finest Hour* (Boston: Houghton Mifflin, 1949), 115.

86. See *New York Times*, 8 April 1971, 6; and Kissinger, 1003.

87. Davidson, 699.

88. Fulghum and Maitland, 91.

89. *USAF Operations in Laos*, 106–7.

90. Ibid., 112.

91. John L. Frisbee, "USAF's Changing Role in Vietnam," *Air Force Magazine*, September 1971, 42.

92. Phil Chinnery, *Air War in Vietnam* (New York: Exeter Books, 1987), 149.

93. Kissinger, 1041.

94. Ibid.; Chinnery, 149.

95. Morrocco, 101.

Chapter 5

"It Was a Loser"

A few years after leaving office, Robert C. Seamans, Jr., the secretary of the Air Force during the Nixon administration, was asked if during his tenure there was a feeling that the Vietnam War was over. He responded, "No, it wasn't that it was finished, it was a loser."[1] By 1971 the question for the Americans was how to end the war so that the United States could withdraw its remaining forces, secure the return of American prisoners of war (POW), and leave South Vietnam reasonably secure.

Certainly there was a sense within the Air Force that the war was over, although those who served in Southeast Asia (SEA) during these last years may not have felt that way. The focus was on molding the kind of Air Force for the 1970s that had existed prior to the 1960s: one equipped and organized to fight the Soviets. After 1970 the United States had lost the large advantage in nuclear weaponry it had held since 1945. The Air Force Association (AFA) warned that there had been "an unprecedented shift in the balance of military power caused by the deteriorating defense posture of the United States." [2] In his 1971 address to the annual meeting of the Air Force Association, entitled "Improving Things for People," Secretary Seamans's only mention of Vietnam was to boast that a mere 1 percent of Air Force personnel assigned to Southeast Asia used heroin.[3] Vietnam was slipping to the periphery of Air Force interests.

Meanwhile, back at the war, "Vietnam as an anachronism" had a deleterious effect on operations. By 1970 a pilot shortage and an experience gap were evident throughout the Air Force. Many of the senior officers with combat experience in World War II and Korea as well as Vietnam had retired. The officers most likely to lead younger flyers within the wings and squadrons, the majors and lieutenant colonels who had served in Korea, began to retire after reaching the 20-year point in their careers. The airlines were hiring, and many younger flyers opted for the "friendly skies" rather than the possibility of a second tour in SEA.

To boost retention of experienced aircrews and enlisted personnel, the Air Force adopted a policy of no involuntary second tours in SEA. The result was that by 1971 and early 1972, an ever-increasing number of newly trained pilots and navigators were assigned to combat units. While this policy addressed retention and morale, it had major drawbacks. Col Stanley M. Umstead, Jr., commander of the 388th Tactical Fighter Wing (TFW), lamented that 25 percent of his F-4 aircraft commanders were recent graduates of pilot training classes (called under-graduate pilot training—UPT). He added that although these aircrews were "highly motivated and [possessed] the basic skills, they were deficient in formation flying . . . and maneuvering." [4] According to another wing commander, Col Lyle E. Mann, "aircrews graduating from UPT need considerably more air-to-air training." [5]

Not only was the fighting force young and inexperienced, it was overworked. Despite the fact that men were flying, fighting, killing, and dying, the United States was not officially at war. Thus, units in the Pacific Air Forces (PACAF) were manned at the same levels as those in Europe or the United States. Normally, the peacetime manning for the F-4 was 1.5 aircrews per seat per aircraft. But because of the servicewide pilot shortage F-4 units were manned at a rate of 1.25 aircrews per seat per aircraft and F-105 units at the rate of 1.21 per cockpit in that single-seat fighter-bomber. [6]

The realities of war seemed not to matter. Although aircrews in Southeast Asia flew more often than those in Europe or the United States, the peacetime manning policy limited the ability of wings in Southeast Asia to respond to surge efforts like Proud Deep Alpha in December 1971. The director of base medical services at Korat Royal Thai Air Force Base (RTAFB) complained that "people were often changed from flying nights to flying days and vice versa . . . crewmembers are often called several times a night while they are asleep to notify them of a new schedule."[7]

Peacetime manning in a wartime situation caused problems among ground crews as well. In the 56th Special Operations Wing, a unit flying only propeller-driven aircraft, the QU-22B line chief in 1971 came to his job from a B-52 wing. Most of the mechanics working on the T-28s and A-1Es flown by the 56th had previously worked only on jets.[8]

Also because of the limited manning, Air Force fighter pilots had to become jacks-of-all-trades rather than specialists. After the F-105s—the workhorses of Rolling Thunder—were withdrawn in October 1970, F-4 Phantoms took over the air-to-ground mission in addition to their air-to-air mission. The young, relatively inexperienced crews, who were already overworked, had to master an increasingly wider range of skills. Because experienced crews were retiring, the Air Force was having to shift to the use of generalist rather than specialist pilots, which resulted in a less capable combat force.

If overwork was a problem, there were plenty of ways to unwind. At Udorn RTAFB, all the snack bars on base, including the one by the Olympic-size swimming pool, were refurbished. The outdoor theater was expanded to accommodate 850 people, while the indoor theater was overhauled with new air conditioning and rocking-chair seats. For those who wanted more exertion than flying combat missions over Laos or working on the flight line in 12-hour shifts provided, newly resurfaced and expanded tennis courts, a new golf driving range, and an expanded archery range were available. Udorn was, however, exceptional as air bases went. Perhaps that is why this showcase base hosted the 1971 All-Thailand Slow Pitch Softball Tournament.[9]

Marking Time along the Ho Chi Minh Trail

At the end of 1971 fighting had declined throughout Southeast Asia to the point that the decreased effectiveness of the Air Force

217

was not readily apparent. Since the end of Rolling Thunder in late 1968, Commando Hunt had been the focus of the air war. The "truck count" reflected tactical successes, thus obscuring the strategic bankruptcy of the operation. Commando Hunt VII was the final effort in this three-and-a-half-year campaign.

The plan for Commando Hunt VII was to bottle up the transportation system in Laos, using B-52s to close the passes leading from North Vietnam into Laos and from Laos into South Vietnam and Cambodia, thus forcing the vehicles to congregate in truck parks where they could be attacked more profitably. Simultaneously, B-52s obliterated sections of some roads so that traffic would be diverted onto specific routes where gunships and tactical bombers stalked them with increasingly predictable success, at least that was the Air Force's official view of this campaign.[10]

Official optimism notwithstanding, Commando Hunt as an interdiction campaign was failing. The North Vietnamese moved men and supplies southward at a steady rate. In mid-1971 a major expansion program got under way along the Ho Chi Minh Trail. Several factors contributed to the North Vietnamese's continuing success in moving supplies to People's Army of Vietnam (PAVN) units in the South. Keeping the trail open was Hanoi's number one priority. Thousands of young men and women lived in work camps throughout the trail network. At night and in bad weather, when there was less danger from air attack, they repaired the roads, bridges, and fords. They were continuously extending the bypass system—a network of small roads that wound through the dense jungle underbrush. Air Force claims to the contrary notwithstanding, Commando Hunt never successfully coupled intelligence to operations. The interdiction effort was fragmented into bureaucratic fiefdoms—the gunship program, the night-bombing effort with B-57Gs and A-26s, the Strategic Air Command's (SAC) interdiction box program, and the intelligence gathering and collation effort at Task Force Alpha—that never came together under the aegis of a strategy devised to work toward a common end. Since each program seemed to have to validate its own existence, a truly coordinated effort never quite emerged. Because of the bombing halt over North Vietnam, troops and trucks loaded with supplies had the advantage of getting into the 250-mile long transportation system where they could spread out over several thousand miles of roads, bypasses, and trails before the Air Force had a chance to attack them. The Air Force approach was reactive, devolving into something analogous to trying to decrease the flow through a fire hose by inflicting a thousand tiny pinpricks. Finally, by 1971 the scope of the air war had diminished as Vietnamization proceeded. The monthly average for fighter attack sorties for Commando Hunt V was 14,000, about half what it had been for Commando Hunt I in 1969.[11]

Commando Hunt became an exercise in the extravagant application of resources to problems—planes to targets as trucks—and as such was exploitable by an enemy who learned to game the system. Before 1971, trucks took to the roads at dusk, with the peak in traffic coming in the early evening at about 8:00 P.M. As the gunships and B-57s arrived on station, traffic would subside until just before dawn, when the gunships and night bombers returned to their bases. Then the trucks started rolling again, to reach another peak in traffic at around 6:00 A.M. as drivers hustled to get to a truck park before sunrise and the arrival of the morning wave of fighter-bombers.

In early 1971 the cadres who ran the trail system got inside the Air Force's "managerial loop." They figured out the sortie scheduling system so that they understood that fighter-bombers returned to base in the late afternoon to stand down before ground crews changed shifts. Also, between 5:00 P.M. and 7:00 P.M., gunships were not yet on station. They did not usually begin their orbits until after sunset in order to gain the protection from antiaircraft gunners that darkness provided. The result was a two-to-three-hour window in which enemy traffic moved with relative safety. The men and women who ran the intelligence and communications centers changed shifts between 4:00 and 6:00 P.M. Higher ranking officers worked day shifts and by 5:00 P.M. were headed for their quarters, the tennis courts, or the officers club. In the morning, shift changes took place between 4:00 and 7:00 A.M. The night shift began winding up its work about 4:00 A.M., and when the day shift arrived, its first order of business was to review the night shift's work so that higher ranking officers could be briefed. Meanwhile, the gunships were heading for home. Fighter-bomber crews were preparing for the first missions of the morning and would not launch until after dawn.[12]

As with Rolling Thunder, the Air Force view of Commando Hunt was that it was another in an unbroken string of unmitigated air power victories. After Commando Hunt VII, the Air Force Intelligence Service claimed 51,500 trucks and 3,400 antiaircraft artillery (AAA) guns destroyed or damaged throughout the seven campaigns. While "allowing an inflationary factor of 50 percent," the report continued, "the effectiveness of air power in finding and destroying these difficult targets is unique in aerial warfare."[13] Or so the story went.

Maj Gen Alton D. Slay, director of operations at Seventh Air Force in Saigon during the final Commando Hunt campaign, had a view different from those shared by most high-ranking Air Force officers. He was convinced Commando Hunt had failed and that it had done so for two reasons. First, while the US was expanding the air war to Cambodia and intensifying operations over northern Laos, the Air Force was simultaneously redeploying units to Europe and back to America. Second, SAC was reluctant to use B-52s where there was any danger from SA-2 missiles. This restriction meant that the passes leading from North Vietnam into Laos were off-limits to B-52 strikes since the North Vietnamese began placing surface-to-air missile (SAM) sites near them in 1971.[14]

The strongest evidence against the reputed success of Commando Hunt was North Vietnam's launching of a major invasion of South Vietnam in late March 1972. In scope, that invasion dwarfed anything since the Korean War. The invasion prompted battles larger than those that had taken place during the Arab-Israeli War of 1967. That this offensive happened despite the fact that well over two million tons of bombs had fallen on the Ho

Chi Minh Trail should have dampened the sanguinity of all but the most avid air power enthusiasts. For the Air Force, however, Commando Hunt had become production-line warfare, and the managers at the top of the corporation interpreted the figures to suit their own preconceived notions of victory.

Spring in the Air

After the 1971 Army of the Republic of Vietnam (ARVN) invasion of Laos failed, Le Duan—the first secretary of the Indochinese Communist Party and former head of the Central Office for South Vietnam (COSVN)—and Gen Vo Nguyen Giap pushed for a large-scale offensive in the South. There were seemingly good reasons to do so. Although the ARVN had been mauled during Lam Son 719, it broke only when overwhelmed by a force three times its size. The fighting qualities of the ARVN had improved since the mid-1960s, intimating that Vietnamization might be working. Because of Vietnamization, the bulk of American ground forces had withdrawn, so the PAVN would face mostly ARVN units. Additionally, peace activists visiting Hanoi had assured their Communist hosts that antiwar sentiment was such that the American president would be in real trouble in the upcoming elections. Coupled with the way the American media was presenting the antiwar movement, the North Vietnamese leadership concluded that public sentiment and political pressures would prevent President Richard Nixon from taking concerted action in 1972. Finally, Le Duan, General Giap, Troung Chinh (chairman of the National Assembly), Prime Minister Pham Van Dong, COSVN head Pham Hung, and Foreign Minister Le Duc Tho were all over 60 years of age. If protracted any longer this already long war might extend beyond their lifetimes.* They wanted to see their life's work completed.[15]

---

*Ho Chi Minh had died in 1969.

There were plenty of indications that something was brewing. Since the summer of 1971 the North Vietnamese air force (NVNAF) had been more aggressive. They deployed units to the southern panhandle with more regularity. MiGs operating from Quang Lang and Vinh made several quick but shallow penetrations into southern Laos in an attempt to shoot down the airborne command and control center (ABCCC) C-130s or other propeller-driven aircraft.[16]

The AAA deployment pattern changed as well. In past years most antiaircraft guns and virtually all SAMs were redeployed to the Hanoi and Haiphong areas at the beginning of the rainy season. In 1971, however, the guns stayed in place, and by September additional SAM sites were reported near the passes. Simultaneously, a large buildup of supplies was noted in all the staging areas.[17]

Along the Ho Chi Minh Trail the movement of supplies and men to the South went on uninhibited during monsoonal rains that began in May and lasted through October. The North Vietnamese took advantage of the overcast skies, which grounded the jet fighter-bombers during the day, to move supplies. They also built an estimated 140 miles of new all-weather roads and expanded the number of AAA guns to include more than 350 23-mm and 37-mm guns in the southern regions of the trail, concentrating these weapons around the staging areas near the passes through which infiltrators and supplies moved into South Vietnam. At the end of 1971 an estimated 96,000 PAVN troops were in Laos, 63,000 in Cambodia, and well over 100,000 inside South Vietnam.[18]

This buildup continued despite Proud Deep Alpha, a concentrated five-day bombing campaign conducted in Route Pack I in late December (see chapter 4). By January the SA-2 threat had extended into airspace south of the demilitarized zone (DMZ) for the first time. All this prompted Gen Creighton W. Abrams, commander of the Military Assistance Command, Vietnam, to warn that an invasion was imminent. Abrams's staff predicted the invaders would strike in early February, just before President Nixon was scheduled to make his historic trip to Peking. On 20

**NORTH VIETNAM
(Route Packages)**

January, Abrams asked for the authority to bomb targets north of the DMZ and, if and when the attack developed, permission to hit whatever targets inside North Vietnam he and his commanders thought necessary without having to go through the complex request and authorization procedures that plagued Rolling Thunder.[19]

To forestall the invasion, Air Force, Navy, and Republic of Vietnam Air Force (VNAF) aircraft staged a large attack on a suspected buildup area in the Central Highlands on 12 and 13 February, and another "24-hour maximum effort" bombing spree just south of the DMZ on 16 and 17 February. The results were unimpressive. After no attack developed, the drawdown of US forces continued.[20] By the end of February the wolf apparently had passed the door.

Vietnamization, of course, continued. Nixon wanted most, if not all, American combat troops out of Vietnam by election day. At the beginning of 1972 the United States Air Force had only three squadrons of F-4s and a single squadron of A-37s, a total of 76 fighter-bombers in South Vietnam. Another 114 jet fighter-bombers were stationed at various bases in Thailand and 83 B-52s were located at Andersen AFB, Guam, and U Tapao RTAFB, Thailand. During Rolling Thunder up to four aircraft carriers had steamed off the coasts of North and South Vietnam. In early 1972 only two were still on station—with a total of 180 aircraft.[21] Although the VNAF was larger than ever with 168 attack and fighter aircraft, 36 gunships, and 500 helicopters, its larger size hardly made up for the same 400 jets and propeller-driven aircraft that the US had withdrawn since 1969.[22]

Given the scope of the PAVN buildup, President Nixon recognized that the South Vietnamese could not handle the coming offensive on their own. A massive redeployment that more than doubled the number of Air Force and Navy planes in Southeast Asia by May 1972 began on 29 December 1971 when 18 F-4s were requested for deployment to Korat RTAFB under operation plan Commando Flash. Six Phantoms flew immediately from the Philippines to Korat. On 8 February the rest of the squadron deployed, with 12 planes divided evenly between Ubon and Udorn RTAFBs in Thailand and Da Nang AB in Vietnam.[23]

On 2 February 1972 Henry Kissinger and Nixon met with the National Security Council (NSC). Kissinger reports that he urged Nixon to beef up the number of B-52s in Thailand and on Guam, to send additional all-weather aircraft to Thailand, and to add one or two aircraft carriers to the Gulf of Tonkin. That evening, after examining all the intelligence reports, Nixon agreed and issued the appropriate orders. Three days later, eight B-52Ds deployed to U Tapao and 29 B-52Ds flew to Andersen. Bullet Shot I was under way.[24]

The Shoe Falls

The shoe fell at the end of March. Hanoi dubbed the invasion "the Nguyen Hue offensive" in honor of a Vietnamese emperor who, in 1789, moved his troops hundreds of miles through the jungle to attack and destroy an invading Chinese army. Fourteen divisions and 26 separate regiments invaded the South, leaving only one division to protect Laos and four at home in North Vietnam.[25]

The attack started at the end of the rainy season, thus limiting what air power could do in response. The Air Force had 76 fighter-bombers and five AC-119 gunships in South Vietnam and about 200 jet fighters and bombers in Thailand, but for the first few days rain and clouds kept most of these planes grounded. On 1 April, the day after the offensive began, President Nixon authorized air attacks on military targets inside North Vietnam up to 25 miles above the DMZ. However, poor weather hampered operations. Henry Kissinger, frustrated with the inability of the Air Force and the Navy to respond, facetiously suggested to Adm Thomas Moorer, chairman of the Joint Chiefs of Staff (JCS), that if the weather was too bad to fly, perhaps the planes could taxi north for 25 miles to unload their bombs.[26] With fighter-bombers and helicopters grounded, only B-52s and Navy A-6s were available. Meanwhile, the ground situation became confused. ARVN and PAVN units commingled as the North Vietnamese advanced and the South Vietnamese forces disintegrated, making it difficult to use the B-52s and A-6s effectively.

After years of guerrilla and quasi-conventional warfare, in one of the many ironies of this war, Hanoi launched precisely the kind of attack American advisors had been anticipating since 1956. The attack developed on three fronts. On 29 March three divisions supported by 200 tanks crashed across the DMZ. Because Hanoi had thus far respected the demilitarized zone, only the ARVN's 3d Division—a new and inexperienced amalgamation of separate units, raw recruits, and arrested deserters pressed into punishment battalions—faced the onslaught. They performed miserably.[27] In addition to the thrust across the DMZ, the PAVN attacked in two other areas: in the Central Highlands, in an attempt to bisect the country and out of the Parrot's Beak region of Cambodia, with Saigon as the ultimate objective.

To the north in Quang Tri Province, the ARVN's 3d Division abandoned fire bases as it disintegrated before the advancing PAVN. By the end of the first week in May, the North Vietnamese had captured Quang Tri City and secured most of the rest of the province. To protect Hue, the ancient capital, the ARVN 1st Division redeployed from Khe Sanh and took up a blocking position west of the city. The bad weather continued to curtail air operations.[28]

Despite the lousy weather, some planes responded. B-52s flew a total of 1,398 Arc Light sorties hitting PAVN base camps, bivouac areas, troop concentrations, and antiaircraft artillery sites throughout Quang Tri Province. The ARVN's poor ground-to-air coordination procedures made it difficult, however, to use these planes to support South Vietnamese units engaged with the enemy.[29] During breaks in the weather, which increased in frequency as the monsoon season waned, F-4s used laser-guided bombs to drop bridges and crater roads in front of the advancing PAVN. In one three-day period in April, the Air Force destroyed 48 bridges in northern Quang Tri Province. Soviet PT-76 and T-54 tanks, with their amphibious capability, were slowed but not stopped.[30]

Clearing weather brought out the fighter-bombers and gunships. Their effectiveness was hampered, however, by the SA-7 shoulder-fired missiles. The SA-7s first appeared when Aerospace Rescue and Recovery Service helicopters, along with Army choppers and Air Force A-1s and OV-10s, were engaged in a massive effort to recover Lt Col Iceal E. Hambleton, an electronics warfare officer who ejected from an EB-66 downed by an SA-2 on 2 April. In their debut the SA-7s brought down two Skyraiders, one OV-10, and an Army CH-46 helicopter.[31]

Close air support missions for the ARVN in the initial days of the invasion were vastly less effective than those flown in support of American units earlier in the war. South Vietnamese forward air controllers (FAC) flying above the battlefield and the forward air guides with the ground units were not of the same caliber as their American counterparts and predecessors. A legacy of French colonialism came home to roost. Under the colonial regime only the lowest class Vietnamese sought to become "middlemen" between the French bureaucrats (who rarely bothered to learn Vietnamese) and the people. These middlemen learned French to translate the orders of colonial officials to the Vietnamese. Too often the middlemen translated both the demands of the administrators and the "needs of the people" to serve their own ends. The legacy was that those who served in that capacity were despised. Forward air controllers and air guides inherited this legacy to the detriment of operational effectiveness.[32] One Air Force wing commander noted, "Vietnamese FAC's are at the bottom of the military and social totem pole . . . the ALOs (air liaison officers) that are assigned to direct FAC operations are often selected because of previous shortcomings."[33]

Consequently, Americans took over the lion's share of the FAC mission. The SA-7s, however, forced FACs to fly between 7,500 and 10,000 feet, much higher than their officially sanctioned minimum of 3,500 feet. The SA-7 threat also prompted the FACs to jink while searching for targets. As General Slay put it, "If you are looking for a launch, you are not looking for targets."[34]

Despite the weather, SA-7s, antiaircraft guns, and a confused ground situation, air power dealt the PAVN a major setback by preventing a rout from turning into the total collapse of the northern front. It soon became apparent that air power alone would not defeat the PAVN. However, coupled with barely satisfactory resistance by the ARVN, it staved off total defeat. To stop the invasion, targets in North Vietnam had to be bombed.

Deciding to Go North Again

First, more planes were needed. Between 1 April and 13 May, 189 F-4s, 12 F-105s, and eight EB-66s deployed from bases in the United States, Japan, and Korea to South Vietnam and Thailand. In April the Air Force sent 54 additional B-52s to

Andersen.[35]   Additional Bullet Shot B-52 deployments to Guam and to U Tapao brought the number of B-52s to a total of 210 in theater. By the end of May the US had 374 F-4s at bases throughout Thailand and South Vietnam.[36]

On 4 April the president decided to bomb North Vietnam to stop the invasion. Two days later Nixon, Kissinger, and Gen John Vogt (the Seventh Air Force commander) met in the White House to work out the specifics of an aerial campaign. The president told Vogt, "I want you to get down there and use whatever air you need to turn this thing around." [37] Vogt asked only that President Nixon not repeat the mistakes of the Johnson administration in overcontrolling the targeting process. Nixon had no intention of doing that and, in fact, noted in his diary, "The bombing proposals sent to me by the Pentagon could at best be described as timid." [38] Perhaps Vogt and the other generals had become *too* used to getting their operational orders from the White House.

Linebacker One, as it was eventually called, would halt the invasion and so devastate North Vietnam's military capabilities that Hanoi would be compelled to negotiate seriously for the first time since peace talks began in 1968. Before Linebacker began on 8 May, air action was already increasing over North Vietnam. Initially dubbed "Rolling Thunder Alpha," the bombing of North Vietnam above the 20th parallel began on 5 April with Operation Freedom Train. Initial attacks concentrated on SAM sites just north of the DMZ but after 24 hours shifted to bridges and petroleum storage areas around Hanoi and Haiphong. The infamous Paul Doumer Bridge was among the first hit and destroyed by laser-guided bombs (LGB). In a single mission, 32 F-4s dropped 29 laser-guided bombs on the bridge and an additional 84 500-pound bombs on the Yen Vien railway marshalling yard, damaging both targets heavily. Later, on 27 April, in Operation Freedom Dawn, eight Phantoms dropped 16 2,000-pound LGBs on the Thanh Hoa Bridge to take it out of action. Another dramatic mission, Operation Freedom Porch Bravo, involved a weekend of B-52 attacks on 15 and 16 April aimed at oil storage facilities around Hanoi and Haiphong. These attacks marked the first use of the heavy bombers north of the 19th parallel.[39]

B-52 releases bombs during Linebacker. The Air Force's strategic bombers were used north of the 19th parallel for the first time in Linebacker One.

Destroying fuel storage depots and bridges around Hanoi and Haiphong had little immediate impact on the fighting inside South Vietnam because the buildup of supplies prior to the invasion had been so tremendous. By the beginning of May, the fighting on the northern front had stabilized, although the tide had not yet turned. Fighting on the central front increased throughout early April with thrusts toward Dak To and Tan Canh and in Binh Dinh Province. The objective there was to cut South Vietnam in two, while simultaneously capturing Kontum, a major provincial capital. By mid-May, Kontum was surrounded and under siege. Air Force C-130 transports kept the defenders supplied with food and ammunition despite the threat of SA-7s. On 16 May a PAVN column, supported by tanks moved south along Route 14 toward Kontum. At the last moment the ARVN defenders withdrew into the city so three cells of B-52s could strike the enemy column. When they did, the PAVN force ceased to exist. Ten days later the North Vietnamese began their final attack on Kontum. The assault lasted three days and some North Vietnamese units got into the city. However, the ARVN, with help from B-52s, outlasted the attackers.[40]

Meanwhile, Giap's third thrust developed just to the west of Saigon. By the end of the first week of the offensive, the Vietcong's 5th Division had taken Loc Ninh, a town on the Cambodian border approximately 20 miles north of An Loc on Route 13. Simultaneously, the Vietcong's 7th Division cut highway 13 south of An Loc. The plan was for the 9th Vietcong Division to take An Loc so that the Communists could establish a provisional government there. On 6 April President Nguyen Van Thieu dispatched the ARVN's 21st Division from the Mekong Delta, along with the 5th Division from Saigon, to join in the defense of An Loc. The battle for this key provincial capital turned into a long, bloody struggle. Before the siege was broken, the three Communist divisions pounded the city with 70,000 artillery and mortar rounds.[41]

On 6 May a North Vietnamese prisoner of war revealed that an attack would develop from the eastern side of the city. A document found on a dead Vietcong officer supported the prisoner's story, further stating that the final push would begin at 5:30 A.M. on 11 May. Starting at 5:00 A.M., B-52s began pounding the eastern approaches to the city, striking hourly for the next 25 hours. One PAVN unit, confident that B-52s would not bomb the same place twice, moved into craters from an earlier attack. Upon learning of this development, Maj Gen James F. Hollingsworth, the US Army III Corps advisor, directed another raid on the original coordinates; the second air strike devastated the entire Communist regiment.[42]

Fighter-bombers and gunships joined the battle for An Loc. Phantoms from the 49th Tactical Fighter Wing, which had just arrived at Takhli RTAFB from Holloman AFB, New Mexico, flew their first combat sorties over An Loc at midday on 11 May. After their initial bomb runs, the Phantoms headed for Bien Hoa to refuel and rearm so that they could bomb the PAVN again on the way back to Takhli. During the next nine days, these shuttle bombing missions became standard operating procedure for the 49th TFW's 269 sorties.[43] At night AC-119s and AC-130s orbited over An Loc to maintain what had become a protective ring of firepower around the city. During the daylight, C-130s dodged SA-7s and intense antiaircraft fire to keep the defenders supplied with food, water, ammunition, and medicine.[44]

Still, the PAVN attack continued. On 12 and 14 May the North Vietnamese probed at the outskirts of the city. Finally, on the 15th, a few tanks entered An Loc but the PAVN infantry did not advance with them. According to one US advisor, South Vietnamese troops, and even local police officers, were lining up to fire LAWs (light antitank weapons) at the T-54s.[45] The struggle for An Loc was over.

Up in I Corps the PAVN offensive stalled before Hue. On 13 May the South Vietnamese counterattacked. Eleven days later the ARVN undertook a combined helicopter and amphibious assault behind PAVN lines. In this bold and imaginative effort, designed to draw the PAVN back from its forward positions around Hue, ARVN rangers raided ammunition dumps and fuel depots and attacked command posts and repair facilities deep in the enemy's rear. By the end of June the momentum had swung to the ARVN and South Vietnamese marines, along with airborne units, moved back into Quang Tri Province.[46]

The scale of the air power response equalled the scope of the invasion; both were awesome. In April, May, and June the Air Force, Navy, and Marines and the VNAF flew 18,000 sorties in I Corps. Nearly 40,000 tons of bombs fell on enemy forces around An Loc. B-52s dropped 57,000 tons of bombs in Quang Tri Province alone. The Air Force lost 20 planes, the Navy two, and Marines one and the VNAF 10 in air action over South Vietnam.[47] These losses, though regrettable, were not excessive.

By early May it was clear that the invasion had not toppled the Saigon government. Still, the fact that 14 new divisions of North

Vietnamese troops had joined about 100,000 PAVN troops already in South Vietnam not only posed a considerable military threat but also constituted a grim political reality for the Saigon regime. Even after the successful South Vietnamese counterattack, the PAVN held more ground at the end of the summer than the Vietcong and North Vietnamese forces had controlled before the offensive. Nevertheless, Quang Tri City was back in government hands, and not a single provincial capital was occupied by the Communists.

One of Hanoi's major objectives was to influence the American elections by discrediting Nixon's Vietnamization policy. Ironically, the fact that a summer of partisan political campaigning was under way probably did Hanoi more harm than good. President Nixon was relatively certain that he could defeat the Democratic candidate, Sen George McGovern, especially after McGovern replaced his vice presidential candidate, Sen Thomas Eagleton, only a week after the nominating convention because Eagleton revealed that he had sought psychiatric help during a bout with mental depression. What Nixon was unsure of, however, was how much longer Congress would support his Vietnam policy.

The prisoner of war issue became a two-edged sword. On the one hand, hawks used it to urge support for administration efforts to "bring our POWs home." However, at the end of 1971, 30 dovish members of the Senate favored settling for an unconditional deadline to complete the removal of American forces in the expectation that Hanoi would respond by freeing American captives; about 40 senators favored withdrawal contingent only upon Hanoi's agreeing to free the POWs. By the end of 1971 a majority of senators endorsed the latter policy, and that number seemed to grow in the early months of 1972. Nixon was convinced that it was only a matter of time until the Senate would cut off funds for the war.[48]

Meanwhile, diplomatic developments presented the president with new opportunities and pressures. A new relationship was being forged with the People's Republic of China. The fear that Chinese troops would enter the conflict had long been laid to rest. Nixon was going to Moscow to sign the Strategic Arms Limitation

Talks treaty (SALT I) in early May. He did not want to go to Moscow on the heels of a defeat in South Vietnam.

Given the developing international situation, stalemate was not acceptable. Because North Vietnam had attacked South Vietnam so blatantly, the United States had to respond strongly. By the end of April, the attack had been blunted. Nixon, however, wanted it defeated—the North Vietnamese divisions inside South Vietnam could not be allowed merely to stand down while additional supplies reinvigorated them for some future effort.

Linebacker One

Pocket Money preceded Linebacker. Precisely at 8:59 A.M., Hanoi time, 9 May 1972, six US Navy A-7 Corsairs and three A-6s began sowing mines at the entrance to Haiphong harbor. Each jet dropped four 2,000-pound Mk-52 or Mk-55 mines which sank to the channel floor. These mines contained sensors that monitored underwater signals caused by a ship's magnetic field, engine noise, propeller wash, and the decreased pressure from a ship's wake. The right combination of signals would spark an explosion powerful enough to rip out the steel hull of most cargo vessels. One minute after the first mines splashed into the water, President Nixon went on national television to announce that they would be activated at 6:00 A.M., Saigon time, on 11 May. This warning provided ample time for any vessel in North Vietnamese ports to depart safely. Two minutes into the broadcast, the Navy aircraft turned east and headed back to the USS *Coral Sea*. Simultaneously, other A-7s and A-6s were sowing mines off Cam Pha, Hon Gai, Vinh, and Thanh Hoa as well as in inlets and estuaries where vessels might off-load cargo.[49] Coinciding with the president's address, an executive message was transmitted to military forces in Southeast Asia ordering the beginning of Operation Linebacker.[50]

Richard Nixon liked football and it may be that the code name Linebacker was chosen to please him. Whether true or not, the name fit. A linebacker is a defensive football player who attacks the offense, disrupting the opposing backfield before the play can develop. The military's Linebacker was designed to cripple North Vietnam's ability to conduct offensive operations inside South Vietnam. Its objective was to destroy war-related resources such as petroleum storage facilities and power-generating plants; to reduce or restrict the importing of supplies by ships through the harbors and by rail and road from China; and to impede the flow of men and supplies by destroying the internal transportation system.[51]

Deciding on how to take the war to the North had not been easy. President Nixon first suggested a three-day B-52 attack on critical targets around Hanoi and Haiphong. Henry Kissinger thought this might cause too much public outcry, which would be embarrassing as the Moscow summit got under way. General Abrams was opposed to diverting the B-52s from the still critical southern battlefields where their all-weather capability gave him a ready source of massive aerial firepower.[52]

The president then turned to the JCS for a plan for attacking North Vietnam but was disappointed at what they gave him. He seemed particularly peeved at their reluctance, perhaps their inability, to come forth with the kind of aerial campaign the generals had been demanding for the past seven years. Considering the Pentagon's bombing plan to be "timid," Nixon turned to his assistant, Army Gen Alexander Haig, who outlined the campaign that began with the mining of Haiphong and moved on to wider bombing of the North.[53] The campaign had two objectives: first, to blockade North Vietnam, sealing it from outside sources of supply; and, second, to destroy North Vietnam's ability to support the 14 divisions of soldiers that had recently entered the South. Taken together, if these objectives were achieved, North Vietnam would be compelled to negotiate a peace plan acceptable to the United States.[54]

By May the battlefield situation in South Vietnam was no longer critical. Although South Vietnam's condition remained serious, the invasion had been blunted. Air power became increasingly effective at supporting the ARVN as the weather cleared and the battle lines stabilized. Linebacker's first objective was to destroy those resources inside North Vietnam most directly related to sustaining the offensive in the South. Bombing of supply caches and bridges in Route Pack I had already affected the PAVN units in South Vietnam. Wrecking the transportation system in the heartland was the next stage, and that was the first objective of Linebacker. This transportation system relied on harbors, highways, and railroads to import war material. Mining closed the harbors. The railroads were next.[55]

Laser-guided bombs were used to great effect in destroying bridges and tunnels along the northeast and northwest rail lines leading from Hanoi to the Chinese border. Because of the changing relationship with China, fear that the People's Liberation Army might intervene no longer constrained the targeting process. Laser-guided and electro-optically guided bombs made short work of the bridges and tunnels in the mountains north of Hanoi— bridges over mountain gorges were not as easily repaired as those in the flatlands of the southern peninsula.

By the end of June the Air Force and Navy had destroyed or damaged more than 400 bridges in North Vietnam, including the infamous Thanh Hoa Bridge and the Doumer Bridge outside Hanoi. Additionally, guided bombs along with conventional iron bombs caused more than 800 road cuts, many of these starting landslides along the twisting, mountainous roads near the Chinese border. These could not be easily circumvented nor quickly repaired. Trucks were backed up along narrow roads or forced into truck parks where supplies were off-loaded and carried around the craters and landslides. While concentrations of trucks made inviting targets, the objective was not so much to destroy vehicles as it was to hamper the movement of supplies to the South.

Once the bridges were down and the railroads and highways interdicted, the Air Force and Navy turned to other targets: petroleum storage facilities, power-generating plants, military barracks, training areas, and military headquarters. The targeting plan called for the petroleum storage facilities to go next.

235

Accordingly, on 18 May, Air Force F-4s struck a large petroleum storage facility three and one-half miles north of Hanoi, destroying 5.5 million gallons of fuel. For several years, petroleum supplies had been dispersed throughout North Vietnam, often in small caches of a hundred barrels or so, many times located close to schools and hospitals or in the center of villages where they could not be struck. But precision-guided bombs greatly reduced the risk of collateral damage to nonmilitary structures, and, since fewer bombs were needed, enhanced the feasibility of destroying even small petroleum storage areas in comparison to the costs and potential risks.

Weather remained a constant problem but it did not have the same impact that it had had during Rolling Thunder, when, if a particular target was obscured by clouds on the day scheduled for attack, the entire mission had to be scrubbed. In Linebacker, planners worked with a list of approved, validated targets. If a petroleum storage facility was blanketed by clouds, then an alternate target could be struck. On 20 May the Haiphong petroleum storage area was weathered in, so Air Force and Navy planes diverted to the Hanoi electrical power station. Again, on 26 May, weather precluded a strike in the Haiphong port area, so the Son Tay warehousing complex was bombed. When the weather cleared over Haiphong a few days later, there was no need to resubmit the oil storage target for validation as would have been the case during Rolling Thunder. Rather it was struck and destroyed by Navy fighters, which not only blasted storage tanks but destroyed the main pumping station as well.[56]

By June it was clear that the Republic of Vietnam would survive the invasion; thus, the complexion of Linebacker operations began to change. Bombing continued to deprive the PAVN units in the South of needed supplies, but beyond that the focus turned to degrading the enemy's long-term potential for making war. To be sure, North Vietnam had few factories, none of which produced tanks, trucks, or warplanes. However, it did have facilities—many of them small shops—for repairing trucks and other machines needed to keep the war effort going. Destroying repair facilities meant that once the trucks, railcars, and locomotives needed to support the war in South Vietnam were worn out or damaged, they could not be fixed easily. Again, laser-guided bombs proved important because the repair facilities usually were no larger than a neighborhood service station in the United States, and they were often located in the middle of villages or city neighborhoods.[57]

The bombing was working. By September imports into North Vietnam were estimated at 35 to 50 percent below what they had been in May.[58] The news did not get better for the Communists as that month progressed. The pace of the air war quickened in September to make it the most productive month of the Linebacker campaign—more than 27,500 tons of explosives were delivered to the North Vietnamese heartland.[59] By the first week in October, the immediate threat to South Vietnam was ended. Again Linebacker changed its complexion. Now the objective was to compel Hanoi to sign an acceptable peace agreement.

Bombing and Diplomacy

During their talks with Soviet Premier Leonid Brezhnev in May, Kissinger and Nixon offered Hanoi, through the Soviets, a new framework for negotiations. Washington's position had been that since American troops were going home, North Vietnamese forces should too. Hanoi had always maintained that their forces were not heavily involved in South Vietnam. Moreover, as the Communists claimed, Vietnam was one country and distinctions between northern and southern Vietnamese were contrived. However, after the Nguyen Hue offensive got under way, it was impossible to claim that the PAVN was anything but heavily involved in the fighting. So, when Kissinger told Leonid Brezhnev that the United States would accept a cease-fire in place in exchange for the removal of *only* those North Vietnamese forces that had entered South Vietnam since the start of the offensive, a major obstacle in the negotiations was removed.[60]

The Paris peace talks had broken down on 2 May. Ten days later, after the harbors were mined, Le Duc Tho responded positively to Kissinger's suggestion for renewed talks. A summer of dancing diplomatic minuets remained and the pace of the air attacks continued even when Hanoi seemed conciliatory. The breakthrough, however, did not come until after the intense bombings of September. On 8 October, Le Duc Tho put forth substantially new terms, including a cease-fire prior to any political settlement. For the first time, Hanoi dropped its demand that the United States dump President Nguyen Van Thieu and sack his entire government prior to any truce.[61] They also agreed that military aid to Saigon could continue in a postagreement period at "replacement levels of armament." Most importantly, perhaps, Hanoi promised not to send additional troops into the South.[62]

Between 8 and 23 October a peace agreement that had eluded negotiators for four years took shape very quickly. It was, to be sure, quite complex and both sides had legitimate concerns about its terminology and provisions. Still, by the third week in October, the expectation that an agreement would be reached seemed reasonable. On 23 October, President Nixon ordered a bombing halt above 20 degrees north latitude and Linebacker ended. On 26 October Henry Kissinger told reporters, "Peace is at hand." It was not.

Linebacker One as a Tactical Success

From April through October 1972, 155,548 tons of bombs fell on North Vietnam.[63] Indeed, Linebacker was a watershed in aerial warfare. All bombing, from the Italo-Turkish War of 1912 through Rolling Thunder, can be lumped into one category: explosives delivered by airplanes. Linebacker was the first modern aerial campaign in which precision-guided munitions changed the way air power was used.

Linebacker succeeded where Rolling Thunder failed and for four reasons. First, President Nixon was decisive in his actions.

Lyndon Johnson had been overly cautious, taking a small war and fretting about it until it was too big a war for the solutions he felt were viable. Nixon's task was more defined: get the United States out of the war. Whereas Johnson sought consensus, Nixon cared little for what the press, the American political left, or the European allies thought of the way he conducted the war. Furthermore, the international situation had changed. Johnson feared that one stray bomb might spark a third world war; Kissinger's diplomatic maneuvering with China and the Soviet Union diminished that fear.

Second, air power had been used forcefully and appropriately during Linebacker. The strategy was tailored to defeat North Vietnam's initiative, which had established the parameters for this stage of the conflict by putting 14 divisions inside South Vietnam. This large force was on the offensive, consuming fuel, ammunition, food, and medicine at an accelerated rate. Since Hanoi was clearly the aggressor, the political and diplomatic pressures for restraint were less than might otherwise have been the case. The cautious, graduated bombing policy of Rolling Thunder would have been useless in the face of the offensive. In the earlier campaign, the Vietnamese leaders in Hanoi had gotten used to Washington's timidity; they were not prepared for the sheer force of Linebacker. Peace activists visiting Hanoi, the antiwar messages emanating from the American press, and the assumption that Nixon would be constrained by election-year politics led the politburo into a major miscalculation.

Third, Nixon gave the military greater latitude in targeting. After establishing guidelines and the general rules of engagement, he encouraged the generals and the planners—in fact ordered them— to devise a targeting approach that kept the North Vietnamese off balance. This latitude made it possible for the offense to "string out" the defense by focusing on one set of targets for a day or so and then shift to another set of targets in an entirely different part of the country. The Air Force had the initiative and the North Vietnamese could not depend on the predictability in operations that had marked Rolling Thunder.

239

Fourth, the immense difference in the technology used made Linebacker the first bombing campaign in a "new era" of aerial warfare. Rolling Thunder was, conversely, the last major bombing campaign of the "old era." The F-105s that carried the brunt of Rolling Thunder operations dropped bombs in much the same way that Sopwith Camels had 50 years earlier. True, the F-105s dropped bigger bombs and hauled them much faster and to more distant targets, but in the end the same principles applied. During Linebacker, the introduction of laser-guided bombs (LGB) and electro-optically guided bombs (EOGB) completely changed the way the Air Force conducted the operation. Fewer bombs caused greater damage because of increased accuracy. Night and all-weather bombing capability had improved because of advances in loran bombing techniques and because of the arrival of 48 F-111s in late September as a part of Operation Linebacker Sherry.[64] Loran technology and the F-111s added to the all-weather bombing capability provided by the B-52s.

Enemy defenses had improved too. Although they had gained in their bombing capabilities, US aircrews faced a more threatening array of North Vietnamese air defenses. During Rolling Thunder, aircrews claimed that defenses around Hanoi and Haiphong were worse than those encountered over Nazi Germany. Between 1968 and 1972, the North Vietnamese almost doubled the number of SAM sites to around 300, though not all were occupied at any one time. The NVNAF grew in size from a handful of MiGs to a force of nearly 250 MiG-17s, -19s, and -21s. The North had improved its air defense communications system dramatically, integrating SAM sites with the over 1,500 AAA batteries throughout North Vietnam and the dozen or so air bases capable of launching MiGs. In the four years of Rolling Thunder, North Vietnamese fighter crews increased not only in number but also in ability. After they returned from basic pilot training in the Soviet Union or China, they practiced almost continuously with ground controllers who guided them to "intruders." Additionally, MiG crews engaged each other in mock aerial combat to sharpen dogfighting skills.[65]

The increased proficiency of the MiG force soon became evident. During May, entire squadrons, as many as 15 interceptors, would launch against US planes. The kill ratio, which had stood at 2.2 to 1 in favor of the USAF during Rolling Thunder, dipped to 2 to 1.5 during the first stages of Linebacker. By June, when the MiGs downed seven Air Force fighter-bombers while losing only two of their own, the North Vietnamese had gained the upper hand.[66]

During Rolling Thunder, AAA claimed up to 85 percent of the aircraft downed. To deliver bombs accurately, the F-105s had to dive into the effective fire envelope of deadly 23-mm and 37-mm guns before releasing their bombs, pulling out of their dives at below 3,000 feet. Laser-guided bombs changed all that. During Linebacker, LGBs were normally dropped from around 10,000 feet, well above the effective range of all but the largest AAA guns. Additionally, because of the effectiveness of guided bombs, fewer strike aircraft were needed, meaning more planes were free to jam enemy radars and to attack the SAM sites, both of which had proliferated since 1968. Accordingly, force composition changed dramatically. During Rolling Thunder, 60 percent of the planes going north carried bombs while 40 percent engaged in MiG combat air patrol (MiGCAP), SAM suppression, jamming, and search-and-rescue combat air patrol (SARCAP). Only 20 to 40 percent of the planes on any given Linebacker mission carried bombs, while 60 to 80 percent were used for support.[67]

The distribution of losses also changed. Most of the Linebacker losses were among the support force rather than the strike aircraft. The Air Force lost 46 planes over North Vietnam between 10 May and 23 October. Surface-to-air missiles claimed 14, antiaircraft fire bagged three, and MiGs shot down 27 planes. Two F-111s either flew into the ground while using their terrain-following radar or were shot down by AAA in the target area since they normally "swooshed" in low to drop retarded bombs. Thirty-five of the 46 losses occurred among the support force.[68]

The losses to MiGs were worrisome, especially since the Air Force had always prided itself on prowess in aerial combat. Still, no one should have been surprised. The US pilot force was younger and less experienced than it had been in the 1960s. Furthermore, since the Korean War, the Air Force increasingly relied on air-to-air missiles for aerial combat; dogfighting skills, considered passé, were either forgotten or not acquired. North Vietnamese crews, on the other hand, stressed air-to-air combat. Their MiGs were dogfighters, designed to turn quickly and tightly. Among their aircrews were veterans who had flown against Americans earlier in the war and, because North Vietnamese believed theirs was a "total war," pilots had not been retiring or leaving the service to pursue airline or other civilian careers. Finally, for the Vietnamese the years between 1968 and 1971 represented only a lull in the fighting. Conversely, after 1968 the United States was clearly disengaging from the war—which for the Air Force tended to become an afterthought. In short, the air war had turned into a contest between a peacetime air force and a highly motivated wartime air force. At that particular place and time, the North Vietnamese air force was, at least in air-to-air combat capabilities, superior to the US Air Force.

What the US Air Force had, however, was the ability to apply technology to make up for tactical and operational shortcomings. One example was the establishment of Teaball, a weapons control center that proved indispensable in overcoming the challenge posed by MiGs in the summer of 1972. Throughout the war, compartmentalization of intelligence had been a problem. One analyst might be cleared for SR-71 photography but not for the photography and signals intelligence gathered by earth-orbiting satellites. Most officers cleared for all levels of intelligence were usually those associated with the headquarters. They tended to be nonflyers who briefed the generals. Intelligence officers at the wing and squadron levels were not usually cleared for higher levels of intelligence. That applied to most combat aircrews. Consequently, a nonflying lieutenant preparing and delivering the general's morning briefing might know, for example, that four MiG-21s had moved to Vinh airfield in the southern panhandle and that they had scrambled to shoot down a slow-moving C-130

242

lumbering over Laos. But that information could not be passed to the crewmen on the C-130 or to the fighter crews on MiGCAP who might respond. Teaball finally addressed this problem.

Using a combination of radar and other intelligence-gathering sources and the down-linking capabilities on aircraft platforms like the KC-135 Combat Apple and Olympic Torch or the EC-121 code-named Disco and the Navy radar picket ship called Red Crown (all involved in gathering or monitoring various electronic signals), up-to-the-moment information was sent to a central clearing house at Nakhon Phanom RTAFB. There Teaball analysts used all the information to plot and track enemy aircraft so that tactical decisions could be made based on the latest intelligence. Then, Teaball controllers passed the information that was needed directly to the aircrews so they could take whatever action was necessary.[69]

This command and control link proved crucially important to the support force. The F-4 Phantoms had advantages in thrust and range of radar, but the MiGs were more maneuverable and most models had guns. If the MiGs took the initiative going into aerial combat they gained several advantages. If the MiG pilot could force the Phantom into a maneuvering contest, the American pilot would find himself dueling with a foe who was probably better trained for this particular kind of combat and who was flying a more agile airplane. Furthermore, because the North Vietnamese had practiced coordination between controllers and aircrews, the MiGs often entered the fray positioned for an initial stern attack with the Atoll heat-seeking missile, a Soviet version of the AIM-9E Sidewinder. With Teaball the Phantom crews could take the initiative and maneuver their aircraft so that the MiGs were forced to react to their opening gambit. Given that advantage, the F-4's extra power and more capable radar could be used to minimize the MiGs' greater maneuverability.

Enhancing Teaball was Combat Tree, a device placed on a limited number of F-4Ds that could identify MiGs by interrogating their identification, friend or foe (IFF) equipment. This device told the Phantom crews who and what they were dealing with so that

F-4 equipped with air-to-air missiles.

In encounters between Air Force Phantoms and MiGs during Linebacker One, the North Vietnamese pilots shot down 27 US planes—for a while the air-to-air kill ratio shifted in favor of North Vietnam.

MiG-21

they could prepare themselves for the encounter. With Teaball and Combat Tree, the kill ratio swung back to favor the USAF with five Phantoms lost to 19 MiGs downed between August and the end of Linebacker on 23 October 1972.[70] General Vogt summed up the effect of these innovations:

> You can talk to our fighter pilots and they'll tell you how they tightened up on their air discipline. They can cut down on their air chatter. They practiced air-to-air combat among themselves. They went from fluid four to something else. They all didn't work before Teaball, and they all worked after Teaball.[71]

Technological advances like Teaball and Combat Tree helped the support force do its job, which was to protect the strike force. The introduction of guided bombs forced changes in the tactics employed by the strike force. Laser-guided and electro-optically guided bombs had been used in Laos since 1968 to blast AAA guns and to cause landslides across roads in mountainous areas. They had knocked out tanks and dropped bridges during the early days of the spring offensive. Still, their use had been more of a novelty and the impact on tactics had been minimal.

During Linebacker, for the most part, two aircraft were needed to deliver LGBs: one to lase the target and the other to drop the bomb. Over North Vietnam and Laos, typically an F-4D equipped with a laser ranging device dubbed Pave Knife illuminated the target while a second F-4 maneuvered to drop the bomb. Although two Phantoms were put at risk, the danger was minimal since the illuminating and the bombing aircraft operated at between 10,000 and 14,000 feet and might be up to four miles away from the target during this process.[72] Because aircraft had engaged in dive-bombing almost exclusively during Rolling Thunder, the North Vietnamese had positioned their antiaircraft guns close to potential targets, such as bridges and railroad switching yards. These guns were useless against aircraft four miles away and two miles high.

The two aircraft involved in lasing and bombing flew in an orbit over their targets. The Pave Knife F-4 "painted" the desired point of impact while the bombing F-4 got into the right position to drop the bomb "into the basket" where the sensor could acquire and follow the laser to its mark. That required concentration and both planes were vulnerable to SAMs or attack by MiGs. The risk was reduced with the introduction of gimbaled Pave Knife pods that enabled the F-4 carrying the bombs to do its own lasing. Furthermore, because gimbaled pods were rotatable, the pilot could engage in a limited amount of maneuvering and jinking while the backseater kept the pod trained on the target. However, only a small number of these pods were available, and they were allocated to F-4Ds in the 8th Tactical Fighter Wing at Ubon. Still, the use of gimbaled pods meant fewer aircraft were put at risk because a single F-4 equipped with a gimbaled Pave Knife pod could accompany several F-4s to the target, and after dropping its own bombs remain to lase for the others.[73]

All in all the laser-guided bomb became the weapon of choice for the air-to-ground mission. Its accuracy was phenomenal when compared to "iron bombs," as unguided bombs became known. For instance, it took an average of 14.3 Mk-82 500-pound bombs to be sure of a hit on a tank but only 2.4 LGBs to get the same result.[74] The big advantage of LGBs over EOGBs was cost. The Pave Way II EOGBs consisting of a KMU-353B guidance kit—a minitelevision camera—wedded to the bomb of choice was about $16,000 as compared to only $3,400 for an LGB kit and Mk-84 bomb together.[75]

Bad weather limited the effectiveness of both the LGBs and EOGBs. Clouds or overcast diffused the laser beam, making it impossible to mark a target. These conditions also lessened the sharp contrasts between shade and light needed to aim an EOGB effectively. The North Vietnamese figured out these limitations and began using smudge pots to obscure highly valued targets, but with only limited success.[76]

These precision-guided bombs opened up targets that had been off-limits because they were located in densely populated areas. One such target was the command and control center for North Vietnam's air force, which was located in a residential neighborhood near Bac Mai airfield. It was a system of underground bunkers where air operations were coordinated with SAM defenses and antiaircraft guns. Using a gimbaled Pave Knife pod, a single F-4 put a 2,000-pound bomb with a delayed fuse into the middle of the complex. Poststrike photography showed a shallow lake where the entrance used to be, indicating that the bomb had exploded deep underground, collapsing the ceilings and rupturing water pipes.[77]

The strike packages were composed differently in Linebacker. The typical Linebacker package consisted of the strike force of 16 to 24 F-4s carrying LGBs or EOGBs or 32 F-4s hauling 500- and 750-pound bombs, rockets, or cluster bombs (CBU). If the weather was good the laser-guided bombs would be the weapon of choice and an appropriate target could be selected. Some targets, however, were more vulnerable to attack with a larger number of 500-pound bombs than with a few precision-guided weapons. These included truck parks and most storage areas.[78]

Attacks began with the flights of four to eight F-4s or A-7s dispensing chaff. When the chaff hit the plane's slipstream it created a corridor of radar reflecting foil. Next came the F-4s and F-105s in the Wild Weasel SAM suppression role. Since Rolling Thunder, "weaseling" tactics had evolved into hunter-killer teams of two F-105 "hunters" to seek out the SAM sites and two F-4 "killers" to destroy them. The F-105s carried either the AGM-45 Shrikes or the more expensive but more accurate AGM-78 standard antiradiation missiles. These homed on the Fan Song radar emissions and, if all went well, would hit the van housing the controllers. Under the hunter-killer team concept, if the F-105s prompted the North Vietnamese to shut down their radars, the F-4s would streak to the site to obliterate vans, launchers, and missiles with cluster bombs and napalm.

Behind the chaff and Weasel flights came the MiGCAP, usually one or two flights of four F-4Ds or F-4Es (equipped with a nose-mounted 20-mm cannon). Because MiGs now posed a greater threat than ever, the role of the MiGCAP increased in importance. If possible at least one Combat Tree-equipped F-4 would be among the MiGCAP aircraft to give them every added advantage technology could provide.[79]

Linebacker One, as it would soon be known, was the most successful aerial campaign of the Vietnam War. It was successful not because more than 150,000 tons of bombs were dropped in a six-month period or because laser-guided bombs destroyed certain key targets. It was successful because it took place under the aegis of an appropriate and viable strategy. Linebacker epitomized conventional air power used to stop a conventional invasion and, beyond that, it qualified as a "strategic" use of air power in that it compelled Hanoi's politburo to negotiate seriously for the first time since peace talks started in 1968.

By late summer 1972 Hanoi had good reason to want the Americans out of the war. Their invasion had failed to deliver victory and the homeland was suffering the kind of damage which, if it continued, would make the future bleak even if the goal of uniting Vietnam was eventually realized. The bombing forced Hanoi's leaders to take a longer view of history if they ever wanted to realize their ultimate goal of a single, Communist Vietnamese state. First, they had to get the United States military out of South Vietnam and make it difficult, if not impossible, for the American air forces to return. Second, the North had to retain a viable fighting force inside South Vietnam and eastern Laos. From Hanoi's point of view, while political forces in Washington might eventually remove US troops, including the air forces, there was no guarantee that this course of events would happen before air power had decimated the PAVN forces to the point they might be incapable of successful combat. By October, Hanoi was ready to deal.

Saigon Balks

The focus shifted to Saigon. That warfare is more than bombs on targets, dead enemy troops, wrecked bridges, and debilitated harbors became evident. The peace that South Vietnamese soldiers and American airmen had fought so hard to win in the spring of 1972 was not to be, at least not yet.

And the problem was not with Hanoi or Washington. Both sides had made concessions to reach agreement. Washington's big concession had been to allow at least 100,000 PAVN troops to remain inside South Vietnam; Hanoi's was to drop its demand that Thieu be ditched in favor of a coalition government. Instead, Hanoi proposed and Washington had accepted a "national council of national reconciliation" that would exist simultaneously with the regime in Saigon until a new government could be elected. From 26 September both sides had moved far enough forward with other provisions of the agreement that 31 October was tentatively set as a signing date.[80]

In its basic outline the agreement reached between Hanoi and Washington went as follows. There would be an in-place cease-fire. The United States would withdraw its remaining forces from the South in exchange for the return of American POWs held in North Vietnam and Laos. All four parties—the United States, North Vietnam, South Vietnam, and the Vietcong—would refrain from violating the territories of Laos and Cambodia. Elections under international supervision would be held in South Vietnam to determine a new government. A national council of national reconciliation would be established to implement the agreement and organize elections. The United States could provide economic and military aid to the existing government of South Vietnam, with a ceiling on military aid set at the level existing when the agreement was signed.[81] What was left was for Kissinger to fly to Saigon to secure Thieu's approval. That was scheduled for 18 October. Three days later, according to a schedule worked out between Kissinger and Le Duc Tho, American bombing of the North would stop. On 21 October, Kissinger was scheduled to be in Hanoi initialing the formal agreement to be signed by all parties in Paris on Halloween.

That Washington and Hanoi had reached this stage was significant. Saigon had been left out and President Thieu had substantial objections to what Washington had negotiated in his interest, and in his stead. He rejected the in-place cease-fire because the PAVN, despite having its offensive blunted, still stood on substantial territory and, more significantly, controlled the access corridors contiguous to the Ho Chi Minh Trail, along with northern Quang Tri Province adjoining the DMZ. Additionally, Thieu viewed the council of national reconciliation as a thinly disguised coalition government; he wanted no part of it. He also insisted that Hanoi acknowledge the 17th parallel—the demilitarized zone—as a political boundary. Furthermore, the wording of the agreement disturbed Thieu. It stated that there were *three* Indochinese states: Laos, Cambodia, and Vietnam. Thieu insisted that there were *four*, and to imply otherwise was to legitimize Hanoi's goal of uniting Vietnam under a Communist system. On 21 October, instead of landing in Hanoi, Kissinger was still in Saigon where South Vietnam's foreign minister was handing him a list of 69 changes, some 23 of which were significant enough to warrant renegotiation of the agreement.[82] At the very least, Thieu's insistence that Hanoi withdraw all its forces from the South would not be acceptable to Hanoi.

Meanwhile, there was the question of a bombing halt over the North. Hanoi, after all, had reached agreement with Washington. It seemed fair that they not be punished for Saigon's intransigence. For several reasons, however, Nixon was not inclined to stop the bombing. He recalled that Lyndon Johnson had stopped bombing North Vietnam the week before the 1968 elections. Nixon felt that action had been a craven political act that had deprived him, as the new president, of the option of continuing or expanding a bombing campaign already in existence. Nixon feared that stopping the bombing so close to the 1972 elections might make it appear he was playing politics with bombs. Kissinger argued the president into a compromise so that the bombing above 20 degrees north latitude was ended while missions into the panhandle continued. So on 23 October, Linebacker formally concluded.[83]

By 22 October, Thieu's demands for textual changes had increased to 129, although the substantive objections focused on the presence of North Vietnamese troops in the South, the composition and function of the proposed national council of national reconciliation, and the nature of the DMZ.[84]

That Hanoi agreed to reopen negotiations must be construed as a backhanded compliment to the effectiveness of the bombing. While there was no agreement, B-52s and fighter-bombers were pounding the North's army inside South Vietnam and the curtailment of bombing above 20 degrees north latitude only meant that more planes were available to bomb farther south. The next round of negotiations was set to start on 20 November.

Meanwhile, Richard Nixon defeated George McGovern. The Democratic candidate never posed a significant threat to Nixon, but the forthcoming Congress was quite another matter. Due to convene in January, the new Congress, with Democrats in control of both the House and Senate, posed a substantial threat in Nixon's view. The president feared Congress would impose peace by cutting off funds for the war, and Saigon's behavior only made that more likely.

Part of the plan to convince Thieu to sign the agreement was Operation Enhance Plus. Under way since mid-1972 to prepare the South Vietnamese armed forces for that day when they would be on their own, Enhance Plus was accelerated and expanded. The US transferred more than 300 fighter-bombers, including all the A-1 Skyraiders in the Air Force and the Navy, additional transport planes, and 277 helicopters to South Vietnam in a six-month period. In addition, the Nixon administration rerouted twin-engine Northrop F-5 fighters, including the newest versions scheduled for delivery to the Imperial Iranian Air Force—painted in tan and brown desert camouflage—to Saigon. Some 200 additional tanks and armored personnel carriers and nearly 2,000 trucks were also sent, many of them after 1 November.[85]

The United States took several other steps to reassure Thieu. In late November, Kissinger and Nixon outlined a contingency plan to update targeting information after the cease-fire. A communications net would link each military headquarters in South Vietnam with the soon-to-be established US military headquarters at Nakhon Phanom. South Vietnamese generals supposedly could phone in daily updates of targeting information so, if need be, American planes could respond quickly and effectively to any violations of the cease-fire agreement.[86] Air power, or its promise, was compelling Saigon toward signing a peace agreement.

On 21 November, Kissinger laid the changes demanded by Thieu before Le Duc Tho. He added 44 thought up by the US delegation. Much of this was for effect, to establish a bargaining position from which concessions could be made. Kissinger had four major goals for this renewed round of talks: first, to obtain a strong statement defining the DMZ as an international boundary and to get Hanoi to agree not to send military forces or supplies across it; second, to obtain at least a token withdrawal of North Vietnamese troops beyond the ones they had already agreed to send home; third, to write a commitment to an Indochina-wide cease-fire into the agreement so that peace might come to Laos and Cambodia as well; and fourth, to obtain a strong international force of 6,000 to 7,000 men to supervise and enforce the cease-fire.[87]

Hanoi's opening gambit was to ignore these demands and withdraw most of the concessions made in October. Le Duc Tho then submitted a number of new demands, including the release of thousands of "political prisoners"—Vietcong POWs held in Saigon's camps and jails—with their release tied to the return of American POWs held in Vietnam and Laos. Talks lasted three days and then recessed until 9 December, when they resumed. This round lasted until 13 December. Both sides quickly discarded most of their new demands, but Le Duc Tho would not budge on the sensitive issue of the DMZ nor would he consider any further withdrawal of PAVN troops. Furthermore, he would accept only a token force of 500 men for the International Commission of Control and Supervision. The United States was willing to compromise on all of these points and, in Kissinger's words, "There was no intractable, substantive issue separating the two sides, but rather an apparent North Vietnamese determination *not to allow the agreement to be completed*."[88] In his opinion, Hanoi believed that both the split between Washington and Saigon and the imminent return of the Democratic-controlled Congress worked to their advantage. Kissinger and Le Duc Tho ended the talks on 13 December, promised to keep in touch, and went home.

Linebacker Two

From April through October the US bombing had sought first to halt the North Vietnamese offensive and then to cripple Hanoi's ability to sustain military operations over an extended period. These objectives were achieved by isolating North Vietnam from its sources of supply and by wrecking its internal transportation system, not by smashing industries in the grand style of World War II–era raids on factory complexes like those that existed in Hamburg or Kobe. In South Vietnam the PAVN was mauled by American bombs and decimated by a stubborn ARVN resistance. Still, Hanoi's leaders seemed to hope for a peace settlement even better than the one Saigon considered so abhorrent.

In mid-December, Hanoi's hope was Richard Nixon's fear: Congress would legislate the United States out of the war. In the president's mind, time was short since Congress would be back in session in a little more than a month. Linebacker Two was aimed at Hanoi's will—the willingness to continue to stall in hopes of getting a better peace agreement by default.

The United States had anticipated the need for continuing air operations into the winter months (November–March). In August, Seventh Air Force targeteers had begun planning for a fall and winter aerial campaign. During the spring and summer monsoons, the weather had been bad enough. While maximum rainfall occurred during summer, the storms usually occurred in the middle of the day and diminished in the late afternoon, providing periods of relatively clear weather, especially in the morning. In contrast winter precipitation took the form of a continuous drizzle, with overcast skies that would severely limit the use of precision-guided weapons.[89] Therefore, in early August, the targeteers reviewed the target lists to select those against which B-52s and Navy A-6s, as well as loran-directed fighter-bombers, could be used. Of necessity these targets would have to be of the sorts susceptible to "area bombing": railway marshalling yards, airfields, and warehouse complexes.

After the first of September the commanders in chief of the Strategic Air Command (SAC) and the Pacific Command (PAC) had settled on those targets with sufficient radar return and vulnerability to area bombing to warrant strikes by three-ship cells of B-52s. B-52s and A-6s were selected for this phase of the bombing for three reasons. First, these planes, especially the B-52s, could deliver more destructive firepower than any other planes, even in their conventional configuration. Second, B-52s provided the kind of bomb dispersal pattern that, with proper targeting, would cause maximum damage to large areas. Third, the B-52s and A-6s were not inhibited by bad weather or darkness.[90] Thus, when President Nixon needed a bombing plan, while it was not exactly "on the shelf," the fundamentals had been addressed. The B-52, in addition to having the right combination of accuracy and capability to destroy targets, also possessed an attribute the A-6 lacked: the ability to shock the mind and undermine the spirit.[91]

When Kissinger returned to Washington on 13 December from the Paris peace talks Alexander Haig met him at Andrews AFB. Haig briefed him on the planned bombing campaign as the two men drove to the White House. On 14 December, Nixon ordered that mines be reseeded in Haiphong harbor and that the bombing of North Vietnam's heartland be renewed, the campaign to commence in 72 hours.[92]

On 18 December, Linebacker Two got under way. Sixteen targets had been identified around Hanoi and 13 in and around Haiphong. That first night, three waves of B-52s struck. The first wave bombed Kep, Phuc Yen, and Hoa Lac airfields along with the Yen Vien warehouse complex. A surface-to-air missile downed one B-52 over Yen Vien. During the second wave, striking at midnight, 30 Guam-based B-52s hit targets around Hanoi. A second B-52 was heavily damaged by SAMs, but limped to Thailand before it crashed. Just before dawn a third wave of B-52s struck near Hanoi and a third bomber went down.[93]

During Linebacker One, MiGs had proven more troublesome than SAMs. Since Linebacker Two would be conducted almost entirely at night, the MiG threat had lessened, but SAMs proved an unpleasant surprise. Given the kind of "jungle-bashing" missions SAC had flown in Southeast Asia and its ongoing commitment to the nuclear mission, that the B-52 crews were shocked by their sudden exposure to this threat is understandable.

Since 1965 the effectiveness of the SA-2s had been steadily degraded not only by the application of electronic countermeasures and the employment of Wild Weasels but also through maneuvers devised, tested, used, and passed along among aircrews of the Tactical Air Command. SAC crews, however, had little experience with the SA-2s. Not until November 1972 was a B-52 lost to a SAM. While the North Vietnamese used a new electronic band for missile tracking during Linebacker, that was not the problem. Poor tactics and a good dose of overconfidence combined to make the first few nights of Linebacker Two nightmarish for the B-52 crews.

The three B-52s lost on the first night, given that 121 sorties were flown, represented an acceptable loss rate. Two of the losses could be rationalized. There were high winds over North Vietnam that boosted the B-52s' speed to over 600 miles an hour on the inbound leg but slowed them to around 400 miles an hour on the way out. Furthermore, the winds dispersed the chaff so that the second and third waves were "naked." With losses two and three conveniently blamed on the weather, the lone remaining loss on the first wave was not only acceptable but, all things considered, not bad. With two of the three losses factored out, one plane out of 121 was less than a 1-percent loss rate. On the second night of Linebacker Two, no aircraft were lost despite the fact that the North Vietnamese defender fired 200 SAMs. A false sense of security set in, only to be shattered the next night when six B-52s were downed in a nine-hour period.[94]

Initially, Linebacker Two was supposed to last only three days. But on 21 December the president ordered it extended indefinitely. Crews, shocked by the losses on the third night, protested the tactics, which were ill-suited to the defenses around Hanoi and Haiphong.[95]

Only the most ardent apologist for air power could argue that a 6-percent loss rate was acceptable, especially in a limited war and for a weapons system as precious as the B-52. To understand how those losses occurred, one has to look into the holy of holies—Headquarters Strategic Air Command. There, mission planning, focused as it had been on getting the bombers over the target, failed to consider the differences between traditional Arc Light missions—which entailed dumping bombs on undefended jungle areas—and flying into what Air Force intelligence had rated as the world's third best air defense, ranked after that of the Soviet Union and Israel. On jungle-bashing Arc Light missions, fragmentation orders were written to consider fuel consumption in relation to bomb load, turn points, bomb release points, and altitudes. The fact that Linebacker Two missions were to be flown at night may have lessened concern about enemy defenses since darkness negated both the MiG and AAA threat. Furthermore, SAC mission planners may not have had enough regard for the SA-2s that ringed Hanoi and Haiphong. They were accustomed to considering missions that would take the B-52s into the Soviet Union where defenses consisted of much more sophisticated missiles than the old SA-2s given to North Vietnam. The critical differences were that B-52s would penetrate Soviet air space at low altitude, after US missiles presumably had already taken a toll on the Soviet defenses. In contrast, the B-52s, with their large radar returns, would be flying at about 30,000 feet over North Vietnam and would fly within parameters that would allow the SA-2 to operate at maximum effectiveness. This oversight led to flawed tactics in North Vietnamese airspace. Years of jungle bashing and the routines of planning for nuclear war had fostered a mind-set within SAC that nearly led to disaster.

Whereas Linebacker One was the first modern bombing campaign in aerial warfare, Linebacker Two was more of a throwback to World War II's era of B-29s ambling over their target cities in long bomber streams. The bomber streams during the first three nights of Linebacker Two were up to 70 miles in length. In three-plane cells, the B-52s lumbered toward North Vietnam in what was described as "an elephant walk," flying one after another into one of the world's best air defense systems. This queuing up of the attackers made it relatively easy for the SAM operators. If they knew where the first 25 bombers had gone, it was pretty easy to tell when and where to expect number 26 to show up.[96]

Because of crew dissatisfaction and the possibility that losses at the rate experienced on the third night would have proven unacceptable, SAC had to make some changes. As a "quick fix," on the fourth night, 21 December, only U Tapao B-52Ds, older models with upgraded ECM, flew against North Vietnam. Newer B-52Gs, many of which had not been modified with ECM to counteract the less sophisticated SA-2s, reverted to Arc Light missions over South Vietnam. Also on the fourth night, the B-52s approached the targets from different directions, with cells reaching their bomb release points within a few minutes of each other, thus lessening the predictability that had resulted from the elephant walk of the first three nights. Additionally, the bombers flew at varying altitudes and the immediate turns after bomb release were eliminated in favor of longer, more shallow turns which did not make for the kind of bright radar returns a B-52 can give off in a 45-degree bank. Exits from North Vietnam were quicker and the crews were authorized to make random changes in altitude to further complicate the job of the SAM operators below.[97]

On the fifth night of Linebacker Two, B-52s pounded Haiphong's petroleum storage areas and nearby railroad yards. Using new tactics, the B-52s escaped battle damage completely. Only one B-52 was lost the next night and one more on Christmas Eve, bringing the total to 11 losses when a 36-hour stand down for Christmas took effect.

Both the North Vietnamese and the Americans used the 36-hour respite in the bombing to prepare for the next round. While the Vietnamese restocked their SAM sites, planners and staff officers at Andersen, U Tapao, Saigon, and Omaha came up with the next phase of Linebacker Two: an all-out attack on the North Vietnamese air defenses.

B-52 crews on Guam. Although Air Force crews on Guam during Linebacker Two did not "mutiny," they were disturbed over the rigid tactics that dominated the first three days of operations—tactics which resulted in the loss of nine B-52s.

B-52 taking off on bombing mission in Southeast Asia. During Linebacker Two, B-52s from Andersen AB, Guam, flew 739 sorties over North Vietnam and dropped 15,000 tons of explosives. North Vietnamese air defenses claimed 15 of them.

The shift to attacking the enemy's air defense had both tactical and strategic objectives. Tactically, those defenses had to be degraded to preclude further losses of B-52s. Losing a B-52 was symbolically, as well as operationally, more significant than losing any number of fighter-bombers. Had B-52 losses continued to mount, it might have been necessary to abdicate the campaign to North Vietnam's defenses—in other words, accept defeat. But, if Hanoi's defenses were destroyed, not only could B-52s bomb with very little threat to themselves but also North Vietnam would be totally at the mercy of the United States, thus making a strategic victory possible. The B-52s could continue attacking what was left of North Vietnam's war-making capacity and, if the president so desired, they could move on to bombing neighborhoods and dikes.

By Christmas most of the legitimate targets in North Vietnam were in pretty much of a shambles. Linebacker One had inflicted considerable damage; Linebacker Two only intensified the devastation. Since the 18th of December an additional 350 railcars and a few more locomotives had been destroyed. Linebacker Two "rerubbled" railway marshalling yards and storage areas that had been devastated earlier. Harbors were resown with fresh mines and the port facilities at Haiphong and the river port at Hanoi were in ruins. Petroleum storage facilities were obliterated, except for the small depots of a hundred or so barrels each—certainly not enough to sustain 14 divisions of troops 500 miles away.[98]

Still, Hanoi gave no indication it was ready to sign an agreement. The essence of deterrence is to make the other side fear what *might* happen. So far, from 1965 to Christmas Day 1972, air power had not had that effect on Hanoi's politburo. And, as long as North Vietnam's defense could exact a high price in downed bombers, Hanoi had a chance. As Christmas night fell, North Vietnam's leaders could still hope that if enough B-52s were brought down, if too many new prisoners of war were added to the rolls at Hoa Lo Prison, and if they could hold out until the new Congress convened in late January, what had been lost on the battlefield might yet be attained.

Were North Vietnam left defenseless, however, the possibilities might be ominous. With all legitimate targets such as railroad marshalling yards, storage areas, military barracks, and ports gone, what was left? The dikes and the neighborhoods?

Beginning the day after Christmas, the Air Force and the Navy went after airfields, SAM sites, and communications centers. Prior to each night's B-52 raids, F-111s struck the MiG fields to keep the MiGs on the ground. During these raids three MiG-21s were destroyed along with an Il-28 Beagle bomber and several transports. These attacks were designed to force the North Vietnamese to "keep their heads down" and not to destroy the NVNAF. After the F-111s swooshed in at low altitude to drop their cluster bombs and Mk-82 retarded bombs, B-52s then lumbered over to crater the runways and blast the support facilities. At Bac Mai, for instance, two F-111s wiped out a score of buildings before a cell of B-52s obliterated the runway.[99] Similar attacks took place at nine other airfields. MiGs, however, were not the immediate problem. Throughout Linebacker Two, the North Vietnamese launched only 32 MiGs. Still, destroying the MiG bases had a double impact. First, it boosted morale among all aircrews, TAC as well as SAC. Second, it was an investment in the future in that this leg of North Vietnam's defense system was broken.[100]

SAMs were the immediate problem. New tactics had diminished the threat; however, to make Hanoi's leadership feel vulnerable, the SAM leg of the defense system had to be broken as well. Iron Hand flights struck more than 30 SAM sites on 26 December, while B-52s hit two SAM support facilities. However, these attacks only fended off the SAM threat since new missiles could be trucked to repaired sites, or new sites could be built with relative ease.[101]

North Vietnam had no SAM production facilities. It imported the missiles by rail or sea, and then assembled them. The largest SAM assembly facility was in the heart of a Hanoi neighborhood where an attack by B-52s could have caused a prohibitive number of civilian casualties. Only precision-guided bombs were accurate enough to destroy the assembly plant without causing extensive collateral damage to surrounding buildings and houses. But the weather was overcast, precluding the use of LGBs and EOGBs.

Since virtually all the B-52 operations were conducted at night, the limited visibility due to bad weather had little effect on their missions. While the weather remained lousy, it cleared enough so that on 26 December 16 F-4s using loran bombing techniques could drop conventional bombs through the overcast into the SAM assembly area. They destroyed the facility completely.[102]

The war may have come down to one day: 26 December. If air power took the day and destroyed enemy defenses rendering North Vietnam defenseless, then its cities and dikes would be vulnerable to attack. Whether or not the United States would have bombed them is highly questionable, but that decision would have been entirely up to Washington. If, on the other hand, the defense system had survived to claim many more B-52s, it might well have been that Hanoi could have gained the upper hand long enough to stall the talks until Congress mandated an end to the fighting. It was a power game. Hanoi's hope rested on actions that might be taken on perceptions that the bombing had become too costly and, perhaps, too barbaric for the American people and their Congress to support. Washington's advantage was in its military arsenal and the options it afforded *if* used imaginatively and innovatively.

During the night of 26 December, 120 B-52s hit a variety of targets nearly simultaneously. The raids were over within a 15-minute period. An additional 100 aircraft, including F-111s, F-4s, and Navy A-6s struck SAM sites and radar sites before, during, and after the B-52 raids. One B-52 was shot down near Hanoi. A second one was damaged but struggled back to Thailand, only to crash just short of U Tapao's runway. All in all, the "eighth day of Christmas" was a rousing success, quite possibly the single most successful day of bombing in the history of aerial warfare when you consider it led to the end of America's longest war.[103]

Although air attacks continued for three more days, Hanoi had blinked, perhaps fearing that the war could be lost forever. Before the 26th had ended, Washington received a message from Hanoi that both condemned "extermination bombing" and proposed that peace talks resume in Paris on 8 January. Nixon's return message demanded that technical talks begin on 2 January with formal negotiations getting under way on the eighth. He added that as soon as arrangements were made to begin the technical talks, the bombing above 20 degrees north latitude would end. Meanwhile, the bombing of the heartland continued, albeit at a reduced rate. On 27 December two more B-52s were lost, but these were the last. North Vietnam had depleted their SAM supply, F-4s had wrecked their largest missile assembly facility, their command and control system was degraded, and the primary MiG bases were unusable: North Vietnam was virtually defenseless against B-52 attacks. Hanoi and Washington completed arrangements for the technical talks to begin. The bombing above 20 degrees north latitude stopped on 29 December.[104] Linebacker Two was over.

- - - - - - - - -

The "Eleven-Day War" became shrouded in myth and the subject of controversy. Within the Air Force in the post-Vietnam Era, it was an article of faith that Linebacker Two had "brought Hanoi to its knees." Simultaneously, "the Christmas bombing" gained near iconographic status in antiwar theology, especially among those who would hold that it constituted "another Dresden." Both interpretations were wrong.

During the eleven days of Linebacker Two, B-52s flew 729 sorties north of 20 degrees latitude and 10 sorties into the southern panhandle. They dropped 15,237 tons of bombs over 34 targets.[105] Fighter-bombers added another 5,000 tons of bombs. The damage to targets hit by B-52s was significant. Rail yards, storage areas, and airfields were destroyed, but while the damage and destruction were extensive in terms of rubble created, it had little immediate operational impact on the PAVN units inside South Vietnam. Most of these targets had been bombed during Linebacker One, and the transportation system was already a shambles. What Linebacker Two contributed was much more in accordance with traditional concepts of strategic bombing in that it had a psychological impact on Hanoi's leadership. That, coupled with the destruction of North Vietnam's air defense system, finally compelled a return to meaningful peace negotiations.

On 2 January technical talks resumed. Le Duc Tho and Henry Kissinger met on 8 January. Before the first session had concluded, all points of contention except the issue of the demilitarized zone and the method for signing the documents had been resolved.[106] These were not, however, insignificant issues.

Meanwhile, B-52s continued bombing south of 20 degrees latitude, and in South Vietnam Arc Light strikes focused on PAVN encampments and staging areas. This bombing was to encourage Hanoi to negotiate expeditiously. Certainly, however, the politburo knew that on 2 January, the day the technical talks resumed, the House Democratic caucus voted 154 to 75 to cut off all funding for military operations in Indochina contingent only on the safe withdrawal of remaining American forces and the return of the

POWs. Two days later, the Senate Democratic caucus passed a similar resolution.[107] While these were only party resolutions and did not carry the force of law, the Communist old guard could still hope. However, if it had no viable army inside South Vietnam, victory might never come, not even over the long haul of history.

On 9 January the peace was won or lost, depending on one's perspective. The DMZ issue was "resolved," albeit more to Hanoi's liking than Washington's or Saigon's. The North Vietnamese acknowledged that such a place existed; the United States agreed to a clause stating that whatever the DMZ might be, it was "not a political or territorial boundary."[108] The issue of who would sign the peace agreement cut to the heart of the matter, as did the issue of whether South Vietnam had a legitimate political boundary. Saigon refused to dignify the national liberation front (NLF) by signing the agreement in their presence. Hanoi refused to acknowledge that the Saigon regime existed as anything other than an American puppet. So who signed what and in whose presence was significant. Washington and Hanoi agreed to sign on separate pages with their "clients" the NLF and the Thieu regime signing with them.[109]

Otherwise, the peace agreement was pretty much what had been negotiated the previous October. It was still hardly palatable to President Thieu. Nixon, Kissinger, and Haig had cajoled, reassured, and finally intimidated Thieu into accepting it. In a personal letter of 5 January, Nixon promised, "We will respond with full force should the settlement be violated by North Vietnam."[110] Since American ground troops were all but gone, "full force" could only mean American air power. Furthermore, "full" implied the kind of force used in Linebacker Two. Air power, marvelous in its flexibility, had succeeded in bombing a United States ally into accepting its own surrender.

Thieu knew that but he did not accede easily. In a letter on 17 January, Nixon told Thieu that the United States would initial the Paris Agreement on 21 January and sign the formal documents on the 27th, with or without South Vietnam. Nixon threatened "a total cutoff of funds," if Saigon did not sign the agreement.[111] Given no viable choice Thieu capitulated, and on 27 January the United States and the Republic of Vietnam, along with the People's Democratic Republic of Vietnam and the national liberation front, signed the Agreement on Ending the War and Restoring the Peace in Vietnam. It provided for the final withdrawal of US forces from the South, the return of American prisoners of war, and little else. The bombing of North and South Vietnam, however, came to an end.

FM JCS/NMCC
TO AIG 707A6

> THIS IS AN EXECUTIVE MESSAGE. EFFECTIVE 272359Z JAN 73, AN INTERNATIONALLY SUPERVISED CEASE-FIRE IN SVN AND THE DMZ WILL BE INSTITUTED. AT THAT TIME, DISCONTINUE ALL ACTS OF FORCE INITIATED BY US FORCES IN NVN AND SVN AND THE DMZ. ALL AIRSTRIKES, ARTILLERY FIRE, AND NAVAL BOMBARDMENT AS WELL AS OTHER FIRE OR MUNITIONS EXPENDITURE TARGETED AGAINST NVN OR SVN AND THE DMZ ARE PROHIBITED.[112]

Secretary Seamans has said it best: "It wasn't that it was finished, it was a loser."

Notes

1. Dr Robert C. Seamans, Jr., interviews with Lt Col Lyn R. Officer and Hugh N. Ahmann, September 1973, November 1972, and March 1974, Washington D.C., interview 687, US Air Force Oral History Program, 149, K239.0512, USAF Historical Research Center (USAFHRC), Maxwell AFB, Ala.

2. "Air Force Association's 1970–1971 Statement of Policy," *Air Force Magazine*, November 1970, 8.

3. Dr Robert C. Seamans, Jr., "Improving Things for People," *Air Force Magazine*, November 1971, 64.

4. Col Stanley M. Umstead, Jr., wing commander, 388th Tactical Fighter Wing, end-of-tour report, April 1971–August 1972, 26 December 1972, 6, K717.131, USAFHRC (hereinafter Umstead, EOTR).

5. Col Lyle E. Mann, commander 432d Tactical Fighter Wing, end-of-tour report, 7 November 1970–6 November 1971, 1 November 1971, 15, K717.131, USAFHRC (hereinafter Mann, EOTR).

6. Umstead, EOTR, 6.

7. Maj Edward W. Parker, Jr., director of base medical services, Korat Royal Thai Air Force Base (RTAFB), end-of-tour report, 1 July 1971–1 July 1972, 10 July 1972, 2, K717.141, USAFHRC.

8. Col E. J. Walsh, commander, 56th Special Operations Wing, end-of-tour report, August 1970–16 July 1971, 21 July 1971, I-3, K717.131, USAFHRC.

9. Col Theodore M. Katz, commander, 432 Combat Support Group, Udorn RTAFB, end-of-tour report, 28 April 1970–2 May 1971, 1–3, K717.131, USAFHRC.

10. Maj Gen Alton D. Slay, deputy chief of staff for operations, Seventh Air Force, end-of-tour report, August 1971–August 1972, August 1972, 20, K740.131, USAFHRC (hereinafter Slay, EOTR).

11. See Jack S. Ballard, *Development of Employment of Fixed-Wing Gunships, 1962–1972* (Washington, D.C.: Office of Air Force History, 1982), 111; and "USAF Operations in Laos: 1 January 1970–30 June 1971," Headquarters Pacific Air Forces (PACAF), 30 May 1972, 22–25, K717.0423-6, USAFHRC.

12. Slay, EOTR, 30. From my personal observation as an intelligence officer at Headquarters Seventh/Thirteenth Air Force in 1970–1971, I can attest to the routines and priorities of shift workers who monitored trail movements at night while preparing for the morning briefings.

13. History, Air Force Intelligence Service, FY 1973, AFIN Linebacker Two Summary, vol. 3, supporting documents, 6, K142.01, USAFHRC.

14. Slay, EOTR, 21.

15. See Sir Robert Thompson, *Peace Is Not at Hand* (New York: David McKay, 1974), 82–84; and David Fulghum and Terrence Maitland, *South Vietnam on Trial: Mid 1970 to 1972*, The Vietnam Experience (Boston: Boston Publishing, 1984), 116.

16. Mann, EOTR, 30.

17. Ibid., 29.

18. See *The United States Air Force in Southeast Asia, 1961–1973: An Illustrated Account*, ed. Carl Berger (Washington, D.C.: Office of Air Force History, 1977), 172; and *Airpower and the 1972 Spring Invasion*, ed. A. F. C. Lavalle (Washington, D.C.: Government Printing Office, 1978), 34.

19. Henry Kissinger, *The White House Years* (Boston: Little, Brown, 1979), 1099–1100.

20. Lavalle, *Airpower*, 3.

21. Lt Gen Phillip B. Davidson, *Vietnam at War: The History, 1946–1975* (Novato, Calif.: Presidio Press, 1988), 701–2.

22. John L. Frisbee, "VNAF Meets the Test," *Air Force Magazine*, June 1972, 53.

23. "History of Linebacker Operations," 10 May 1972–23 October 1972, Headquarters PACAF, 1973, 3–5, K740.04-24, USAFHRC.

24. Ibid.

25. Davidson, 673.

26. Kissinger, 1098.

27. See Dave Richard Palmer, *Summons of the Trumpet: U.S.-Vietnam in Perspective* (San Rafael, Calif.: Presidio Press, 1978), 250–51; and Fulghum and Maitland, 128.

28. Davidson, 687–88.

29. Slay, EOTR, 42.

30. John L. Frisbee, "The Air War in Vietnam," *Air Force Magazine*, September 1972, 51–52.

31. See Earl H. Tilford, Jr., *The United States Air Force Search and Rescue in Southeast Asia, 1961–1975* (Washington, D.C.: Office of Air Force History, 1980), 118–19; and Slay, EOTR, 68.

32. Edward Doyle and Samuel Lipsman, *Setting the Stage*, The Vietnam Experience (Boston: Boston Publishing, 1981), 107.

33. Col Howard B. Fisher, quoted in Lavalle, *Airpower*, 46.

34. Slay, EOTR, 69.

35. See "History of Linebacker," 3–5; and Lavalle, *Airpower*, table II-2, Summary of B-52 Deployments, 27.

36. Mark Clodfelter, *The Limits of Air Power: The American Bombing of North Vietnam* (New York: Free Press, 1989), 154.

37. See Vogt's account of his conversation with the president in Fulghum and Maitland, 142.

38. Richard Nixon, *RN: The Memoirs of Richard Nixon* (New York: Grosset and Dunlap, 1978), 606–7.

39. See "History of Linebacker," 7–8; *The Tale of Two Bridges and the Battle for the Skies over North Vietnam*, ed. Maj A. J. C. Lavalle et al., vol. 1, monographs 1 and 2, USAF Southeast Asia Monograph Series (Washington, D.C.: Government Printing Office, 1974), 84; and Kissinger, 1121–23.

40. See Davidson, 692–93; Fulghum and Maitland, 156; and Slay, EOTR, 156.

41. See Davidson, 697; and Thompson, 108.

42. Lavalle, *Airpower*, 98.

43. Ibid., 99.

44. Slay, EOTR, 51.

45. Thompson, 109.

46. Slay, EOTR, 42.

47. Lavalle, *Airpower*, 58.

48. Kissinger, 1306–7.

49. See John Morrocco, *Rain of Fire: Air War, 1969–1973*, The Vietnam Experience (Boston: Boston Publishing, 1985), 130; Melvin F. Porter, "Linebacker: Overview of the First 120 Days," Project CHECO, Headquarters

PACAF, 27 September 1973, 16–17, K717.0414-42, USAFHRC; and Fulghum and Maitland, 170.

50. Porter, 11.

51. Ibid., 1.

52. Kissinger, 1178.

53. Nixon, 606.

54. Kissinger, 1178.

55. Gen John W. Vogt, Jr., commander, Seventh Air Force, interview with Claude G. Morita, 12 November 1972, interview 723, USAF Project CHECO Office, 58, K717.0414-42, USAFHRC.

56. Porter, 36–37.

57. Ibid., 31.

58. Guenter Lewy, *America in Vietnam* (New York: Oxford University Press, 1978), 411.

59. Morrocco, 131.

60. Nguyen Tien Hung and Jerrold L. Schecter, *The Palace File: Vietnam Secret Documents* (New York: Harper and Row, 1986), 58.

61. See Kissinger, 1195 and 1309; and Thompson, 125.

62. Kissinger, 1344.

63. Clodfelter, 166.

64. Walter P. Schlitz, "Aerospace World," *Air Force Magazine*, November 1972, 26.

65. Lavalle et al., *Tale of Two Bridges*, 156–57.

66. "History of Linebacker," 14.

67. "Analytical Notes on Support/Strike," PACAF/DOA briefing script, 11 October 1972, unnumbered pages, K239.031-51, USAFHRC.

68. "History of Linebacker," 75; and "The Battle for the Skies over North Vietnam" (Maxwell AFB, Ala.: Air Command and Staff College), 71–72.

69. "History of Linebacker," 51–52.

70. Clodfelter, 165.

71. Vogt interview, 68.

72. Col Patrick J. Breitling, "Guided Bomb Operations in SEA: The Weather Dimension, 1 February–31 December 1972," Project CHECO, Headquarters PACAF, 1 October 1973, 7–9. The laser-guided bomb was a standard 500-, 2,000- or 3,000-pound bomb mated to a laser sensor. The Mk-82 500-pound bomb produced too little blast to warrant the $1,600 investment needed to turn it into a precision-guided bomb. The 3,000-pound bomb provided a good blast, but its fins were too small for the size and weight, meaning that while it fell in a straight trajectory the bomb was difficult to maneuver. Its size and shape created a great deal of drag on the aircraft hauling it to the target, thus cutting speed and range. The Mk-84 2,000-pound bomb became the weapon of choice as an LGB. It was large enough to inflict considerable destruction and was relatively maneuverable. The F-4s could carry two Mk-84s without significantly reducing range or inhibiting aircraft handling characteristics.

73. Vogt interview, 59.

74. Slay, EOTR, 81–82.

75. Edward Ulsamer, "Airpower Halts an Invasion," *Air Force Magazine*, September 1972, 67.

76. Breitling, 36.

77. Vogt interview, 62–63.

78. Slay, EOTR, 89.

79. "Battle for the Skies," 57–58.

80. Samuel Lipsman and Stephen Weiss, *The False Peace: 1972–1974*, The Vietnam Experience (Boston: Boston Publishing, 1985), 9–10.

81. Thompson, 125.

82. Kissinger, 1378; and Bui Diem and David Chanoff, *In the Jaws of History* (Boston: Houghton Mifflin, 1987), 301.

83. Kissinger, 1390.

84. Lipsman and Weiss, 16.

85. See Walter Scott Dillard, *Sixty Days to Peace: Implementing the Paris Accords, Vietnam 1973* (Washington, D.C.: National Defense University Press, 1982), 115; Dana Bell, *Air War over Vietnam*, vol. 3 (London: Arms and Armour Press, 1983), 49; and Lipsman and Weiss, 18.

86. Hung and Schecter, 136–37.

87. Lipsman and Weiss, 21.

88. Kissinger, 444.

89. Harvey Smith et al., *North Vietnam: A Country Study* (Washington, D.C.: Department of the Army, 1967), 12.

90. W. Hays Parks, "Linebacker and the Law of War," *Air University Review* 34, no. 2 (January–February 1983): 16–17.

91. Kissinger, 448–49.

92. Nixon, 734.

93. "Battle for the Skies," 88–89.

94. See John T. Greenwood, "B-52s: Strategic Bombers in Tactical Role," in *The Vietnam War: The Illustrated History of the Conflict in Southeast Asia*, ed. Ray Bonds (New York: Crown Publishers, 1979), 206; and Kenneth P. Werrell, "Linebacker II: The Decisive Use of Air Power?" *Air University Review* 38, no. 2 (January–March 1987): 53.

95. To say the crews mutined, as some have suggested, is a gross overstatement. The general feeling among B-52 crews—a very subjective thing to gauge—was what it seemed to be throughout SAC and the Air Force: air power was, at last, going to be used as it was meant to be. Of course, crews going into combat were apprehensive and afraid. The number of patients reporting for sick call at the dispensary at Andersen AFB, Guam, rose from an average of 35 a day to 55, but not all of the patients were B-52 crewmen. Considering the number of people at Andersen and that they were working long shifts, this increase is not remarkable. In any event, this trend hardly constitutes a rebellion. See Clodfelter, 193.

96. Morrocco, 149.

97. "Battle for the Skies," 95.

98. House Committee on Appropriations, Subcommittee on the Department of Defense, *DOD Appropriations: Bombings of North Vietnam Hearings before the Subcommittee on the Department of Defense*, 93d Cong., 1st sess., testimony of Adm Thomas H. Moorer, chairman, Joint Chiefs of Staff, 9 and 18 January 1973, 7–10 (hereinafter Moorer testimony).

99. Air Force Intelligence Service briefing script, "Linebacker Two, 18–29 December, 1972," in History, AFIS, FY 73, 11–12 (hereinafter AFIS Linebacker Two Briefing).

100. Moorer testimony, 9 January, 11.

101. AFIS Linebacker Two Briefing, 12.

102. Parks, 20.

103. See Clodfelter, 188; and Greenwood, "Strategic Bombers in a Tactical Role," 208.

104. Admiral Moorer reported to Congress that 350 railroad cars and 200 storage buildings had been destroyed. Electric power generating capability was reduced to between 17,000 and 24,000 kilowatts from 92,000 kilowatts. (Moorer testimony, 9 January, 10). For the sequence of events leading to renewed negotiations, see Kissinger, 1458–59; and Nixon, 741.

105. Moorer testimony, 18 January, 40–41.

106. Kissinger, 1463.

107. Nixon, 742.

108. Lipsman and Weiss, 29.

109. Kissinger, 1465.

110. See Richard Nixon to Nguyen Van Thieu, 5 January 1973, in Hung and Schecter, appendix A, letter 18, 392.

111. Nixon to Thieu, 17 January 1973, ibid., 393.

112. See 42d Bombardment Wing History, 1972, vol. 2, supporting documents, message file, K-WG42HI, USAFHRC.

Chapter 6

Completing the Setup

Contrary to what many believed and hoped, the fighting did not end with the signing of the cease-fire agreement in Paris on 23 January 1973. Although the bombing stopped in North and South Vietnam, it continued over Laos and Cambodia. Because the cease-fire in Vietnam released a large number of sorties, the bombing in the rest of Indochina increased accordingly.

Meanwhile, US policy unraveled with each passing day. The role President Richard M. Nixon played in the 1972 election year burglary of the Democratic party headquarters in the Watergate, a fashionable Washington condominium and hotel complex, became apparent as the political scandal unfolded. The power of the presidency, fundamental to the effective employment of air power in Indochina that year, waned. A Congress intent on disengagement from Vietnam, old political foes who sensed a wounded Nixon, and a public sapped of its will by years of frustration over the war combined to confound the direction of American policy in the months after the penning of the Paris Accords.

Laos: Coming Full Circle

When a circle is drawn, it ends at the same point where it began. Similarly, when the bombing stopped in Vietnam, American policy was where it had been a dozen years before, focused on Laos. As was the case during the Kennedy presidency and in the early months of the Johnson administration, the Air Force was bombing Laos and doing so to affect Hanoi's behavior. Interdiction had become, at best, a secondary objective since the

United States had already agreed that Hanoi could maintain an army of 100,000 inside South Vietnam.

The North Vietnamese, however, violated the Paris Accords by funnelling additional soldiers into South Vietnam. In northern Laos the Pathet Lao and their ally, the People's Army of Vietnam (PAVN), moved west, gobbling up as much territory as possible in anticipation of a cease-fire. In Vientiane, Premier Souvanna Phouma searched for a way to keep his country independent after the United States completed its withdrawal from Indochina. Despite a decade of fighting, the civil war in Laos had not changed in its dynamics—it had only become bloodier as a result of participation by the North Vietnamese, Thais, and Americans.

There were certainly valid reasons for the United States to continue bombing Laos in the early months of 1973. Hanoi blatantly violated article 20 of the Paris Accords, which specified that all foreign troops be withdrawn from Laos and Cambodia and forbade the use of those countries as corridors of infiltration or staging areas for attacks on South Vietnam.[1] Air Force B-52s and fighter-bombers stationed in Thailand, so recently engaged in Linebacker Two, stood down for a few days after the signing of the Paris Accords. However, by mid-February the sortie output rivaled that of the "Eleven-Day War." Before the month was out, B-52s had flown 1,147 sorties in Laos. They hit 286 targets in northern Laos, including truck parks and storage areas. Along the Ho Chi Minh Trail and in areas west of the infiltration corridor, B-52 crews flew 948 Arc Light sorties and bombed 426 targets, including truck parks, storage areas, and staging bases—from the Mu Gia Pass south to the Cambodian border. In addition, Air Force aircraft bombed PAVN and Pathet Lao units massing for an attack on Paksong, the last Royal Laotian stronghold on the Bolovens Plateau—the strategic high ground overlooking the Mekong River.[2]

While the fighting and the bombing of Laos continued, Henry Kissinger and Le Duc Tho, along with the various Lao parties, moved toward a cease-fire there. A cessation of hostilities in Laos, at least a temporary one, worked to Hanoi's advantage. It required the United States to stop bombing. Given the weakened condition of the Nixon presidency, the North Vietnamese were savvy enough to know that once a major step had been undertaken, it would be nearly impossible for the beleaguered president to reverse it. They also knew that the American public was beginning to learn more about the "secret war" in Laos. A sensationalized but flawed account of the narcotics trade in Indochina, *The Politics of Heroin in Southeast Asia*, by Alfred G. McCoy, Cathleen B. Reed, and Leonard P. Adams, accused the Central Intelligence Agency, its contract airline Air America, and the Air Force of working with Laotian drug lords to produce and smuggle heroin from the Golden Triangle area of northwestern Laos. These revelations, however inaccurate or overstated, weakened the administration's already damaged credibility. All things considered, it was to Hanoi's advantage to compel their Pathet Lao clients to sign the cease-fire agreement, which took effect at noon Vientiane time on 22 February 1973.[3]

Two days after the cease-fire was signed, Pathet Lao and PAVN units occupied Paksong. Over the next two days, there were 28 violations of the cease-fire, most of them initiated by the Communists. On 24 February B-52s and fighter-bombers returned to action over Laos for two days of bombing.[4] The bombing stopped again on 26 February after Hanoi halted the ground offensive and returned to moving as many troops and as much tonnage in supplies as possible down the Ho Chi Minh Trail and into South Vietnam prior to the beginning of the monsoonal rains. By mid-April they had moved an estimated 40,000 additional troops, 300 tanks, 150 heavy artillery pieces, 160 antiaircraft guns, and 300 trucks into South Vietnam.[5]

Henry Kissinger pushed for a renewed bombing of the trail. His efforts foundered when the Joint Chiefs of Staff insisted that any attack on targets in southeastern Laos would have to be coupled with bombing of adjacent areas in North and South Vietnam from which newly established SA-2 sites might menace B-52s bombing the trail. Nixon did order the B-52s back into action on 16 and 17 April, but their targets were Pathet Lao and PAVN encampments in northern Laos around Ban Tha Vieng—a key town south of the Plain of Jars—and not the Ho Chi Minh Trail.[6] Sending B-52s back over Laos caused considerable outcry, but restarting the bombing of North Vietnam and South Vietnam was politically infeasible and Nixon hesitated to do so.

Although not of the proportions of the 1968 Tet offensive or the spring invasion of 1972, April 1973 was another watershed in America's Vietnam experience. By not reacting forcefully to Hanoi's violations of the Paris Accords, Washington abdicated its role as guardian and guarantor of South Vietnam's independence. The deteriorating domestic political scene took away Nixon's ability to use bombing as an effective stick. Simultaneously, Congress withdrew the carrot by forbidding payment of the $3 billion in aid the administration had promised Hanoi in January so that it could rebuild its shattered industries. Stories of torture related by returning prisoners of war and Hanoi's disregard for the Paris Accords led Sen Harry Byrd to sponsor an amendment barring assistance to North Vietnam unless specifically authorized by Congress. It passed by a vote of 83 to 3.[7] Consequently, the administration had neither the threat of bombing to compel nor the promise of aid to induce Hanoi into abiding by the accords. By April 1973 Hanoi, not Washington, had the initiative in Indochina and the fates of South Vietnam and Cambodia were sealed.

Cambodia

While the North Vietnamese controlled events in Laos, and increasingly took charge of defining Saigon's future, their claim to have had no influence over Cambodia's Khmer Rouge turned out to be true. From 1970 to 1972 the North Vietnamese army and the Vietcong carried the brunt of the war against the Lon Nol government. Beginning in 1972, however, the Khmer Rouge took over the bulk of the fighting and the conflict became much more of a civil war.[8] Furthermore, the Khmer Rouge hated Vietnamese Communists about as much as they hated any other Vietnamese, maybe more since matters of ideological interpretation were involved. Reports of Khmer Rouge and Communist Vietnamese units clashing in the border regions increased in number. The cease-fires in South Vietnam and Laos did not lead to any decrease in the fighting in Cambodia. And, when the bombs stopped falling elsewhere in Indochina, the air forces of the United States focused all their efforts on Cambodia, and the Khmer Rouge suffered accordingly. Despite the bombing, the war was not going well for the Phnom Penh regime. The capital was, by early 1973, surrounded by the Khmer Rouge. The FANK (*Forces Armée National Khmer*) had abandoned much of the countryside, holding onto only a few larger towns.[9] Air power probably saved the Lon Nol government in 1973, but by then the bombing was more the death rattle of a failed American policy than it was part of any coherent strategy to preserve the independence of Cambodia.

After the cease-fire in Laos, fighter-bombers from Air Force units in Thailand began operating over Cambodia, many for the first time. Until then the 432d Tactical Reconnaissance Wing at Udorn Royal Thai Air Force Base (RTAFB), for instance, had not sent planes as far south as Cambodia. However, between 24 February and 15 August (the latter the congressionally mandated date that the bombing was to halt), the wing's F-4s and RF-4s flew 7,557 sorties over the Khmer Republic, a sortie rate approximated by other tactical wings based at Ubon and Korat RTAFBs.[10]

On 25 and 26 February, 60 B-52s struck targets around the Chup rubber plantation, marking the beginning of one of the more intense bombing campaigns in a war that had produced a plethora of record-setting bombing efforts. Air action over the Khmer Republic increased through mid-March, when Arc Light sorties averaged 60 per day. By April B-52s were flying an average of 80 sorties per day.[11] This bombing undoubtedly helped FANK units reopen major highways linking Phnom Penh to the provincial capital of Battambang in the north and the main port of Kompong Som in the south. B-52s and fighter-bombers also struck Khmer Rouge units entrenched along the Mekong River where they had been firing rockets and recoilless rifles at ships carrying essential supplies from Saigon to Phnom Penh.

Because there were no American advisors with the FANK, and because few Cambodians spoke English, close air support missions like those flown in South Vietnam hardly ever occurred. Instead, the bombing focused on troop concentrations and Khmer Rouge base camps identified by various American intelligence agencies. Furthermore, Cambodia presented unique problems for mission planners and targeteers.

Recall that the secret bombing missions conducted in Cambodia in 1969 and 1970 depended on Combat Skyspot radar stations located in South Vietnam. These stations were dismantled and the controllers withdrawn in early 1973. They had been important because Cambodia's flat, marshy landscape rendered few distinctive radar returns for the B-52 navigators to use as aiming points. The Air Force devised two ways to remedy this situation. First, B-52s began using loran bombing techniques previously employed by fighter-bombers. Second, radar beacons were placed in key towns and villages (for a while one was located on top of the US embassy in Phnom Penh) for airborne radar navigators to use in calculating their bomb release points.

Loran bombing was given the code names Pave Phantom and Pave Buff. It involved a procedure employing highly accurate loran systems in F-111s and F-4s, as well as those installed in a handful of B-52D models, to lead bombers and fighter-bombers to their targets. In effect the Pave Phantom (F-4s or F-111s) and Pave Buff (B-52Ds) aircraft were pathfinders for other aircraft. Pave Buff operations were conducted primarily at night and continued with increasing intensity until the end of the campaign.[12]

The navigator-bombardier in the B-52 plotted the bomb release point off a radial from one of the beacons and fed that information into a computer that directed the plane to the release point. Otherwise, the computer, if tuned to a specific beacon, homed in on it. As an unfortunate consequence of the "fog" of war, on 7 August 1973 a navigator using the beacon placed in Neak Luong, a town on the Mekong River approximately 50 miles southeast of

Phnom Penh, forgot to flip a switch that would have directed the computer to fly the bomber to the offset bombing point and 20 tons of bombs fell on the town. More than 400 people were killed or wounded.[13] The "Neak Luong short round," as the incident was known within the Air Force, was a needless tragedy since only eight more days of bombing remained before the 15 August deadline.

The mandated end of the bombing was the whimper with which America's longest war, and the largest aerial campaigns in the history of warfare, ended. The controversy generated by the bombing throughout Indochina contributed in no small measure to the ultimate fate of Cambodia, as well as to the fates of Laos and South Vietnam. By the late spring of 1973 Congress only reflected the mood of the American people. War weariness and pessimism concerning not only the way the war was fought but how the country was governed had taken a toll on the administration, inhibiting its ability to prevent Congress from ending the bombing. The compulsion to legislate the country out of the war manifested itself on 10 May 1973 when the House of Representatives voted 219 to 188 to block funds for a supplemental appropriations bill needed to fund the air war. President Nixon was so crippled by the mushrooming Watergate scandal that he could not muster the support needed to stop Congress. The best the administration could do was to effect a compromise in the Senate that specified 15 August as a cutoff date. On 29 June the president signed the bill.[14]

By 1973 many Americans were all too willing to view their soldiers, sailors, and airmen jaundicedly. Terms like *warmonger* were much in vogue. It seemed to many in uniform, this writer included, that the public had started hating the warriors as much as they hated the war. Popular perceptions of a military marching in lockstep notwithstanding, the US Air Force was never a monolith in support of the Vietnam War, most especially the way the war was fought. Tensions that tore at the larger society were present in the Air Force. By 1973 there was a feeling within the Air Force that the war had long since been over. Linebacker Two, to be sure, fostered a kind of high among the force. It was welcomed by many who were excited at being "turned loose" to go downtown to Hanoi and Haiphong. If going downtown in a B-52 was dangerous, it was also purposeful. By comparison, bashing paddies in Cambodia seemed as pointless as the bashing of jungles in Vietnam had seemed a year or two before, especially so to "BUFF" crews who had so recently gone downtown.

According to an official SAC history, Col James R. McCarthy, commander of the 43d Strategic Wing, spent half his time meeting with different groups of aircrew members in an effort to address morale problems. He attended crew briefings and met formally and informally with delegations of pilots, navigators, and gunners to discuss their concerns. He invited individual crew members to dine with him at virtually every meal to talk over factors affecting morale. McCarthy attended social functions—barbecues and picnics—to mingle with the men. He also ordered a formal study of their grievances.

The study indicated that B-52 crews were, first and foremost, tired of their indefinite status under Bullet Shot. They wanted to know how long they would be staying on Guam and whether or not they would be forced into another temporary duty (TDY) to U Tapao RTAFB when TAC units in Thailand were withdrawn. Because their TDY deployments under Bullet Shot came up quickly, personal and family matters were left unsettled and those needed attention. Another irritant was that TDY assignments to Southeast Asia did not count as a remote or short tour, meaning the personnel center in San Antonio, Texas, might send them back to Andersen AFB, Guam, or U Tapao RTAFB, to some other Thai base, or to a remote spot elsewhere in the world for a one-year tour. Furthermore, they were dissatisfied with the mission and with the rigors of flying long hours across the Pacific to drop bombs on rice paddies—targets hardly resembling anyone's concept of a vital center. The fact that by the summer of 1973 all bombing would stop on 15 August did little to convince them that their mission had much efficacy.

Additionally, officers fretted about their careers. They perceived that Arc Light TDYs hindered rather than helped their chances for promotion. Traditionally, SAC pilots—even navigators—enjoyed better promotion rates than their counterparts in TAC or MAC, but that was changing. Officers on a six-month TDY received a letter of evaluation (LOE) rather than an officer effectiveness report (OER) for their promotion folders. The LOEs did not seem to carry the same weight with promotion boards as OERs, especially since they were not normally written or endorsed by higher ranking officers. Finally, crews assigned to B-52D and G models were sent on Bullet Shot deployments while those assigned to the B-52H, a model designated for the nuclear mission, were not. Some felt that B-52H crew members, despite the fact that they spent long hours on nuclear alert, had an unfair advantage by being assigned state-side where they could arrange future assignments more easily.[15]

It was not only the relatively junior officers flying the missions who were concerned about bombing Cambodia. Colonels and generals at Headquarters Strategic Air Command were worried as well. Those responsible for personnel matters were alarmed by the increasing number of pilots who were leaving the Air Force for the airlines once their service commitments were over. Planners worried especially about accomplishing the nuclear mission while half the B-52 force was deployed to Andersen and U Tapao. Maintenance specialists fretted about the wear and tear on the already aging B-52s caused by years of hauling large loads of 500-pound and 750-pound bombs on jungle- and paddy-bashing missions. Those officers with an eye on doctrine and the future of the manned bomber were concerned about the ramifications and implications that might arise should the Khmer Rouge take Phnom Penh—in effect, win the war—while B-52s were bombing Cambodia. The future of the manned bomber, which seemed to be constantly under scrutiny in some quarters of the Congress, might be less secure if critics asked what good such expensive and sophisticated airplanes were if they could not deny victory to a third-world guerrilla army. Most of these concerns dissipated after 15 August, when a sigh of relief rose from Omaha because the capital of the Khmer Republic had held out for the duration of the aerial campaign. To be sure, aircrew morale improved when B-52s began returning to their stateside bases.

While Cambodia received less bomb tonnage than any of the other Indochinese states, some 539,129 tons between 1969 and 1973, it was still one of the most intensely bombed countries in the history of aerial warfare. One only has to consider that nearly half those bombs, some 257,465 tons, fell between 24 February and 14 August 1973. Even though much of this energy was wasted in paddy bashing or in bombing fictitious underwater storage areas in the Tonle Sap, a big lake in the middle of Cambodia, it was still an imposing figure—the significance of which was enhanced because it was divorced from a coherent strategy devised to secure the long-range security of Cambodia.[16]

Mayaguez as a Microcosm of the War

While the air war in Indochina ended on 15 August 1973, many more years of fighting and dying lay ahead for the peoples of Vietnam, Laos, and Cambodia. At the end, all the bombs that had fallen throughout nearly 14 years of the American commitment had not prevented the Communists from coming to power. Cambodia was the first to fall when, on 12 April 1975, the Khmer Rouge marched into Phnom Penh. American air power, in Operation Eagle Pull, covered the evacuation of the capital as Marine Corps CH-53 helicopters hauled 276 people, including 82 Americans, 159 Cambodians, and 35 foreign nationals to the safety of US Navy assault carriers in the Gulf of Tonkin.[17] Eagle Pull was the harbinger of things to come. Saigon was evacuated on 28 and 29 April in the much larger Operation Frequent Wind.

Like a nightmare that would not end, the fall of Saigon on 29 April did not mean an end to Americans dying in Indochina. On 12 May several Khmer Rouge patrol boats seized the American-registered cargo ship *Mayaguez*. After its 39-man crew was taken to the Cambodian mainland, President Gerald R. Ford ordered Air

Force units based in Thailand and Navy and Marine forces still in the Gulf of Tonkin following the recently conducted evacuations of Phnom Penh and Saigon to take back the ship and recover its crew. An Air Force CH-53 carrying 18 security policemen from Nakhon Phanom RTAFB to U Tapao RTAFB for possible use in the rescue operation crashed, killing them and the five-man crew.[18]

The *Mayaguez* rescue operation got under way on 14 May. American intelligence erroneously estimated that a company of Khmer Rouge guerrillas was holding the crew on Koh Tang, an island off the Cambodian coast. While a helicopter from a Navy assault carrier took 60 Marines to the decks of the *Mayaguez* to secure the by then totally abandoned vessel, a force of up to 600 Marines at U Tapao prepared for the assault on Koh Tang. The plan called for an Army interpreter, in the first helicopter load of leathernecks, to tell the Khmer Rouge that the Marines had landed and that their only hope of survival lay in immediately handing over the crew of the *Mayaguez*.[19] It did not work out that way.

The Marines landing on Koh Tang island ran into real trouble. The opposition was far greater than expected, and three of the first four helicopters to reach the island were shot down; the fourth, having suffered considerable battle damage, crash landed on the coast of Thailand. Meanwhile, the crew of the *Mayaguez*, having been released from a jail in the port of Kompong Som, was making its way back to the vessel on board a fishing boat. While no Americans were being held on Koh Tang, an estimated force of more than 300 well-entrenched Khmer Rouge was dug in there. An hour after the assault began 54 Marine and Air Force helicopter crewmen were pinned down on the beaches of Koh Tang. Three helicopters were down in the surf off the island, one had crashed in Thailand, and another had been severely damaged but made it back to an assault carrier. Worse, 14 Americans were dead or missing, and what started as a rescue operation for the *Mayaguez* crew turned into a recovery operation to disengage and rescue the assault force.[20]

As Air Force jets and AC-130 Spectre gunships strafed and bombed Khmer Rouge positions, Air Force and Marine choppers carried in a total of 202 additional Marines to recover those trapped on the beaches. Before the day was over, four helicopters were lost and nine others severely damaged. More important, 52 American servicemen had died, three were missing and 49 were wounded during the *Mayaguez* operation.[21]

The *Mayaguez* affair could be construed as a microcosm of America's larger, recently concluded involvement in Indochina. A miscalculation led to the employment of too limited a force to accomplish a mission which, given that the crew had already been released, did not need to be undertaken in the first place. That initial deployment resulted in a situation demanding the deployment of additional forces to avoid disaster, and then the employment of more force and firepower to disengage. In colloquial parlance, the *Mayaguez* recovery operation was a "goat rope," but that did not keep it from becoming a part of the evolving mythology of the Vietnam War.

The Setup Completed

Professor Thomas C. Thayer, in his book *War without Fronts: The American Experience in Vietnam*, argues that the Vietnam War was, in terms of resource allocation and expenditure, first an air war and second a ground war of attrition. Thayer points out that the Air Force built up its forces the fastest, reaching nearly 90 percent of its peak strength by the end of 1966, and remained in the theater the longest of any service, not totally closing down its Thailand-based headquarters until January 1976. Approximately half the money spent on the Vietnam War—about $200 billion (in 1973 dollars)—went to support Air Force, Navy, and Army aerial operations.[22] The air forces of the United States and its allies dropped nearly eight million tons of bombs on Indochina, well over twice the tonnage dropped by the Allied powers in all of World War II. The Air Force, by its own accounting, dropped 6,162,000 of those tons.[23] For all this expenditure of effort, firepower, and resources—not to mention lives—the air war was occasionally pivotal but *it was never decisive.*

In April 1975, when 20 divisions of North Vietnamese troops were headed toward Saigon, with columns of tanks and trucks strung out along Route 1 and other major highways, a perfect situation existed for the effective use of air power. Fighter-bombers and B-52s could have decimated those forces and, perhaps, temporarily averted doom for the Thieu regime. But President Ford did not—indeed, could not—order those planes into action, except to cover the final, ignominious withdrawal from Saigon. After 15 years of costly warfare, which divided and frustrated the American public while it sapped the national will, President Ford found it politically impossible to send American forces back into action for a cause which had been lost long before April 1975. The fact that Saigon was falling despite the expenditure of effort implicit in dropping eight million tons of bombs, contributed to Washington's inability to act to avert the final collapse of Thieu's government. Consequently, the Vietcong flag went up over Ho Chi Minh City—as the victorious Vietcong and North Vietnamese had renamed Saigon.

Why Did Air Power Fail?

There were no witch hunts in America after 1975. President Ford urged the nation to look to the future. That was good enough for the Air Force, which made a conscious effort "to put Vietnam behind it" just as two decades before it had put Korea behind it when Secretary of the Air Force Thomas K. Finletter had declared that the Korean War was a unique, never-to-be-repeated diversion from the true course of strategic air power. As was the case in the mid-1950s, the post-Vietnam US Air Force returned its attention to preparing to counter the Soviet threat in the more familiar environs of Europe and, to a lesser extent, the rim of the Pacific Ocean. Thus, the Air Force, to a greater extent than the Army, failed to learn from the Vietnam War—except, of course, for matters relating to air tactics, especially as they were affected by the requirements of the emerging "age of electronic warfare." From the top to the bottom, Air Force officers preferred to focus on Linebacker Two as a reaffirmation of traditional doctrines and strategies, thus indulging in self-induced anesthetization against the uncomfortable implications of a failure which, if not recognized, could at least be ignored.

If, as Thayer suggests, the Vietnam War was first and foremost an air war, then the failure of the United States to achieve its admittedly tenuous, ill-defined, and limited goals is also a failure of air power. In other words—words that are anathema to many in the Air Force—we lost! While the reasons for that failure are many and complex, Air Force professionals need to address five which are peculiar to their service (although elements of them apply to other services as well), and two others which are generically inherent in air power.

History

The Air Force was a victim of its history. More than the study of the past, history is part of a dynamic linking yesterday to today and defining the future. From the 1920s air power enthusiasts within the Army, however well intentioned, engaged in subterfuge and intrigue to promote their case for an independent Air Force. Like an illegitimate child at a family reunion, the Air Force felt less than fully comfortable with its origins, and all the more so since its primary reason for being was based on the unproven doctrine of strategic bombing. Wedded to strategic bombing, the Air Force neglected other missions, particularly close air support, which tended to tie air assets to the needs of ground commanders. This single-mindedness exacerbated interservice rivalries because, while the Air Force did not especially want the close air support mission, neither did it want the Army to co-opt that mission and thereby avail itself of the opportunity to procure combat airplanes.

Doctrine

Strategic bombing—flying to the enemy's heartland to lay waste to industrial vital centers—dominated Air Force doctrine from the first AFM 1-series in 1953 to its latest published edition of AFM 1-1, *Basic Aerospace Doctrine of the United States Air Force*. This doctrine led Air Force leaders to believe that North Vietnam, a preindustrial, agricultural nation, could be subdued by the same kind of bombing that helped to defeat industrialized nations like Nazi Germany and Imperial Japan.

Technology

The strategic bombing doctrine espoused by the USAF fit well with the Eisenhower administration's policy of massive retaliation, itself driven more by economic than military reasons. Thus, the nation's newest service was able to gobble up the largest slice of each budget pie between 1954 and 1961. The B-52, the B-58, the XB-70, and intercontinental ballistic missiles were all at the leading edge of technology, as were the century-series fighters obtained by the Tactical Air Command. This fascination with technology in the 1950s transferred to Vietnam in the 1960s, where the Air Force was ever in search of a technologically inspired silver bullet. Airmen assigned to the first units sent to South Vietnam urged the deployment of F-100s and B-57s, jets which they felt would quickly "finish this thing." Cluster bombs, napalm, herbicide defoliants, Task Force Alpha, and electro-optically guided and laser-guided bombs all promised much. While some delivered a great deal of destruction, in the end technologically sophisticated weapons proved no substitute for strategy. What technology did do, however, was to foster a managerial mind-set.

Management

The managerial ethos, proven during World War II and institutionalized in the 1950s, took hold in the 1960s and turned the air war into a production-line affair. High-tech weapons, after all, demand effective and efficient management and do so from initial research and development through procurement and deployment. In seeking efficiency, the tendency is to look for definable and objective criteria for assessing effectiveness. The managerial ethos, implemented during the massive buildup of the Air Force in the 1950s, dominated the service in the 1960s. It promoted the objectivity of the quantifiable at the expense of the subjectivity of the creative but unpredictable.

War, however, being inherently more subjective than objective, proved both unpredictable and, in its larger aspects, unmanageable. That was especially true in Vietnam, where the art of unconventional warfare practiced by the enemy was not susceptible to the rigid approaches fostered by the Air Force's managerial elite. For the Air Force, the Vietnam War came to resemble production-line warfare where success was assessed on statistical compilations, which became an end unto themselves. Statistics, however, proved a poor substitute for strategy. Moreover, this numbers game produced perceptions of success and only the illusion of victory, fooling many into thinking that air power was winning the war.

Decreased Intellectual Acumen

The 1950s and 1960s witnessed a steady decline in the intellectual quality of articles appearing in the *Air University Quarterly Review*, which along with its bimonthly successor the *Air University Review*, served as the Air Force's professional journal. This decline was especially evident in articles signed by general officers.[24] Doctrinal thinking was not aided by the attitude implicit in Gen Curtis E. LeMay's statement before Congress in 1961 that doctrine written in 1935 was still appropriate. One result was that air power leaders abdicated strategic thinking to civilian think tanks like the Air Force-sponsored Rand Corporation. Consequently, when Presidents John F. Kennedy and Lyndon B. Johnson turned to their military leaders for a strategy to follow in Vietnam, the generals could not devise one appropriate to the war as perceived by the civilian leaders. Instead of operating within parameters of a limited war, air power leaders sought to refight World War II—a conflict for which the doctrine of strategic bombardment was better suited. In Vietnam, the Air Force along with the other services was rarely outfought, but like the other services it was often *outthought*.

Some Generic Reasons

Two attributes of air power are generic and beyond the control of the Air Force. First, air power is awesome in its destructive potential, and that is intimidating. Bombs and missiles, like bolts from Zeus, come from above. Since most people know about as much about air power as the ancients knew about the less notable inhabitants of Olympus, aerial warfare inherits many of the awe-inspiring attributes of the gods. Thus, when the Vietnam War began to frustrate and frighten them, many Americans were ready to believe what the Air Force had been telling them for a generation: their Air Force could win any war. However, when the public was disappointed, it turned rather quickly to an almost opposite point of view: the Air Force was unleashing its cruel technology on a peaceful and peace-loving people. Hanoi's propaganda apparatus found it easy to promote images of schools, pagodas, churches, hospitals, and dikes being obliterated by bombs. When the public's perceptions about air power were thus skewed, an American strength was turned against itself.

Second, aerial warfare is inherently technical and difficult for most people to understand. Civilian leaders at the highest levels of the US government did not understand the more technical aspects of bombing. Presidents Kennedy and Johnson, unfortunately, were more inclined to seek the advice of their civilian staffs than they were of their generals even when it came to such operational questions as, Should surface-to-air missile sites be bombed? These presidents turned to civilians because they were more politically astute than the generals. Men like Robert McNamara, McGeorge Bundy, and Walt Whitman Rostow, however, were as ignorant of the technical aspects of bombing as Air Force generals seemed to be of its political implications. Like most people, these civilians believed air power was much more capable than it was, or could have been, and they ascribed to it abilities beyond those attributed to it by the most ardent air power enthusiasts. To the unschooled, it seemed that if X number of bombs could accomplish Y result, one-tenth X would achieve a correspondingly smaller objective. Therefore, limited bombing could achieve limited objectives.

Historians, political scientists, economists, and lawyers are not expected to be masters of the art of war. That they would not understand the factors affecting circular error probable (CEP)—the percentage of any number of bombs falling within a certain distance of the aiming point—and its relationship to force packaging is understandable. Most Air Force generals understood CEP and force packaging. That they were not masters of the art of war, in other words, that they were not capable of integrating the social, cultural, and political aspects of the conflict with its military aspects, was a key factor in the setup that resulted in America's defeat.

Unhealthy Myths

After the American Civil War, myths played a healthy role in healing the war's wounds among defeated Southerners. The war had devastated the South, and its people knew the bitterness of total defeat as no Americans (except Native Americans) have before or since. Southerners had little left but their pride after the Union armies defeated the Confederate forces. The idea that the glorious dead had perished fighting against tremendous odds to defend a noble cause was important to the survivors. The myth that one

Rebel could whip 10 Yankees was important—even healthy—because after Appomattox most Southerners knew that they had been beaten, and virtually all believed secession, in addition to being a dead issue, was also a bad idea. While the great grand-children of the Rebel soldiers revere the past and its symbols, they have been among the country's most patriotic and loyal citizens. Adm Thomas H. Moorer (Alabama), Gen William C. Westmoreland (South Carolina), and Lt Gen Joseph Moore (South Carolina) were among the native Southerners who led American forces in Vietnam.

Unhealthy myths are those which serve to excuse or delude. The stab-in-the-back thesis emerged in Germany after the First World War. It held that a combination of Jews, democrats, and Communists betrayed the cause, selling out the German nation and its army by forcing a surrender while the army was holding its own in the field. The myth deluded the nation and was a factor contributing to the failure of the Weimar Republic and the subsequent rise of Adolf Hitler and his National Socialists. Likewise, in the post-Vietnam US Air Force, several unhealthy myths, including a version of the stab-in-the-back thesis, enforced a kind of institutional self-delusion.

The most popular and most widely accepted Vietnam myth is that Linebacker Two "won" the war. A corollary to the myth holds that if air power had been used with equal resolve earlier, anytime between 1965 and 1969, the war could have been concluded sooner and on more favorable terms. This line of reasoning has contributed to an our-hands-were-tied-behind-our-back thesis similar in its thrust to the stab-in-the-back thesis that held sway in the German officer corps after World War I. The our-hands-were-tied thesis has dominated thinking about Vietnam in the Air Force because it blames the final outcome on a pernicious press, the antics of antiwar activists such as Jane Fonda, and, perhaps most disturbingly, on "interference" by politicians who restrained the military.

As with most myths, the one surrounding Linebacker Two contains kernels of truth. Militarily, Linebacker Two paved the way for a final agreement that allowed the United States to complete its withdrawal from South Vietnam. It also compelled Hanoi to release American prisoners of war (POW). In the euphoria surrounding the signing of the Paris Accords, the withdrawal of the last American troops from the South, and the return of the POWs, there was the illusion of victory. The conclusion that air power delivered that victory appealed to the Air Force.

The Air Force Association led the way in trumpeting the *perceived* accomplishments of Linebacker Two. Editorials in the February, March, and April 1973 editions of *Air Force Magazine* praised Linebacker Two. Not only was it cast as a vindication of long-held tenets of strategic bombing doctrine but also as proof of the enduring role of the manned bomber.[25]

Bolstered by official policy pronouncements and by remarks of high-ranking officers, the myth of Linebacker Two gained in prominence. In a speech before the Navy fighter pilot's annual Tail Hook Reunion in Las Vegas on 8 September 1973, Admiral Moorer, who had served as chairman of the Joint Chiefs of Staff during the Christmas bombing, stated: "Airpower, given its day in court after almost a decade of frustration, confirmed its effectiveness as an instrument of national policy in just nine and a half flying days."[26] Retired Air Force Gen T. R. Milton, lamenting the fall of Saigon in the June 1975 edition of *Air Force Magazine*, stated that the December 1972 bombing of North Vietnam was "an object lesson in how the war might have been won, and won long ago, if only there had not been such political inhibition."[27] In his book *Airpower in Three Wars*, Gen William W. Momyer, former commander of the Seventh Air Force, wrote, "An early Linebacker II campaign (with the enforcing threat of subsequent Line-backers) . . . can be strategically decisive if its application is intense, continuous, and focused on the enemy's vital systems."[28] A decade after the end of the American involvement in Vietnam, Milton wrote, "The Christmas bombings of 1972 should have taken place in 1965."[29]

Returning prisoners of war strengthened the myth. Adm James B. Stockdale wrote of the impact of the bombing: "One look at any Vietnamese officer's face told the whole story. It telegraphed accommodation, hopelessness, remorse, fear. The shock was there; our enemy's will was broken."[30] Brig Gen Robinson Risner wrote, "We could see a definite change in the attitude of the Vietnamese. Before they had been defiant . . . but it was a totally different situation with the B-52s."[31] Virtually all the repatriated POWs credited the Christmas bombing with their release.*

Many air power enthusiasts shared the feelings of the POWs concerning Linebacker Two. They also believed that had a Linebacker Two–type operation been conducted in 1965 the war might have ended then on terms more favorable to the United States and South Vietnam. Although appealing, this assertion overlooks many realities. In 1965 the North Vietnamese would have had much to lose by ending the fighting. Their goals had not been realized, and Washington's demand that Hanoi stop supporting the national liberation front and remove its increasingly larger number of troops from South Vietnam was unacceptable. Furthermore, the guerrilla war in the South probably would have continued because the Vietcong, despite claims by Hanoi and Washington, was not yet controlled by the North Vietnamese.

However, as of May 1972, the situation had drastically changed. During the Nixon visit to Moscow, Kissinger made a key concession when he asked the Soviets to tell the North Vietnamese that the United States no longer insisted on a withdrawal of PAVN forces from the South. By 1972 US goals had changed and American forces were headed home. Hanoi had secured the right to keep a large army in South Vietnam and with time as their ally, the North Vietnamese figured that after the American withdrawal they would eventually win. In December 1972, with most of the North's military and political objectives won, or at least achievable, it made good sense for Hanoi to sign a peace

---

*Post hoc, ergo propter hoc.

agreement, one which President Nguyen Van Thieu of South Vietnam found absolutely abhorrent. Finally, Linebacker Two served very little tactical military purpose other than rearranging the rubble that Linebacker One had caused; Linebacker One, not the "Eleven-Day War," had jeopardized Hanoi's designs on South Vietnam.

The Air Force has no monopoly on Vietnam myths. Some people outside the Air Force believed myths about air power which have been perpetuated by those intent on criticizing America's role in Vietnam. Again, Linebacker Two looms prominently. At the time, the press dubbed Linebacker Two "the Christmas bombing" and some journalists compared it to fire bomb raids on German and Japanese cities during World War II. When one wing of the Bac Mai Hospital was damaged, a cry went up not only from Hanoi but also from many quarters of the world press. No one mentioned that the hospital was located close to a primary North Vietnamese fighter base. No one raised the possibility that the damage might have been caused by a stray bomb aimed at the base or suggested that a spent North Vietnamese surface-to-air missile might have fallen on it. Certainly no one made the point that although the Air Force *could* have targeted the hospital since the roof and grounds had been used by antiaircraft guns during Linebacker One, its targeteers did not do so.[32]

Indeed, Linebacker Two has become as precious to the mythology of the antiwar movement as it has to many within the Air Force. H. Bruce Franklin, the John Cotton Dana Professor of English and American Studies at Rutgers University, stated in a 1988 article in the *American Quarterly* "that during the Christmas bombing of North Vietnam, Hanoi alone was hit with 100,000 tons (of bombs)."[33] His source for this preposterous figure was Gloria Emerson's *Winners and Losers*. Following the footnote trail, one discovers that Emerson's source was an unnamed official in Hanoi.[34] Thus, "somebody in Hanoi said so" becomes sufficient documentation to support assertions in an article published in a respected and prestigious American scholarly publication.

While most scholars consider Professor Franklin's avowed Marxist and Maoist ideological world view when assessing his writing, even highly respected mainstream scholars have occasionally accepted some of the more facile pronouncements concerning Linebacker Two. Professor George C. Herring, a highly respected historian and author of *America's Longest War*, in editions prior to 1986, used Hanoi's figure of 34 B-52s shot down during Linebacker Two rather than the actual figure of 15.[35]

Other icons associated with air power are equally precious to the antiwar viewpoint. Nancy Zaroulis and Gerald Sullivan's monumental study of the peace movement, *Who Spoke Up? American Protest against the War in Vietnam, 1963–1975* (published in 1985), states that "U.S. and South Vietnamese planes dropped *220 million* tons of bombs in the area (around Khe Sanh) during the seventy-seven day siege."[36] No source is cited, but since the United States dropped eight million tons of bombs in Indochina between 1962 and 1973, compared with a total of around four million tons dropped by all the warring nations during the Second World War, it seems safe to estimate that *220 million* tons is a figure well in excess of all the tonnage of bombs manufactured by all nations since the first bombs were dropped from an airplane during the Italo-Turkish War of 1912!

Myths, when they excuse failure or support an ideological proposition, can be dangerous. At the least, as is the case with the numbers so easily tossed about by professors Franklin, Zaroulis, and Sullivan, myths promote an obviously biased and slanted version of history. As is the case with the myth that Linebacker Two brought North Vietnam to its knees, myths can lead to self-delusion. When historians promote a version of history designed to support a particular ideological or political bias, their dishonesty betrays their profession by perpetuating misunderstanding and ignorance. When soldiers adhere to myths to support institutional interests they run risks with potentially greater and more violent consequences.

Victory does not foster the compulsion for self-examination that defeat imposes. With its institutional eyes fixed firmly on the perceived accomplishments of air power, as typified by Linebacker Two, the Air Force returned its attention to the more familiar threats posed by the Soviet Union and its allies. As it had after the Korean War, the Air Force put its recent unpleasant experience behind it. Some took comfort in the simplistic and flawed logic that when the last Air Force units pulled out of South Vietnam though not from Thailand in 1973, the Republic of Vietnam was still an independent nation. Whatever lessons the Air Force sought were tactically oriented and technologically applicable, that is, fighters need an internally mounted gun, outstanding maneuverability, and a bubble canopy for better vision. For too many airmen, the Air Force role in Vietnam nestled in their memories as an unbroken string of unmitigated victories marred only by "political constraints that kept us from winning." Probably because it seemed indelicate or inappropriate, no one dared to ask why a disproportionate number of Air Force heroes from the Vietnam War were men who had been shot down and held captive. At best, Vietnam was ambiguous and not amenable to school solutions that fit comfortably into educating the members of a bureaucratic technocracy.

Study of the Vietnam War, therefore, was slighted at the Air War College and the Air Command and Staff College, two of the professional military education (PME) schools in the Air University, located at Maxwell AFB, Alabama. From 1974 through 1979, the Air War College, the Air Force's premier PME school for specially selected senior officers, devoted only 2.5 hours of study to the Vietnam War in a case study entitled "TACAIR in Vietnam." It focused on the role of air power in Linebackers One and Two. That block comprised a mere 1.4 percent of the 172 hours devoted to studying "general purpose force employment." The same amount of time was allotted for studying air power during the six-day Arab Israeli War of 1967.[37]

The Air Command and Staff College, a 10-month course for majors, offered its first elective on the Vietnam War in 1983, but that year it was cancelled because less than 10 officers out of more than 500 attending the school signed up. The ACSC students packed courses on family financial planning, using personal computers, and physical fitness, however. Since then, while the above listed courses retain their popularity, the Vietnam elective has been filled to its 30-student maximum each time it has been offered.

Some excellent official histories by Air Force officers assigned to the Office of Air Force History notwithstanding, no serving Air Force officer wrote a book to compare with the many fine books on Vietnam written by US Army officers until Maj Mark Clodfelter's *The Limits of Air Power: The American Bombing of North Vietnam* appeared in 1989. That it became mandatory reading at the Air War College is encouraging. While Clodfelter's book can stand with the best produced by serving Army officers, the fact that it took nearly two decades for an Air Force officer to write a book critical of the way the Air Force fought the war is indicative of a larger problem endemic to the service.

Too few Air Force officers in the 1970s and 1980s read history books. That fact was reflected in the service doctrine manuals, the Air Force's "officially sanctioned beliefs" about the way air power should be used. The current version of Air Force Manual (AFM) 1-1, *Basic Aerospace Doctrine of the United State Air Force*, dated 1984, lists the Strategic Aerospace Offensive as the Air Force's first mission and defines this as the ability "to neutralize or to destroy the enemy's war-sustaining capabilities or will to fight . . . through the systematic application of force to a selected series of vital targets." [38] The strategic planners and operations officers who devised the 94-targets list would have been comfortable with this manual. The manual for tactical operations, AFM 2-1, *Tactical Air Operations—Counter Air, Close Air Support, and Air Interdiction*, was not revised between 1969–89.

Perhaps the Air Force has had difficulty dealing with Vietnam because no one could deny that American conventional air power could have obliterated North Vietnam in two weeks. The United States had tremendous advantages in military resources that seemingly dwarfed the capabilities of the Indochinese Communists. Although this disparity was enormous, it also led to the self-delusion that applied firepower, even in lesser doses, could substitute for strategy. What confounded America's primary strength—air power—was that it was used in measured doses through time to pursue limited objectives. Air power leaders, accustomed to thinking of warfare in terms of either a Warsaw Pact versus NATO scenario or a final nuclear face-off against the Soviet Union, could not devise a strategy appropriate to the war at hand under the conditions dictated by political leaders.

Furthermore, the commitment of the North Vietnamese and the Vietcong to objectives that were more total in nature provided them with the moral strength needed to outlast the United States. Given their willingness to fight for an exceedingly long time if necessary, the Vietnamese were able to turn America's advantage in military resources against itself. In the end, dropping eight million tons of bombs was no substitute for a coherent strategy; instead it subverted America's moral position, fostered national and international disapprobation, and contributed to the crippling of America's ability to support the non-Communist regimes of Indochina. Despite the enormous expenditure of firepower, the level of violence employed was neither sufficient nor well focused enough to secure a successful outcome. Short of the total obliteration of North Vietnam, something that was never considered by America's leadership, it is unlikely that there was a level of violence that would have sufficed. In the final analysis, however, the war was not America's to win or lose. It was South Vietnam's war.

The ambiguities of the Vietnam War remain, and this author has no lock on the truth. But what is more certain is that warfare is more than sortie generation and firepower on targets. It incorporates many factors, including some which seem (but are not) beyond the purview of the soldier, such as politics and economics. Geography, the weather, and the many aspects of culture—one's own as well as the enemy's—are factors that determine the way nations fight their wars. Above all, warfare, especially limited warfare, is an art. As such, it requires intellectual sophistication, mental dexterity, and the ability to think abstractly.

As long as air power enthusiasts cling to Linebacker Two as evidence to support the hallowed doctrine of strategic bombing, what history can teach them about Vietnam and air power will go unlearned. If that is so, the setup may not yet be complete.

Notes

1. Henry Kissinger, *Year of Upheaval* (Boston: Little, Brown, 1982), 303.

2. History, 43d Strategic Wing (SW), 1 January–30 June 1973, vol. 1, 65–67, K-WG-43-HI, USAF Historical Research Center (USAFHRC), Maxwell AFB, Ala.

3. Arthur J. Dommen, *Laos: Keystone of Indochina* (Boulder, Colo.: Westview Press, 1985), 97.

4. See Kissinger, 316; and History, 43d SW, 67.

5. "A Trail Becomes a Turnpike," *Time*, 26 March 1973, 34.

6. *The United States Air Force in Southeast Asia, 1961–1973: An Illustrated Account*, ed. Carl Berger (Washington, D.C.: Office of Air Force History, 1984), 135.

7. "The Secret Agony of the POWs," *Newsweek*, 19 April 1973, 30.

8. Elizabeth Becker, *When the War Was Over: The Voices of Cambodia's Revolution and Its People* (New York: Simon and Schuster, 1986), 138–52.

9. See ibid., 169; and History, 43d SW, 67.

10. Col Robert William Clements, commander, 432d Tactical Reconnaissance Wing, end-of-tour report (hereinafter Clements, EOTR), 15 March 1974, 2, K717.131, USAFHRC.

11. History, 43d SW, 70–71.

12. Ibid., 59; and Clements, EOTR, 2.

13. See William Shawcross, *Sideshow: Nixon, Kissinger, and the Destruction of Cambodia* (New York: Simon and Schuster, 1979), 282–83; and Berger, 147.

14. Kissinger, 359.

15. History, 43d SW, 38–39.

16. As an intelligence officer at Strategic Air Command headquarters in Omaha, Nebraska, the author briefed "underwater storage areas" in Cambodia as Arc Light targets. In discussing this with Maj William A. Buckingham, Jr., a colleague at the Office of Air Force History in 1979, Major Buckingham related a story told to him by a former targeteer in the American embassy in Phnom Penh. According to the targeteer, when SAC reached a sortie rate of 60 per day, there were not enough targets in Cambodia to justify that level of bombing. After several incidents when bombs fell on civilians rather than on legitimate military targets, the targeteer started submitting fictitious underwater

storage areas as targets because SAC insisted on flying a certain number of B-52 sorties to Cambodia every day, regardless of whether or not there were any targets suitable for a B-52 strike. In an interview on 1 May 1980, this author asked former ambassador to Cambodia Colby Swank if there was any truth to this allegation. While Swank did not confirm the targeteer's remarks, he said these allegations had "an element of truth to them in that (General) John Vogt had these sorties to be used."

17. "Farewell," *Newsweek*, 21 April 1975, 23.

18. Earl H. Tilford, Jr., *The United States Air Force Search and Rescue in Southeast Asia, 1961–1975* (Washington, D.C.: Office of Air Force History, 1980), 147.

19. Ibid., 148.

20. John F. Guilmartin, Jr., and Michael O'Leary, *Helicopters*, The Illustrated History of the Vietnam War (Toronto: Bantam Books, 1988), 138–44.

21. Ibid., 151.

22. Thomas C. Thayer, *War without Fronts: The American Experience in Vietnam* (Boulder, Colo.: Westview Press, 1985), 26, 37.

23. See Raphael Littauer and Norman Uphoff, eds., *The Air War in Indochina* (Boston: Beacon Press, 1972), 11; and Berger, 368.

24. The decline in the sophistication of articles signed by higher ranking officers, but particularly by general officers, was especially obvious. Early editions of *Air University Quarterly Review* contained articles rich in ideas, many of them flawed but nevertheless vibrant. Generals and colonels proposed new ideas, argued with policy, and articulated their own thoughts on doctrine, strategy, and institutional issues. By the mid-1950s that had pretty much stopped. In part this was the result of Consolidation Directive no. 1, issued in 1949 by Secretary of Defense Louis Johnson, which required that all information emanating from the Pentagon be screened not only for security but also for policy and propriety. The effect was evident by the mid-1950s. Articles by general officers rarely, if ever, dealt with substantive issues in a provocative or innovative way. "It's the World's Greatest Air Force," and "SAC's New Direction" are representative of the titles and reflective of their content. A public relations approach based on "telling the Air Force story" was partly to blame, but no one considered that there were pitfalls in confusing professional thinking and writing with public relations.

25. See John L. Frisbee, "The Phoenix That Never Was," *Air Force Magazine*, February 1973, 4; Frisbee, "Not with a Whimper, But a Bang," March 1973, *Air Force Magazine*, 5–6; and Martin W. Ostrow, "The B-52's Message to Moscow," *Air Force Magazine*, April 1973, 2.

26. "What Admiral Moorer Actually Said about Airpower's Effectiveness in Vietnam," *Air Force Magazine*, November 1973, 2.

27. Gen T. R. Milton, USAF, Retired, "USAF and the Vietnam Experience," *Air Force Magazine*, June 1975, 56.

28. Gen William W. Momyer, USAF, Retired, *Airpower in Three Wars* (Washington, D.C.: Office of Air Force History, 1978), 339.

29. Gen T. R. Milton, USAF, Retired, "The Lessons of Vietnam," *Air Force Magazine*, March 1983, 110.

30. Jim and Sybil Stockdale, *In Love and War: The Story of a Family's Ordeal and Sacrifice during the Vietnam Years* (New York: Harper and Row, 1984), 432.

31. Robinson Risner, *The Passing of the Night: My Seven Years as a Prisoner of War of the North Vietnamese* (New York: Random House, 1973), 237.

32. W. Hays Parks, "Linebacker and the Law of War," *Air University Review* 34, no. 2 (January–February 1983): 25.

33. H. Bruce Franklin, "How American Management Won the War in Vietnam," *American Quarterly*, September 1988, 423.

34. Gloria Emerson, *Winners and Losers: Battles, Retreats, Gains, Losses and Ruins from a Long War* (New York: Random House, 1976), 42.

35. George C. Herring, *America's Longest War: The United States in Vietnam, 1950–1975* (New York: Random House, 1979), 248.

36. Nancy Zaroulis and Gerald Sullivan, *Who Spoke Up? American Protest against the War in Vietnam, 1963–1975* (New York: Holt, Rinehart, and Winston, 1984), 151. Zaroulis and Sullivan (p. 346) also cite the figure of 100,000 tons of bombs as having fallen on North Vietnam during Linebacker Two; incredibly, however, they claim it took only five days for the Air Force to do this, not eleven! No source is cited.

37. Suzanne Budd Gehri, *Study War Once More: Teaching Vietnam at Air University*, CADRE Paper (Maxwell AFB, Ala.: Air University Press, 1985), 6, AU-ARI-CP-85-7.

38. AFM 1-1, *Basic Aerospace Doctrine of the United States Air Force*, 16 March 1984, 3-2.

Index

Abrams, Creighton W.: 222–23, 234
Acheson, Dean: 151
Aerospace Rescue and Recovery
    Service: 226
AFM 1-1, *Basic Aerospace Doctrine
    of the United States Air Force*
    (1984): 285, 295
AFM 2-1, *Tactical Air
    Operations—Counter Air, Close
    Air Support, and Air Interdiction*:
    295
AGM-45 (Shrike): 125–26, 131
AGM-78 (Standard ARM): 131, 247
Agreement on Ending the War and
    Restoring the Peace in Vietnam:
    265. *See also* Paris Accords or
    Agreements
Air America: 193, 273
Air Command and Staff College:
    294–95
Air commandos: 63–64, 66
Aircraft types
    A-1: 66
    A-1E: 67
    A-4: 51
    A-7: 233
    AC-47: 192
    AC-119: 179, 192, 202
    AC-123: 179, 192
    AC-130: 175–76, 178–79, 184,
        202–3, 281
    B-26: 22, 64–65, 77
    B-29: 2, 7, 10, 14, 18, 22
    B-36: 10–11, 13–15
    B-52: 14, 32, 49-50, 100, 107,
        148, 169, 175, 180, 185,
        197–98, 202, 220, 228–29,
        254, 257–59, 263, 273
    B-57: 33–35, 100, 178–79
    B-58: 96

C-47: 61, 71, 171
C-123: 71
C-130: 34, 171
EC-121: 177
F-4: 50, 52, 127–28, 130, 217,
    243–44
F-8: 130
F8F: 61
F-84E: 32
F-100: 33–34, 80, 171, 202
F-102: 67
F-104: 35
F-105: 33, 37, 50, 113, 119, 125,
    127–28, 130–31, 217, 240
F-111: 52, 260
H-19: 61
HC-130: 131
HH-3: 131
HH-53: 131
KB-50: 34
MiG-15: 17, 127, 144
MiG-17: 127, 144, 197
MiG-19: 127, 144
MiG-21: 127, 144, 242, 244, 260
RB-66: 34
RF-4C: 131
RF-101: 34, 60
SC-47: 64
T-28: 65, 67, 69, 77, 100, 114,
    189
XB-70: 32, 48, 50, 285
XF-108: 32
Air deniability: 122–23
Air Force Association: 15, 117, 165,
    167, 215, 290
Air Force Magazine: 14–15, 24,
    29-30, 39, 121, 141, 290
Air forces (numbered)
    Seventh: 109, 118, 139, 183–84,
        191, 201, 220, 253

Seventh/Thirteenth: 183, 190–91
   Thirteenth: 70, 191
Air University Quarterly Review:
   8, 19, 23, 39, 286
Air University Review: 286
Air War College: 36, 294–95
A-loi: 200
An Loc: 230–31
Andersen AFB, Guam: 224, 228,
   257, 259, 278
Annam Cordillera: 153
Anthis, Rollen H.: 67, 71, 78
Arc Light. *See* operations
Army of the Republic of Vietnam
   (ARVN): 64, 68–69, 73, 75, 199,
   201, 231, 253
Arnold, Henry H.: 7
A Shau Valley: 169, 182, 199
Attopeu: 204

Bac Mai airfield: 246, 260
Bac Mai Hospital: 292
Ball, George: 93
Ban Ban: 186
Ban Tha Vieng: 274
Barrel Roll. *See* operations
Base area 353: 195
Battambang: 275
Bay of Pigs: 47
Berlin: 47
Bien Hoa Air Base: 78, 100, 184,
   231
Binh Dinh: 229
Bird and Son: 193
Bolovens Plateau: 204, 272
Brezhnev, Leonid: 237
Brodie, Bernard: 29
Brown, Harold: 89, 136, 152
Bullet Shot. *See* operations
Bullpup: 114
Bundy, McGeorge: 102, 150, 288
Bundy, William P.: 97, 107
Bunker, Ellsworth: 140
Byrd, Harry: 274

Caldara, Joseph D.: 22
Cambodia: 67, 194–95, 197, 199,
   205–6, 274, 277, 279-80
Camp Holloway: 103
Central Office for South Vietnam
   (COSVN): 197, 221
Central Intelligence Agency (CIA):
   22, 111, 115, 118, 133, 138, 151,
   183–84, 191, 193, 273
China: 59, 64, 186, 234
CINCPAC: 58–59, 100, 138
Civil Air Transport: 22
Clifford, Clark: 149–50, 152, 169
Combat Apple: 243
Combat Skyspot: 276
Combat Tree: 243, 245, 247
Commander in chief, Pacific
   Command. *See* CINCPAC
Commando Bolt: 179
Commando Flash. *See* operations
Commando Hunt. *See* operations
Composite air strike force (CASF):
   33–34, 36
Continental Air Services: 193
Counterinsurgency: 61–62, 66, 82,
   90
Cricket. *See* operations

Dak To: 229
Defense Intelligence Agency (DIA):
   111, 115–16, 119, 133
Delaware. *See* operations
Demilitarized zone (DMZ): 61, 250
Dempster, K. S.: 125
Desert Rat. *See* operations
Dien Bien Phu: 21–23
Dirty Thirty detachment: 72
Disco: 243
Dong Ha: 203
Douhet, Giulio: 2–4
Doumer (Paul) Bridge: 228, 235
"Dr Pepper War": 132
Dutch Mill: 172

Eagle Pull. *See* operations
Enhance Plus: *See* operations
Enthoven, Alain C.: 130
Ewell, Julian J.: 170

Fall, Bernard: 23
Fan Song radar: 123–24, 126
Farm Gate. *See* operations
Felt, Harry D.: 64
Finletter, Thomas K.: 16, 21, 26, 283
56th Special Operations Wing
    (SOW): 189, 197, 217
559th Transportation Battalion
    (North Vietnam): 55
Flaming Dart. *See* operations
Flexible response: 49
Forces Armée Nationale Khmer
    (FANK): 197, 275–76
Ford, Gerald R.: 280, 283
4400th Combat Crew Training
    Squadron (4400th CCTS): 63–64,
    66, 73–74
Fowler, Henry H.: 150
Franklin, H. Bruce: 292–93
Freedom Dawn. *See* operations
Freedom Train. *See* operations
Friendship Highway: 194-95
Fulbright, J. William: 141
    Senate Foreign Relations
    Committee: 118, 141

Gavin, James M.: 16
Gia Lam Airport: 148
Gilpatric, Roswell L.: 62, 64
Green, Marshall: 97

Haig, Alexander: 234, 254
Haiphong: 109, 111, 139, 142, 148,
    151, 229, 234, 236, 254, 257
Hanoi: 64, 109, 119, 137, 142, 148,
    187, 204, 229, 234, 239, 250, 254
Harkins, Paul: 70, 75–76
Helms, Richard: 150

Hmong guerrillas: 186, 188–89, 193
Ho Chi Minh: 21, 55, 103–4, 135,
    154
Ho Chi Minh Trail: 91, 113, 172–74,
    177–78, 181–82, 185–88, 191,
    197–98, 201, 204–5, 217, 222,
    250, 272–74
Hoa Lac airfield: 254
Hoa Lo Prison: 260
Hollingsworth, James F.: 230
Honolulu conference: 107–8
Hue: 231
Hurlburt Field, Florida: 63

Igloo White sensor: 177
Infiltration surveillance center
    (ISC): 177
Institute for Defense Analysis
    (IDA): 133, 173
International Security Affairs (ISA):
    100, 135, 140
Iron Hand. *See* operations

Jason Division, ISA: 133, 147, 173
Johns Hopkins University: 108
Johnson, Louis: 11, 13, 38
Johnson, Lyndon: 1, 23, 80, 92, 94,
    100, 103–4, 111, 115, 137,
    147, 151, 165–66, 171, 195,
    239, 287
Joint Chiefs of Staff: 63
Joint United States Military
    Assistance Advisory Group
    (JUSMAAG): 59, 62

Katzenbach, Nicholas: 150
Kennedy, John F.: 45, 47, 51, 53, 56,
    62–63, 72, 78, 151, 287
Kennedy, Robert F.: 151, 165
Kep airfield: 254
Khe Sanh: 167–68, 171–72, 226
Khmer Rouge: 274, 280-81
Khrushchev, Nikita S.: 39, 47

King, Benjamin H.: 66–67
Kissinger, Henry A.: 28–29, 196, 200, 209, 224-25, 228, 236, 238-39, 249–50, 252, 263, 272–73, 291
Knight, Hal: 196
Koh Tang: 281
Kompong Som: 275, 281
Kong Le: 54, 56, 59
Kontum: 229
Korat Royal Thai Air Force Base (RTAFB): 216, 224, 275
Korea: 15–16, 20–21, 23, 25, 142
Kosygin, Aleksey: 102–3

Lam Son 719. *See* operations
Lansdale, Edward G.: 22
Laos: 36, 47, 53, 57–58, 173, 180, 184, 186–88, 198–99, 205, 271
Le Duan: 221
Le Duc Tho: 209, 238, 252, 263, 272
Lebanon: 25, 34–35
LeMay, Curtis E.: 1, 11–12, 31, 39, 48, 50–53, 62, 66, 70, 80, 93, 97, 286
Liddell Hart, Basil: 3
Linebacker. *See* operations
Linebacker Sherry. *See* operations
Loc Ninh: 146, 230
Lon Nol: 274
Long Tieng (LS 20 alternate): 192, 207
Luang Prabang: 54, 186–87, 189

Mann, Lyle E.: 216
Mayaguez: 280–82
McCarthy, Eugene: 151
McCarthy, James R.: 278
McConnell, John P.: 93, 108, 121
McGarr, Lionel: 62, 64
McGovern, George: 251
McNamara, Robert S.: 45, 50, 52, 76, 89, 106–7, 111, 113, 116, 118–20, 124, 133–35, 137, 139, 144–45, 147, 149, 168, 288
McNaughton, John T.: 97, 101, 107, 135, 144
Menu (bombing). *See* operations
Meyers, Gilbert L.: 119, 142
Military Assistance Command, Vietnam (MACV): 68, 70, 138–39, 222
Milton, T. R.: 290
Mitchell, William: 2–4
Momyer, William W.: 79, 93, 114, 129, 139, 142–44, 155, 204, 290
Moonbeam: 178
Moore, Joseph H.: 71, 289
Moorer, Thomas H.: 105–6, 225, 289–90
Moscow: 36, 233, 291
Mule Train. *See* operations
Muong Phalane: 205
Muong Phine: 205
Muong Soui: 99–100, 189

Nakhon Phanom Royal Thai Air Force Base (RTAFB): 172, 175, 177, 243, 281
National Security Act of 1947: 16–17
National Security Council (NSC): 25
Naval Task Force 77: 109
Neak Luong: 276
New Look defence policy: 21, 24–25
Ngo Dinh Diem: 60, 70, 101
Nguyen Hue offensive: 224, 237
Nguyen iron and steel works: 108
Nguyen Van Thieu: 198, 200, 203–4, 230, 238, 249–52, 264, 292
Niagara. *See* operations
94-targets list: 1, 93, 100, 135
Nitze, Paul: 152
Nixon, Richard M.: 111, 165–66, 171, 196, 200, 203–4, 224–25,

228, 233, 236, 238–39, 250–51,
  253, 262, 264, 271, 277, 291
Norodom Sihanouk, Prince: 194, 197
North Vietnam: 59, 64, 67, 89, 92,
  95, 106, 118, 186
NSC-162: 25
NVA. *See* PAVN

O'Daniel, John: 62
Olympic Torch: 243
Operations
  Arc Light: 180, 196, 226, 256,
    263, 272
  Barrel Roll (Laos): 101, 172,
    174–75, 188
  Bullet Shot: 228, 278
  Commando Flash: 224
  Commando Hunt: 153, 172–77,
    182–83, 185–86, 198, 201,
    205, 218–20
  Cricket: 175
  Delaware: 169
  Desert Rat: 205
  Eagle Pull: 280
  Enhance Plus: 251
  Farm Gate: 64, 66–67, 71–74,
    77–78
  Flaming Dart I: 103
  Flaming Dart II: 103–4
  Freedom Dawn: 228
  Freedom Porch Bravo: 228
  Freedom Train: 228
  Iron Hand: 261
  Lam Son 719: 198, 200–1,
    203–5, 221
  Linebacker: 153, 233–36,
    238–41, 245, 247, 250
  Linebacker One: 228, 248, 254,
    292
  Linebacker Sherry: 240
  Linebacker Two: 253–65, 284,
    289, 291–92, 297

Menu
  breakfast, dessert, lunch,
    snack, supper: 196
  Mule Train: 71, 78
  Niagara: 168, 172
  Palace Dog: 192–93
  Pegasus: 169
  Pierce Arrow: 98
  Pocket Money: 233
  Prairie Fire: 192
  Proud Deep Alpha: 208–9, 222
  Ranch Hand: 70, 72, 78, 174
  Rolling Thunder: 89, 95, 104–7,
    111, 122–23, 130, 134, 137,
    140–41, 152–56, 166, 188,
    236, 238–41
  Rolling Thunder Alpha: 228
  Shed Light: 176
  Silver Buckle: 205
  Steel Tiger: 174–75, 189
  Vulture: 22
Operations Plan 34A (OPlan 34A):
  98
OpRep-4: 132
Outside instigator: 35–36, 47, 60,
  92, 103, 105

Paksong: 207, 272–73
Palace Dog. *See* operations
Paris Accords or Agreements:
  271–72, 274, 290
Parrot's Beak: 194
Pathet Lao: 53–54, 56–57, 59, 186,
  272
Pave Buff: 276
Pave Knife: 245–47
Pave Phantom: 276
Pegasus. *See* operations
Peking: 36
People's Army of Vietnam (PAVN):
  91, 146, 167, 169–70, 181,
  185–87, 199, 201, 218, 226, 231,
  236, 249, 253, 272, 291

People's Republic of China: 20, 25, 29–30
Pham Van Dong: 121
Phnom Penh: 64, 67, 194, 280
Phong Saly Province: 55
Phou Pha Thi: 188–89
Phoui Sananikone: 53
Phoumi Nosavan: 53–56
Phuc Yen airfield: 100, 144, 254
Pierce Arrow. *See* operations
Plain of Jars: 56, 99, 176, 186, 189
Pleiku: 78, 93, 103, 170
Pocket Money. *See* operations
Prairie Fire. *See* operations
Projects
    404: 192–93
    Gunboat: 176
    Water Pump: 188, 192
Protocol to the Declaration on the Neutrality of Laos: 59
Proud Deep Alpha. *See* operations

Quang Lang: 222
Quang Tri
    City: 74, 226, 232
    Province: 146, 199, 201, 226, 231, 250
Quemoy Island: 34

Ranch Hand. *See* operations
Rand Corporation: 287
Raven (forward air controllers, Laos): 191–93
Red Crown: 243
Risner, Robinson: 291
Rolling Thunder. *See* operations
Rolling Thunder Alpha. *See* operations
Rostow, Walt W.: 79, 92–94, 121, 150, 288
Route 9 (Laos): 58, 146, 199
Royal Laotian Air Force (RLAF): 192

Royal Laotian Army (RLA): 53–54, 56–57, 186, 188, 191–92
Rusk, Dean: 94, 150

SA-2: 123, 125, 255–56
Saigon: 74, 146, 149, 198, 248
Sam Neua: 55, 186, 188–89
Saravane: 207
Sarit Thanarat, Marshal: 55
Savang Vatthana, King: 186
Savannakhét: 55, 58
Seamans, Robert C., Jr.: 165–67, 215, 265
Search and rescue (SAR) helicopters: 69–70
2d Advanced Echelon (2d ADVON): 67, 69, 74
2d Air Division: 71, 109
Senate Armed Services Committee: 141
Senate Foreign Relations Committee: 141. *See also* J. William Fulbright
Seventh Air Force. *See* air forces (numbered)
Seventh/Thirteenth Air Force. *See* air forces (numbered)
Shank, Edwin G., Jr.: 71, 76
Sharp, U. S. Grant: 103, 105, 107–8, 139, 142, 147
Shed Light. *See* operations
Shrike missile. *See* AGM-45
Sidewinder: 64
Sihanoukville, Cambodia: 112, 194–95
Silver Buckle. *See* operations
Sisavang Vong, King: 54
Sitton, Ray B.: 196
Skybolt: 50
Slay, Alton D.: 220
Slessor, John C.: 29
Smith, Dale O.: 9, 19, 36
Smith, Margaret Chase: 141

Snack. *See* operations
Somsanith, Prince: 53
Souphanouvong, Prince: 53
Souvanna Phouma, Prince: 53–55,
99, 186, 272
Soviet Union: 8, 10, 13, 25, 27,
29–30, 256, 296
Standard ARM (antiradiation
missile). *See* AGM-78
Steel Tiger. *See* operations
Stennis, John: 141
Stockdale, James B.: 291
Strategic Air Command (SAC):
7–10, 12, 27, 35, 47–49, 196,
218, 254, 256
Strategic Arms Limitations Talks
treaty (SALT I): 232–33
Sullivan, William H.: 176
Supper. *See* operations
Surface-to-air missiles (SAMs): 261
Symington, Stuart: 50, 141

Tactical Air Command (TAC): 9,
30, 32, 49
Taiwan: 35
Takhli RTAFB, Thailand: 230–31
Tan Son Nhut Air Base, South
Vietnam: 60, 78, 81, 172
Task Force 116 (United States):
58–59
Task Force Alpha: 177, 218, 285
Taylor, Maxwell D.: 28, 76, 101–2,
107, 150
Tchepone: 55, 58, 146, 180,
198–200, 203
Teaball (weapons control center):
242–43, 245
Tet offensive: 146, 149–50, 167–68,
171, 195, 198
Thailand: 186
Thakhek: 58
Thanh Hoa: 116, 153

Thanh Hoa Bridge: 108, 228, 235
Thirteenth Air Force. *See* air forces
(numbered)
Thurmond, Strom: 141
Tonle Sap: 280
Truman, Harry S.: 23
21st Special Operations Squadron:
193

Ubon RTAFB, Thailand: 184, 275
Udorn RTAFB: 58, 183, 188, 217,
275
Umstead, Stanley M., Jr.: 216
*United States Air Force Basic
Doctrine*: 28. *See also* AFM 1-1
U Tapao RTAFB, Thailand: 203,
224, 228, 257, 278, 281

Vance, Cyrus R.: 107
Vang Pao: 186, 188–89, 192–93,
201, 207
Vientiane: 54–55, 190–91, 272
Vietminh: 21–24, 56, 75–76
Vietcong: 35, 60, 64, 73, 75–76, 91,
101, 112, 146, 149, 169–70, 185,
252, 274
Vietnamese air force (VNAF): 60,
64, 75, 231
Vietnamization: 171, 177, 181, 195,
203, 205, 223
Vinh: 98, 116, 222, 242
Vogt, John: 228, 245
Vulture. *See* operations
Vo Nguyen Giap: 112, 146, 221

Walsh, James H.: 36
Watergate: 271, 277
Westmoreland, William C.: 71, 105,
107, 111, 116, 146, 150, 168,
171, 289
Wheeler, Earle G.: 97, 107, 109,
135, 138, 142, 146, 171

White Star: 57
White, Thomas D.: 31, 50, 58
Wild Weasels: 126

Xom Bang: 106–7

Yalu River: 19
Yankee Station: 109
Yen Vien: 254

Zuckert, Eugene M.: 45–46, 48, 50,
62, 73, 107